普通高等教育"动画与数字媒体专业"规划教材

数字媒体专业英语

桑莉君　高旭　主编

清华大学出版社
北京

内 容 简 介

本书是为数字媒体艺术和数字媒体技术专业英语课程编写的教材。全书按照数字媒体范畴，共分为数字媒体产业、数字媒体艺术、数字媒体技术、数字媒体应用4个部分，17个单元。每个单元都包含课文、词汇、注释、练习和多篇阅读材料。

本书可供应用型本科院校或大专院校数字媒体技术或数字媒体艺术专业师生教学使用，也可供教育技术专业、新闻传播学类专业师生教学参考。

本书封面贴有清华大学出版社防伪标签，无标签者不得销售。
版权所有，侵权必究。举报：010-62782989，beiqinquan@tup.tsinghua.edu.cn。

图书在版编目(CIP)数据

数字媒体专业英语/桑莉君，高旭主编. —北京：清华大学出版社，2017(2024.1重印)
(普通高等教育"动画与数字媒体专业"规划教材)
ISBN 978-7-302-44708-5

Ⅰ.①数… Ⅱ.①桑… ②高… Ⅲ.①数字技术－多媒体技术－英语－高等学校－教材 Ⅳ.①H31

中国版本图书馆CIP数据核字(2016)第185502号

责任编辑：白立军
封面设计：常雪影
责任校对：时翠兰
责任印制：刘海龙

出版发行：清华大学出版社
网　　址：https://www.tup.com.cn,https://www.wqxuetang.com
地　　址：北京清华大学学研大厦A座
邮　　编：100084
社 总 机：010-83470000
邮　　购：010-62786544
投稿与读者服务：010-62776969，c-service@tup.tsinghua.edu.cn
质量反馈：010-62772015，zhiliang@tup.tsinghua.edu.cn
课件下载：https://www.tup.com.cn,010-83470236

印 装 者：三河市人民印务有限公司
经　　销：全国新华书店
开　　本：185mm×260mm　印　张：14.75　字　数：347千字
版　　次：2017年1月第1版　　　　　印　次：2024年1月第8次印刷
定　　价：39.00元

产品编号：070364-02

Foreword

数字媒体专业是我国近年来兴起的热门专业之一。据教育部《普通高等学校本科专业目录(2012版)》，我国的数字媒体类专业主要有数字媒体艺术(专业代码为130508)和数字媒体技术(专业代码为080906)，此外还有在教育技术、视觉传达设计、网络与新媒体等专业下开设的数字媒体方向。数字媒体专业在校学生人数正在逐年增加。

"数字媒体专业英语"是数字媒体类专业的必修课程之一。数字媒体专业是传播、技术和艺术的多学科复合型专业，故"数字媒体专业英语"课程的内容应该能够基本覆盖数字媒体产业、数字媒体艺术、数字媒体技术和数字媒体应用几个方面。本书在此4个方面的基础上，通过划分的17个单元，分别对数字媒体各内容进行了细致、专业的介绍。

本书以提高媒体类学生的英语文献阅读能力为目的，扩展其英语的写、译和专项表达能力。立足于实用性，本书从数字媒体常见的产业、艺术、技术和应用几个方面出发，同时兼顾技术发展热点和媒体文化原则，分别列入17个教学单元：数字媒体现状、数字媒体产业、达达主义、波普艺术、蒙太奇艺术、计算机技术、多媒体计算机、计算机图形学、虚拟现实、增强现实、新媒体广告、用户设计、Web设计、信息设计、建筑动画、视觉传达设计、游戏娱乐。每个单元都包含课文、词汇、注释、练习和阅读材料几个部分，其中课文侧重于展示本主题领域的基础知识和关键内容，阅读材料主要是对主题内容的补充。本书内容的组织不仅有利于学生了解数字媒体的现状及发展，而且可让学生在轻松有趣的阅读中掌握并积累数字媒体专业英语词汇。

本书主要由太原理工大学桑莉君和高旭编写。此外参加本书编写工作的还有郝小星、张琤、刘东霞、李烽、赵慧、王玉文、常林梅、常春燕、樊宁、温芝龙、高永利、吴朋波、赵文慧及大同大学赵慧琴老师。

由于编者水平有限，书中的疏漏、不足在所难免，敬请广大读者不吝赐教。

编　者
2016年4月

Contents

Chapter 1 Industry Background

UNIT 1 Digital Contemporary Life 3

  Text A Disney Buys Pixar 3
  Text B Chinese Make Big Push into Animation 9
  Text C WeChat: The Chat App Stealing Weibo's Thunder 12
  Reading Material 7 Lessons You Can Learn from Shooting
                    with a Camera Phone 15

UNIT 2 The Rise of Digital Media Industry 19

  Text A Digital Art in China 19
  Reading Material Wall Street Has Made Hillary Clinton a
                    Millionaire 22

Chapter 2 Art Background

UNIT 3 Dadaism 27

  Text A Dadaism 27
  Reading Material Duchamp 31

UNIT 4 Pop Art 34

  Text A Pop Art Pioneer Richard Hamilton Dies at the Age
          of 89 34
  Text B Restless Genius: Pablo Picasso 37
  Text C Andy Warhol and the Can That Sold the World by Gary
          Indiana 40
  Reading Material "My Mind Split Open": Andy Warhol's
                    Exploding Plastic Inevitable 44

UNIT 5　Montage	47
Text A　Montage (filmmaking)	47
Reading Material　Taxi Driver (1976)	51
Reading Material　Avatar 3D Film Employs Cutting Edge Visual Effects	54

Chapter 3　Technical Elements

UNIT 6　Overview Of Computer	61
Text A　Evolution of Computer	61
Reading Material　Who Invented the Computer?	68

UNIT 7　Multimedia Computer Technology	72
Text A　Windows Media Player 12	72
Text B　Adobe Fast Facts	77
Text C　Adobe Character Animator	80
Reading Material　We Had No Idea	84

UNIT 8　Computer Graphics	87
Text A　Apple's First Macintosh Turns 25	87
Text B　How Mandelbrot's Fractals Changed the World	90
Reading Material　Listening to Geometry	93
Reading Material　The Backbone of Fractals: Feedback and the Iterator	95

Chapter 4　Professional Outlook

UNIT 9　Virtual Reality	99
Text A　Building a Digital Museum	99
Text B　5 Ways Virtual Reality Will Change Education	102
Text C　Don't Compare Virtual Reality to the Smartphone	107
Reading Material　"China's Google" Baidu is Making Smart Glasses	110

UNIT 10　Augmented Reality	112
Text A　7 Ways Augmented Reality Will Improve Your Life	112
Text B　Can Augmented Reality Help Save the Print Publishing Industry?	117
Text C　(geolocation ＋ augmented reality ＋ QR codes) Libraries	120
Reading Material　GPS App Keeps Drivers' Eyes on the Road	123

UNIT 11　New Media Advertisement 126

Text A　Mobile Advertising Is Soaring While Newspapers Continue Their Inexorable Decline 126
Text B　8 Reasons to Join the Digital Media and Advertising Industry 129
Reading Material　What is Digital Media? 132

UNIT 12　UI 135

Text A　Realism in UI Design 135
Text B　Experience vs Function—a Beautiful UI is Not Always the Best UI 139
Reading Material　Eye-Catching Mobile App Interfaces with Sleek Gradient Effect 142

UNIT 13　Web Design 151

Text A　Design Trend: Ghost Buttons in Website Design 151
Text B　How To Create a Web Design Style Guide 156
Reading Material　11 Web Design Trends for 2016 164

UNIT 14　Information Design 171

Text A　What Is Information Design? 171
Text B　Physical, Cognitive, and Affective: A Three-part Framework for Information Design 176
Reading Material　Audible Information Design in the New York City Subway System: A Case Study 180

UNIT 15　Architectural Animation 184

Text A　Making of Phoenix & Vieques House Animation 184
Reading Material　Architecture Software 197

UNIT 16　Visual Communication 200

Text A　Type Basics 200
Reading Material　Style Tiles and How They Work 205

UNIT 17　Online Game 211

Text A　Angry Wingless Birds are Taking Over 211
Reading Material　Apple Buys Star Wars Tech Firm Faceshift to up Its VR Game 219
Reading Material　Microsoft Pays $2.5bn for Minecraft Maker Mojang 220

参考文献 224

Chapter 1

Industry Background

UNIT 1

Digital Contemporary Life

COMPETENCIES

After you have read this unit, you should be able to:
1. Talking about the digital contemporary life.
2. What is your favorite digital contemporary life?

Text A

Disney Buys Pixar

No one has a monopoly on the understanding of what the headlong rush into digital media means. There are no real gurus, only a great many people grappling with what all the complex interplays of new technologies, new business models and new social responses to media and information add up to. The day of the expert is over. Everyone has a legitimate viewpoint and should feel confident enough to express it. What books like this one try to do, therefore, is not to dictate a point of view as if cast in stone but to think through what is happening and come up with some models for making sense of it. But a process of thinking it through—like keeping the Forth Bridge free of rust—is actually a task without end. In other words, if you do ever think you have reached a final conclusion, it is probably the wrong one! So, a book like this one has to be the author's take on the world at a given moment in time. It is not only a snapshot of a real world of events and activity but also a snapshot of an internal world of mental models, ideas, perception and—it has to be admitted—doubts and uncertainties.

From: An introduction to digital media
Author: Tony Feldman

House of Mouse is teaming up with Pixar in a $7.4 billion deal. Steve Jobs to become board member at Disney(See figure 1-1).

NEW YORK (CNNMoney.com)—Mickey Mouse and Nemo are now corporate cousins. Walt Disney has announced that it is buying Pixar (See figure 1-2), the animated studio led by Apple head Steve Jobs, in a deal worth $7.4 billion.

Figure 1-1 Disney

Figure 1-2 Pixar

  Speculation about a deal being imminent raged on Wall Street for the past few weeks. Disney has released all of Pixar's films so far, but the companies' current distribution deal was set to expire following the release of this summer's "Cars." The merger brings together Disney's historic franchise of animated characters, such as Mickey, Minnie Mouse and Donald Duck, with Pixar's stable of cartoon hits, including the two "Toy Story" films, "Finding Nemo" and "The Incredibles."

  "Disney and Pixar can now collaborate without the barriers that come from two different companies with two different sets of shareholders," said Jobs in a statement. "Now, everyone can focus on what is most important, creating innovative stories, characters and films that delight millions of people around the world."

  As part of the deal, Jobs will become a board member of Disney, the companies said. And John Lasseter, the highly respected creative director at Pixar who had previously worked for Disney, will rejoin the House of Mouse as chief creative officer for the company's combined animated studios and will also help oversee the design for new attractions at Disney theme parks.

  "The addition of Pixar significantly enhances Disney animation, which is a critical creative engine for driving growth across our businesses," said Disney CEO Robert Iger in a written statement.

During a conference call with analysts Tuesday, Iger said that acquisition discussions had been going on for the past several months. Jobs added that after a "lot of soul searching," he came to the conclusion that it made the most sense for Pixar to align itself with Disney permanently instead of trying to distribute films on its own or sign with another movie studio partner.

According to the terms of the deal, Disney (Research) will issue 2.3 shares for each Pixar share. Based on Tuesday's closing prices, that values Pixar at $59.78 a share, about a 4 percent premium to Pixar's current stock price. Shares of Pixar (Research) fell slightly in regular trading on the Nasdaq Tuesday but gained nearly 3 percent in after-hours trading. The stock has surged more than 10 percent so far this year on takeover speculation.

Disney's stock gained 1.8 percent in regular trading on the New York Stock Exchange and was flat after-hours.

Prior to the deal's announcement, some Wall Street observers had speculated that Disney may be paying too much for Pixar. A source tells FORTUNE that some Disney board members also thought the price was too high.

To that end, Disney chief financial officer Thomas Staggs said during the conference call that the deal would reduce Disney's earnings slightly in fiscal 2006, which ends this September, as well as fiscal 2007. He added though that Pixar should add to earnings by fiscal 2008 and that Disney was still on track to post annual double-digit percentage gains in earnings through 2008.

But one hedge fund manager said that the risk of Disney losing Pixar was too great.

"The question isn't did Disney pay too much but how expensive would it have been for Disney if Pixar fell into someone else's hands," said Barry Ritholtz, chief investment officer with Ritholtz Capital Partners, a hedge fund that focuses on media and technology stocks.

Jeffrey Logsdon, an analyst with Harris Nesbitt, agreed with that assessment. He said that Pixar's "success quotient" justified the price of the deal.

Pixar has yet to have a flop with its six animated movies. They have grossed more than $3.2 billion worldwide, according to movie tracking research firm Box Office Mojo.

Disney, however, has struggled in the computer-generated animated movie arena. Even though its most recent CG-animated film, "Chicken Little" performed better than many had expected at the box office, it was not as big a hit as any of the Pixar films.

"Robert Iger has made no secret of the fact that he wanted to get the animated business back to where it was. It's what Disney has known for but the movies they did in-house did not do as well as the ones they did with Pixar," said Michael Cuggino, a fund manager who owns about 100,000 shares of Disney in the Permanent Portfolio and Permanent Portfolio Aggressive Growth funds.

Pixar has yet to announce what movies it is working on after "Cars," however. It is believed that Pixar's next film about a rat living in a fancy Parisian restaurant, tentatively titled "Ratatouille" may be released on 2007 and that a "Toy Story 3" may be in the works as well. Jobs said during the conference call that nothing has been decided about future Pixar releases yet, but added that the company feels strongly about making sequels to some of its previous hits (See figure 1-3).

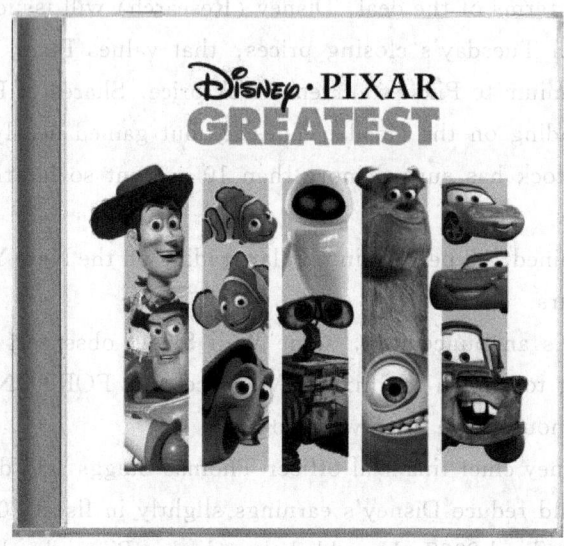

Figure 1-3　Disney buys Pixar

And Iger said that announced plans for Disney-produced animated films, including the release of "American Dog" in 2008 and "Rapunzel Unbraided" in 2009, are still on track.

It would have been unthinkable to imagine Disney and Pixar teaming up just a few years ago. The two companies broke off talks to extend their current distribution agreement in 2004 due to a strained relationship between Jobs and former Disney CEO Michael Eisner. But since Iger succeeded Eisner last year, he has extended an olive branch to Jobs.

Disney and Apple have already announced several online programming deals during the past few months. Disney now has agreements in place to sell hit ABC prime time shows, such as "Desperate Housewives" and "Lost", as well as content from ABC Sports and ESPN on Apple's popular iTunes music and video store.

Cuggino said the addition of Jobs, who will also become Disney's largest individual shareholder, to Disney's board could mean that more innovative digital deals could be in the works. "Jobs is a dynamic personality who knows consumer electronics. It's an opportunity to bring some youthful energetic thinking to Disney's board."

Disney, like many other large media companies, has seen its stock price stagnate during the past year as investors have flocked to more rapidly growing digital media firms such as Apple as well as search engines Google (Research) and Yahoo!.

But Logsdon said the acquisition of Pixar could help Disney increase revenue throughout all of its business lines. So even though some may be quibbling in the short-term about how much Disney had to spend, he thinks Disney made the right move.

"It's a smart strategic deal," Logsdon said. "The benefit in theme parks, consumer products and cable will probably make this deal look a lot smarter a year or two from now."

From: http://money.cnn.com/2006/01/24/news/
Author: Paul R. La Monica, CNNMoney.com senior writer

New Words

Disney *n.* 迪斯尼(美国动画影片制作家及制片人)
Pixar *n.* 皮克斯公司,它制作了世界上第一部全计算机动画电影《玩具总动员》
Animate *vt.* 使有生气;驱动;使栩栩如生的动作;赋予……以生命;*adj.* 有生命的;活的;有生气的;生气勃勃的
Cartoon *n.* 漫画;动画片;讽刺画;草图
Innovative *adj.* 创新的;革新的;富有革新精神的;创新立异
Speculation *n.* 投机活动;投机买卖;思考;推断
Assessment *n.* 评估;评价;(应偿付金额的)估定;(为征税对财产所作的)估价
ESPN (Entertainment and Sports Programming Network),即娱乐与体育节目电视网

Exercises

Translation

1. "Disney and Pixar can now collaborate without the barriers that come from two different companies with two different sets of shareholders," said Jobs in a statement. "Now, everyone can focus on what is most important, creating innovative stories, characters and films that delight millions of people around the world."

2. Even though its most recent CG-animated film, "Chicken Little" performed better than many had expected at the box office, it was not as big a hit as any of the Pixar films.

3. Disney, like many other large media companies, has seen its stock price stagnate during the past year as investors have flocked to more rapidly growing digital media firms such as Apple as well as search engines Google (Research) and Yahoo!.

Reading

Reading the picture(See figure 1-4) about the history of Disney films and the company Walt created, summarize Disney's history.

_____
_____
_____
_____

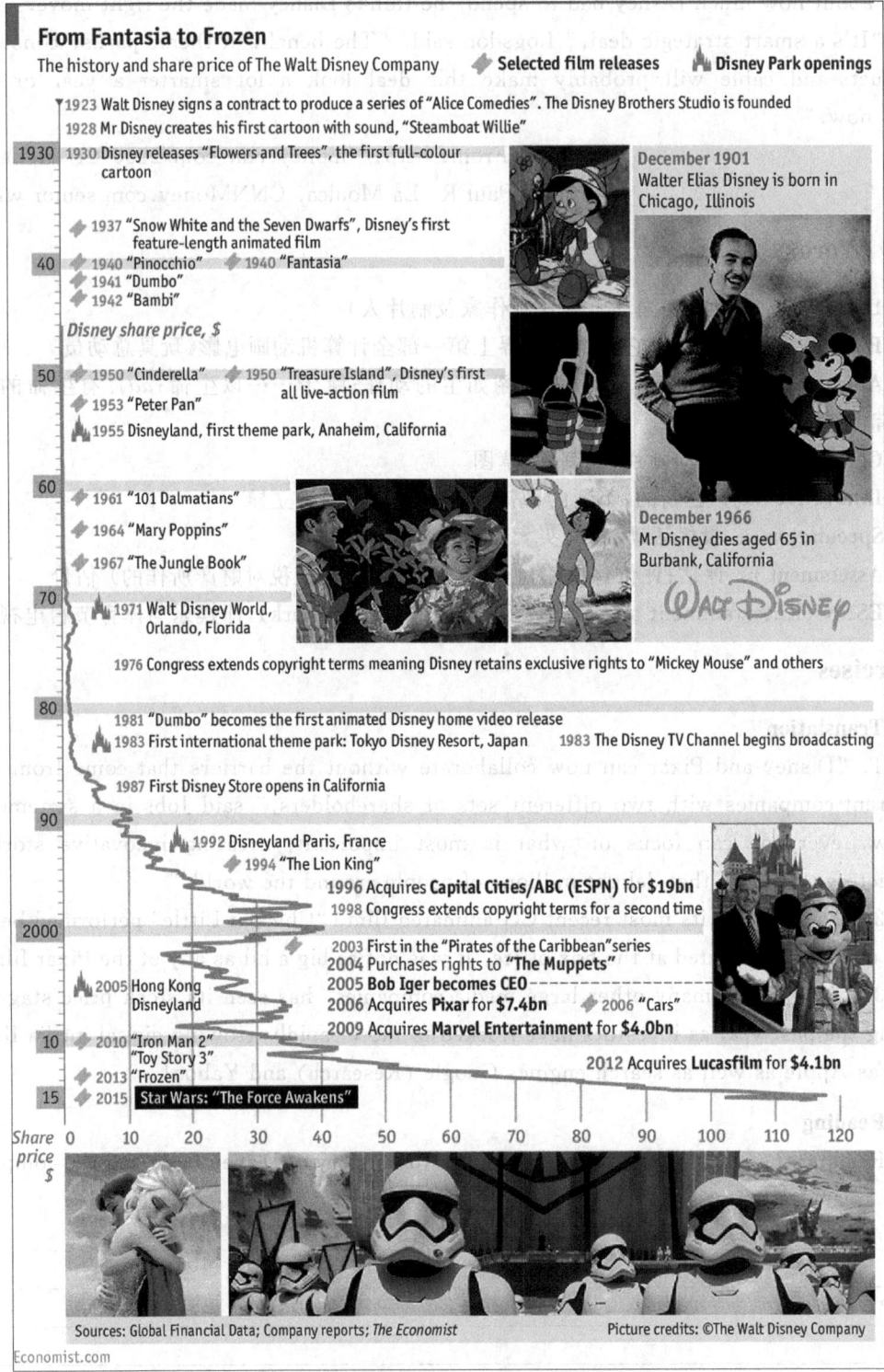

Figure 1-4 A graphical history of Disney films and the company Walt created

Text B

Chinese Make Big Push into Animation

Entering the campus of the largest animation production facility in China, visitors are greeted by life-size statues of Disney and Pixar characters: Belle dancing with the Beast, Mowgli and Baloo sitting on a tree trunk and Buzz and Woody in a classic buddy pose.

But this isn't an overseas outpost of the American studios. Instead, these knockoff statues are meant to inspire a new generation of Chinese animators to make films that can compete with Hollywood blockbusters and classics such as "Beauty and the Beast," "The Jungle Book" and "Toy Story."

The National Animation Industry Park formally opened in May and occupies roughly 250 acres at the Sino-Singaporean Tianjin Eco-City, 100 miles southeast of Beijing. It represents part of the Ministry of Culture's $695-million attempt to spur the national animation industry and make films that can compete on the international market.

Although the facility is managed by the government, film studios from across China can rent space and equipment at subsidized rates—incentives intended to encourage more cartoon production. A company or government agency can even simply present an idea, and animators at the facility will take care of the rest—though of course the content is subject to censorship rules. A number of private companies are expected to establish satellite offices at the park.

The campus boasts the latest in animation technology from around the world, including the largest motion-capture studio in Asia and what it says is the fastest rendering software in the world.

"Some Chinese animators don't have their own thoughts," said Yang Ye, a business manager at the facility. "If you tell them to make something round, they'll make it round, but they won't ask, 'Why is this round?'"

"Children only have a short amount of time to watch TV because their parents are constantly pushing them to study," Yang said. "When every channel is playing 'Pleasant Goat,' of course it's going to do well."

"Pleasant Goat" moved from TV into film. The third "Pleasant Goat" movie was released in China in January and is the top-grossing Chinese-made animated feature ever at $22.7 million, according to EntGroup, a Beijing entertainment research and consulting company. But that's still far behind the Chinese box-office receipts for other types of movies, including dramas and comedies, both foreign and domestic.

Given the rather measly box-office returns for Chinese-made cartoons, investors have been unwilling to spend a lot of money on such projects. That in turn results in films with low production values that are unpopular with the public. (In contrast, live-action films have seen the opposite trend in recent years, with budgets breaking the $100 million mark and investment coming from both private and government entities)

One example is "Xibaipo,"(See figure 1-5) the only other animated feature in theaters at the same time as "Kung Fu Panda 2," produced by DreamWorks Animation SKG Inc. of Glendale.

Figure 1-5　Xibaipo

Chinese firms buy the same technology as many American animation outfits, and a lot of postproduction work for U.S. animated films is already outsourced to China. Inside the Tianjin facility, large signs tout the technology on site, noting that the same equipment was used to make some of Hollywood's biggest animated films. (But even with the tools, a promotional video shown at the facility was jumpy and seemed unfinished.)

One major concern is that films produced at the Tianjin animation park ultimately will suffer from the same problems many live-action films have faced on the international market—mainly story lines that are too entrenched in Chinese culture to make them palatable to audiences abroad.

The $18-million "Legend of a Rabbit," which was made at a smaller animation facility in Tianjin, is China's most expensive animated feature to date. The movie, which arrived in theaters in July and took in $2.4 million in its first two weeks, centers on a hare because 2011 is the year of the rabbit in the Chinese zodiac; in all, a dozen films are planned over 12 years to celebrate each zodiac animal.

Chinese animation studios realize the dearth of originality and are trying to combat it by looking to box-office record holder "Avatar."

"A unique visual style and storytelling is a priority," said Jon Chiew, general manager of Crimson Forest Films, a Beijing company with an in-house animation studio that uses some of the same technology found at the Tianjin animation base. "We've adopted similar filmmaking techniques that were used in 'Avatar,' which allows for a more interesting visual style compared to prior locally made animated films."

Massive government investment in creative sectors has had some disappointing results in the past and in some cases has even harmed it.

"There's a lemming mentality where everyone is trying to follow government patronage," said Duncan Clark, president of Beijing research firm BDA China. "Too many people jump on the bandwagon and that actually ends up stifling creativity."

A 2009 study by the Chinese Academy of Social Sciences found that only one of Chinese teens' favorite 20 animated characters came from China. All the others were Japanese.

Shanghai film critic Wu Renchu sees the industry constantly playing catch-up with animation developed overseas.

"U.S. and Japanese animated films have influenced young people in China and set the standard," Wu said. "When Chinese films don't live up to that level, they don't do well."

Still, if there's any question that this industry is looking to take down Hollywood titans, look no further than "Legend of a Rabbit." The story follows a rabbit, initially a cook with no kung fu knowledge, who learns quickly and must ultimately battle an evil kung fu master: a panda.

From: http://www.latimes.com/business
Author: Benjamin Haas   August 17, 2011

New Words

Animation n. 生气,活泼;动画片制作,动画片摄制;[影视]动画片
Generation n. 产生;一代人;代(约 30 年),时代;生殖
Priority n. 优先,优先权;(时间,序上的)先,前;优先考虑的事;[数]优先次序
Avatar n. 阿凡达;化身

Exercises

Translation

1. Entering the campus of the largest animation production facility in China, visitors are greeted by life-size statues of Disney and Pixar characters: Belle dancing with the Beast, Mowgli and Baloo sitting on a tree trunk and Buzz and Woody in a classic buddy

pose.

2. One major concern is that films produced at the Tianjin animation park ultimately will suffer from the same problems many live-action films have faced on the international market—mainly story lines that are too entrenched in Chinese culture to make them palatable to audiences abroad.

Text C
WeChat: The Chat App Stealing Weibo's Thunder

The exchange of name cards has long been a ubiquitous part of meeting new people in China.

But now it's increasingly likely to be accompanied by the frenzied flourishing of smartphones, as the participants add one another on WeChat(See figure 1-6).

Figure 1-6 Pedestrians in Beijing use their mobile phones as they wait to cross the street

While name cards have yet to be completely supplanted, many now also have a QR code which, when scanned into a mobile phone, adds the card's bearer as a WeChat contact.

The popular function is one reason behind the rise of WeChat—called Weixin in Chinese.

Abandoning Weibo

Ye Jun, a 26-year-old project manager in Shanghai, started using WeChat when she upgraded to an iPhone last May.

By that time, most of her friends were already using the service, although she still preferred Weibo.

That changed in November, when she caught the bouquet at a friend's wedding, and posted pictures of the event on her WeChat activity timeline which, like Facebook, allows users to share photos and status updates with their contacts.

"There were instant comments from my friends. It was fun. I realized that WeChat was a better, more effective social networking tool than Weibo, which has been practically abandoned by most people."

The rise of WeChat

WeChat was launched in early 2011, attracting 100 million registered users in its first 15 months.

This was in part due to Tencent's ability to promote the App to its huge base of over 800 million users of its many other services, including QQ, its desktop instant messaging client.

Tencent has also been quick in rolling out new versions of the App, adding features such as mobile payment, e-commerce integration, games, marketing accounts for brands, a taxi-hailing function and an online investment fund.

Many were quick to gain traction in the day-to-day lives of users. A function that allowed people to give and receive digital versions of Lunar New Year red envelopes saw 20 million exchanged.

As of last September, when Tencent's most recent figures were released, WeChat had 271.9 million active monthly users, up 124% from the previous year.

A report by the China Internet Network Information Center backs the findings of East China Normal University, claiming the number of microblog users, which includes Sina Weibo and similar services, dropped by over 27.8 million last year.

According to Sina's latest figures, Weibo's daily active users are still growing, albeit slowly, with a 4.2% rise in the fourth quarter.

The company says third-party claims of a drop in active users are flawed, and chairman and CEO, Charles Chao said during a recent earnings call that the average time users spent on Weibo did not change over the third quarter of 2013.

Sina seems to be pushing ahead with the long-awaited spin-off and IPO of Weibo, with reports that it recently enlisted Goldman Sachs and Credit Suisse to underwrite an offering of up to $500 million in New York sometime in the second quarter for a share of up to 25%.

Will one replace the other?

The greater control WeChat offers over information sharing looks like one of the factors that makes it appeal more to users.

Posts made to Weibo are public, and therefore can go viral in a very short time, while posts made to WeChat timelines are shared only with contacts, and there is no easy way to forward them.

Mark Englehart Evans, digital strategist and co-founder of Techyizu, a technology and entrepreneurship community in Shanghai, says this means the two platforms are not necessarily mutually exclusive, although a change does seem to be underway.

"Much like Facebook versus Twitter, there seem to be more than enough dual users, or at least people with both Apps on their phones. (But) monthly active users have certainly shifted. I know my Weibo App has gotten dusty," says Evans.

This shift is palpable when speaking to Chinese social media users.

"It is very obvious that fewer people are using Weibo, because I get less feedback when I tweet and retweet," says Duan Wuning, a 29-year-old media professional.

"WeChat status updates are private, so my friends and I prefer to post things about our daily lives there. I have to check WeChat every day to make sure I don't miss important things."

Going global

As Facebook announces its $19 billion acquisition of WeChat competitor WhatsApp, the question of WeChat's potential for international expansion has come to the fore.

Tencent still faces huge challenges in going global. Its functionality could be appealing to users but questions remain over what marketing approach the company will take for a product that already has a 100 million-strong user base abroad.

"This will be new for Tencent and very expensive," says Evans. "It will be interesting to see how hard Tencent is willing to spend to win new users outside of China, and if they can scale up all its advanced features such as mobile commerce and banking to other markets."

From: http://edition.cnn.com/2014/02/27/business

Author: Adam Skuse February 27, 2014

New Words

WeChat *n.* 微信

Weibo *n.* 微博

Ubiquitous *adj.* 无所不在的;普遍存在的

Phenomenally *adv.* 现象上地,明白地

Upgrade *vt.* 提升;使(机器、计算机系统等)升级;提高(设施、服务等的)档次;提高(飞机乘客、旅馆住客等)的待遇

Timeline *n.* 时间轴,时间表

Register *n.* 记录;登记簿;登记,注册;*vt.* 登记,注册;表示;*vi.* 登记,注册;[印刷]对齐
Desktop *n.* 桌面
Media *n.* 媒体;介质
Tencent *n.* 腾讯公司

Exercises

Translation

1. The exchange of name cards has long been a ubiquitous part of meeting new people in China.

2. As Facebook announces its $19 billion acquisition of WeChat competitor WhatsApp, the question of WeChat's potential for international expansion has come to the fore.

Reading Material

7 Lessons You Can Learn from Shooting with a Camera Phone

Given the ubiquity of the camera phone and their ever increasing quality, there are people who are perfectly content having their mobile device also serve as their only camera. I, for one, would likely experience something akin to severe withdrawal if I had to give up my DSLR and shoot exclusively with my cellphone.

But, as with everything in life, I am willing to bet that such a circumstance would present you with at least a few important points that you will want to retain. So no matter where you are on your journey as a photographer, consider the following lessons you can learn from shooting with a camera phone (See figure 1-7).

For most of us, we would rather offer up an internal organ (a kidney maybe, or even better, the actually useful but still totally expendable appendix) than part with our cameras. I guess it makes sense to feel that way, considering we sometimes see our technology-laden cameras as being more important than they are, assigning to them a value directly proportional to the photos we make.

But we're all familiar with the notion that great photographers make great photos regardless of what camera they have in hand. I'm not suggesting that everyone should run around with pinhole cameras just to prove that they are "good" photographers, but it would probably be a fun and worthwhile exercise to undertake. And if you were indeed to put aside your trusty DSLR, your next best alternative wouldn't be so low-tech as a pinhole camera; you'd likely turn to your mobile phone camera.

1. Seeing

Shooting with your phone's camera is going to free up your head. Obviously, you're

Figure 1-7 7 Lessons you can learn from shooting with a camera phone

not going to have any gear to lug around and, perhaps most important, you don't really have any settings to fiddle with. You're free to spend much more of your time simply seeing; you'll eventually find yourself looking at everything and everybody in a different way than if you were using a DSLR. Since you have so little control over settings, you won't be able to fall back on any technical contrivances. You will have to learn to rely solely on your ability to "see" good things in order to make good photos.

2. Using Your Feet

Have you ever used your phone's zoom feature? If you have, then you know the results are appalling. It's a conundrum of engineering: the thinner phones get, the more difficult it is to design a built-in camera with a usable zoom. Zooming in on most phones means it's using digital zoom, just blowing up and cropping in on an image, causing it to appear pixellated and rather ugly. So, forget the zoom. If you want the subject closer to your lens, your best bet is to use your feet. This idea translates well to the DSLR user also, especially when using a prime lens. Sometimes (but not always) it's better to get closer to your subject.

3. Finding the Light

While the sensors found in camera phones improve with each generation of devices, they are still no match for the sensors found in DSLRs and, as such, are prone to struggle when it comes to capturing adequate light. To compensate, you will need to learn to find good lighting, whether natural (wait a moment for that cloud to pass) or artificial (turn on the lights in the room). Applying the same principle to shooting with your DSLR will allow you can keep ISO levels low.

4. Composing Your Shot

Repeat after me: "composition still matters when you're using a camera phone." You may have little to no control over shutter speed or ISO on your phone, but you do have total control over composition. There's no reason to disregard it just because you're shooting with a camera phone; in fact, the camera display on your phone is probably equipped with an optional grid overlay singularly purposed to help you compose your shot according to the classic "rule of thirds". Use it. Strengthening your compositional skills is never a bad thing and it will give you the foundation you need to start breaking the rules of conventional composition.

5. Companionship

Having a cellphone that doubles as a camera is convenient (a gross understatement, I know). It's lightweight, fits in a pocket, doesn't require lens changes—it easily goes everywhere you go, making it possible for you to capture life as it happens. To invoke another old photography adage, the best camera is the one you have with you. Using your camera phone in this fashion just might encourage you to start taking your DSLR with you everywhere, allowing you to document the speed of life in higher quality.

6. Maintenance

Most people I've observed tend to dote over their devices, cleaning and charging them on a very regular basis, and carrying them in protective cases. It's understandable behavior; after all, what good is a dead or broken phone? The lesson here for DSLR users is that you should maintain your camera with the same dedication. Public charging stations for cell phones are becoming easier to find in most cities; I don't think such a thing exists for big camera batteries. Thus, it would be to your advantage to keep at least one fully charged spare battery with you whenever you're out shooting, and when you return home, recharge each battery you used even if it's only partially drained.

7. Appreciation

Despite the advancements being made in mobile phone cameras—better sensors, better lenses, more megapixels—it's never going to be enough to sway DSLR users away from their cameras. But if you have ever spent a significant amount of time shooting exclusively with a camera phone, I can only imagine how eager you were to be reunited with your main camera. No, it doesn't fit in your pocket and you can't make calls or play games on it, but it's your bread and butter. You're an artist and it's your paintbrush. Your camera phone makes a great sidekick, but it can never be the main attraction. Give your main camera the love and respect it deserves (See figure 1-8).

They say good technique is more important than anything else. Is it true? If you think

Figure 1-8 7 Lessons you can learn from shooting with a camera phone

you're up to it, challenge yourself to shooting for a few days with just your camera phone and consider how what you learn along the way can apply to shooting with your DSLR. If you're recently transitioning from a camera phone to a DSLR, have you found anything in particular that has been helpful in making the transition a little easier? Feel free to share.

From: http://gizmodo.com/598278

Author: Jason D. Little

UNIT 2

The Rise of Digital Media Industry

COMPETENCIES

After you have read this unit, you should be able to:
1. Discuss the digital media industry in China.
2. Discuss the digital media in your life.

Text A
Digital Art in China

I proposed the topic *Digital art in China* in 2008, and since then, almost every year we have invited scholars, critics and artists, both at home and abroad, to join seminars and forums on this topic. Though people's understandings and knowledge of digital art are full of contradictions and difficulties, and even suspicion and debate, I think the publicity and uncertainty are precisely the charm of digital art.

Undeniably, the popularity of the Internet and application of the computer in China have gradually removed the veil of mystery of science and technology, and the emergence of a large number of open-source hardware and programs has brought unprecedented creative means and tools to more Chinese artists. Our Chinese ancestors said that the writing brush and ink painting should always embody the changing times. Viewed in regard to the evolution of production tools, digital technology may be a more functional and convenient "toolkit" compared with the writing brush and oil painting brush. Since these have been substituted by the mouse and hand-drawn board, and paper and canvas have been substituted by the screen, then can we say that digital technology is only a tool for us? In my opinion, certainly not. Digital technology brings us a digital way of thinking, whereby artists can carry out information processing and conversion. Artists can be inspired to observe life and society in this unique way.

In the 1980s, after "electronic game"—a kind of interactive game that fascinated people—was introduced to China, changes have taken place in the creation of a number of artists;for example, artists can create paintings by recoding game source programs. The artist Feng Mengbo is representative of this, and I very much appreciate his seemingly casual remark that "these things are actually being played with". It is the great wealth of creative means that promotes the maximum release of performance of concept. Art has been released from depression and has gradually become a game to play, turning from a political, negative, gloomy, human art form into a new relaxed art form. Meanwhile, digital and traditional Chinese art have not only experienced transformational change in creation, but have also experienced dramatic change in spread and influence.

Since 2000, many international and local digital art and new media art exhibitions, arts festivals and forums, large and small, have been held in China, the most significant of which include three International New Media Art Exhibitions held in Beijing from 2004 to 2006; four Electronic Art Festivals held in Shanghai from 2007 to 2009; the large-scale "Synthetic Times: Media Art China 2008" held in the National Art Museum of China in 2008; Coding and Decoding: International Digital Art Exhibition held in CAFA Art Museum in 2010; and Beijing New Media Art Annual Exhibition held in Beijing in 2011.

Over the past few years, the institution I worked in has been more focused on discovery and the display of China's domestic digital art, and our project had the privilege of starting from the cosmopolitan cities of Beijing and Shanghai, but we do not aim to focus our attention only on Beijing, Shanghai, Guangzhou and other first-tier cities in China, we hope that the wider population in China has the opportunity to appreciate the works integrating science with art, which will bring more creativity and innovation to artists. Due to inadequate funding over the past few years, we had to go to Chinese mainland's secondary cities such as Jinan, Chongqing, Hangzhou and Zhuhai, but we still strive to bring our works to Hong Kong and a dozen overseas cities, such as Melbourne, Sydney and cities in Malaysia. Each exhibition always brings me energy, which comes not only from academia, science and technology, and artists, but more from the ordinary audience, who have never seen these works but are full of curiosity and enthusiasm (See figure 2-1 and figure 2-2).

Figure 2-1　Destruction (Miao Xiaochun)

Figure 2-2　Water is deep here in Beijing (Bu Hua)

In view of digital art education in China, some universities set up special programmers related to digital art ten years ago, and now almost all key universities have set up new media art departments or digital art departments. The most satisfying aspect of this is that these universities always encourage interdisciplinary cooperation and exchanges. For example, Tsinghua University and China Academy of Fine Arts have set up cross-media institutes. Thus, an artistic creative team composed of artists, engineers and programmers has emerged in China, who will further explore possibilities between technology and art to create amazing works. I believe that, along with the development of society, all Chinese and western art rules in this field will be changed, while the creative integration of science and art will be an inevitable trend of the development of digital art.

Author: BoQiao Wang

New Words

Digital *adj.* 数字的;数据的;手指的;指状的
Seminar *n.* 研讨会;研讨班,讲习会;研讨小组;培训会
Hardware *n.* 计算机硬件
Program *n.* 程序;节目,节目单
Functional *adj.* 功能的;[数]函数的;有多种用途的;机能性
Interactive *adj.* 互动的;相互影响的;[计]交互式的;*n.* 交互式视频设备
Electronic *adj.* 电子的;电子操纵的;用电子设备生产的

Exercises

Translation

1. Though people's understandings and knowledge of digital art are full of contradictions and difficulties, and even suspicion and debate, I think the publicity and uncertainty are precisely the charm of digital art.

2. Undeniably, the popularity of the Internet and application of the computer in China have gradually removed the veil of mystery of science and technology, and the emergence of a large number of open-source hardware and programs has brought unprecedented creative means and tools to more Chinese artists.

3. In view of digital art education in China, some universities set up special programmers related to digital art ten years ago, and now almost all key universities have

set up new media art departments or digital art departments.

Fill in the Blanks

In the 1980s, after "_____"—a kind of interactive game that fascinated people was introduced to _____, changes have taken place in the creation of a number of artists; for example, artists can create paintings by recoding game source programs. The artist _____ is representative of this, and I very much appreciate his seemingly casual remark that "_____". It is the great wealth of creative means that promotes the maximum release of performance of concept. Art has been released from depression and has gradually become a game to play, turning from a political, negative, gloomy, human art form into a new relaxed art form. Meanwhile, digital and traditional _____ have not only experienced transformational change in creation, but have also experienced dramatic change in spread and influence.

Reading Material
Wall Street Has Made Hillary Clinton a Millionaire

Wall Street has made Hillary Clinton (See figure 2-3) a millionaire.

Figure 2-3 Hillary Clinton

As Clinton tries to talk tough about how she will stand up to America's biggest banks, her Democratic rivals are likely to remind voters just how cozy she's been with Wall Street (See figure 2-4).

Clinton made $3.15 million in 2013 alone from speaking to firms like Morgan Stanley, Goldman Sachs, Deutsche Bank and UBS, according to the list her campaign released of her speaking fees.

"Her closeness with big banks on Wall Street is sincere, it's heart-felt, long-established and well known," former Maryland Governor Martin O'Malley has said on the campaign trail.

While Clinton has given paid speeches to many groups, Wall Street banks and investment houses made up a third of her speech income.

Figure 2-4   Wall street

She even made more money speaking to UBS and Goldman Sachs than her husband Bill did. Goldman Sachs in New York paid Bill $200,000 for a speech in June 2013 and Hillary $225,000 for a speech in October of that year.

Clinton's Wall Street ties likely to be debate issue.

"If the other candidates want to make this an issue, they've got plenty of material," says Larry Sabato, director of the University of Virginia Center for Politics.

Sabato predicts O'Malley or Jim Webb are more likely to go negative on Clinton in the CNN debate Tuesday, but even Bernie Sanders may be able to take a sideswipe when it comes to Wall Street.

Sanders has been outspoken that the big banks are still "too big to fail" and should be broken up.

Clinton's anti-Wall Street policies stop far short of that, with proposals to tax short-term trading and impose a "risk fee" on big banks with assets over $50 billion.

Wall Street's reaction to her plan to regulation big banks was mostly a sigh of relief.

"We continue to believe Clinton would be one of the better candidates for financial firms," one analyst wrote.

Wall Street has been a top supporter of Clinton's career.

As a former senator from New York, it is not surprising that Hillary Clinton would have a close connection to the financial world. But Wall Street continues to be a big contributor to her political career.

In her 2008 run for president, JPMorgan (JPM), Goldman Sachs (GS), Citigroup (C) and Morgan Stanley (MS) employees were among her top campaign contributors, according to the Center for Responsive Politics.

Tabulating campaign contributions for her entire senate political career shows that four of the top five her contributors are Wall Street banks (Citigroup, Goldman Sachs, JPMorgan and Morgan Stanley).

In contrast, Sander's career campaign contribution list is almost entirely made up of union groups.

Republicans likely to have even more Wall Street ties.

Clinton has tried to re-cast herself in this campaign. She shunned Manhattan for her campaign headquarters, opting to locate in hip Brooklyn.

She also did not list out where her speaking fees came from on her 2014 tax return, although she made about the same overall for speeches—around $10 million—as she did in 2013.

Still, her ties to big banks could be a problem in the Democratic primary, making it more difficult for her to appeal to the far left of her party. But if she becomes the Democratic candidate, her banking connections probably won't be as big of a deal on Election Day.

"The GOP candidate is likely to have even more time with, and donations from, Wall Street," says Sabato.

From: http://money.cnn.com/2015/10/13/investing

Author: Heather Long

Chapter 2

Art Background

UNIT 3

Dadaism

COMPETENCIES

After you have read this unit, you should be able to:
1. Discuss your comprehension about Dadaism.
2. Find the other representative figure and their magnum opus.

Text A

Dadaism

Apart from its anecdotal place as a colorful moment in the history of art and aesthetics, Dada, for better or worse, significantly changed the concepts and practices of art in the twentieth century. The noisy debates and wild theatrics of the Dadaists across Europe, and the work and writings of Marcel Duchamp, Man Ray, and Francis Picabia, among others, raised profound conceptual challenges that altered the course of art and aesthetics in the twentieth century. The shift from the idea of art as a selection of attractive visual objects to art as a vehicle for ideas forced artists and aestheticians to reexamine and modify their thinking about the very concept of art, as well as its practice. The upheaval fostered by the Dadaists has called into question all essentialist definitions of art (such as Plato's mimetic theory of representation), as well as the formalist and expressionist theories that were advanced during the seventeenth to the nineteenth centuries. Modern theories espousing the purity of art media such as painting also would have found no favor with the Dadaists. In contrast to modernist purity, their practices fostered the dissolution of the boundaries of the separate art media. The combined assault of wild, irreverent Dadaist experiments with the cool but deadly wit of the likes of Duchamp and Man Ray called into question all assumptions about art.

Dada represents an aesthetic of action grounded in conflicting anarchist sentiments extending from idealism to nihilism. It exhibits a nonconformist human spirit with respect to societal and artistic conventions and traditions. Dada first established its presence in Europe, and was ultimately more successful there, perhaps owing in part to its incompatibility with the progressive and pragmatic sentiments of American culture. It refers to the artistic practices and ideas of gifted émigré writers and artists in Zurich who founded Cabaret Voltaire in 1916 and launched a movement that appeared more or less coincidentally with related happenings in New York and Paris. The German poet-philosopher Hugo Ball, the Romanian poet Tristan Tzara, the German writer Richard Huelsenbeck, and artists Jean (Hans) Arp and Marcel Janco were the principal activists in Zurich. In New York, the main Dadaists were the artists Marcel Duchamp, Man Ray, and Francis Picabia, who also engaged in Dada activities in Barcelona. In Paris the dominant figures were literary: Tzara, the poet Paul Eluard, and André Breton (who later was active with Surrealism), aided by Duchamp, Man Ray, Picabia, and others. Huelsenbeck took Dada ideas to Berlin, where he attracted the support of such artists as John Heartfield and George Grosz. Artist Max Ernst was active in Dada circles in Cologne, and artist Kurt Schwitters was the leading proponent of Dada in Hanover. Officially, Dada was a short-lived enterprise lasting from 1916 to 1924, when it more or less dissolved over differences among the principals active in Paris. Dada action in New York virtually ceased when Man Ray and Duchamp left for Paris around 1920. While relatively brief in duration, the Dadaist spirit and ideas still dominate within the avant-garde forces of contemporary art.

Apart from its underlying message of aesthetic anarchy, Dada warrants serious attention for highlighting certain concepts that have further enriched the field of aesthetics, such as the social role of art, the principle of contradiction, and the principle of chance. At the center of Dada action is contradiction. As Duchamp once remarked, anything that seems wrong is right for a true Dadaist. "It is destructive, does not produce, and yet in just that way it is constructive." Contradiction extends to the Dadaists' views on art. Hence, Dada embraces both anti-art and art. Anti-art, when applied to Dada, refers to the revolutionary art intended to debunk existing concepts and practices of making art. It represents a reaction to these concepts and practices, although it may incorporate them to achieve a different end. By its nature it entails an element of protest. The principal target of this anti-art was the "noble" and "beautiful" art derived from an aesthetic of "art for art's sake" that was being used in bourgeois society to mask social ills. While aspects of the Dada performances and exhibitions in Cabaret Voltaire and elsewhere were considered anti-art, as were Duchamp's shovel and urinal, they were at the same time experiments in advancing the future of art forms such as conceptual and abstract art. In addition to an anti-art component, the events at Cabaret Voltaire regularly included a wide range of art made by the Dadaists and others. African carved sculptures, drawings, and chance collages by Jean Arp; paintings by Paul Klee, Pablo Picasso, Henri Matisse, and others; the sound poems by Ball, a sequence of syllables without rhyme or meaning; bruitisme or noise music borrowed from the Futurists; dance, skits, storytelling, and the reading of texts, including poetry and manifestos—all were integrated into the evening soirées. At the Galerie Dada in Zurich, the works of Heinrich Campendonk, Kandinsky, Klee, and others were shown in March 1917. In the same year, Duchamp attempted unsuccessfully to exhibit his Fountain (See figure 3-1), signed R. Mutt, in Newm York at the first annual exhibition of the Society of Independent Artists. In a Paris Dadaist soirée, paintings by Alberto Giacometti, Juan Gris, and Fernand Léger coexisted with poetry readings by Eluard, Jean Cocteau, and Tzara. On the same program, Breton "performed" the erasing of a Picabia drawing as it was produced on a chalkboard. All of these events suggest that the contradictory elements of art and anti-art remained unresolved in Dada circles.

From: *Dadaism*
Author: Curtis Carter

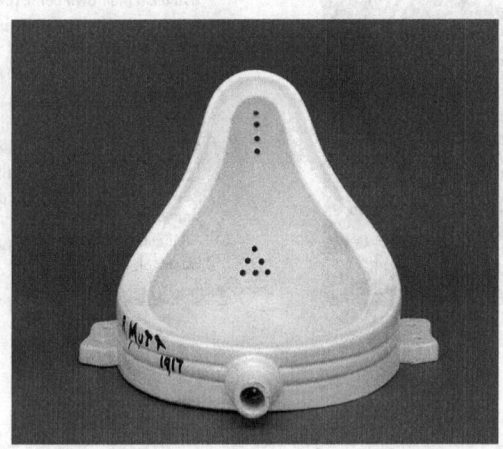

Figure 3-1　Fountain

New Words

Dadaism *n.* 达达主义,达达派
Dadaist *n.* 达达主义的艺术家
Aesthetics *n.* 美学;美术理论;审美学;美的哲学
Reexamine *vt.* 复试,再调查
Definition *n.* 定义;规定,明确
Idealism *n.* 唯心主义;理想主义;理想化
Nihilism *n.* 虚无主义,极端怀疑论
Anti-art *n.* 反传统艺术

Exercises

After reading the following materials, introduce your work to like it.

Hairy Who
Chicago, 1966–1969

As likely to use Plexiglas as canvas and to employ a language based on verbal confusion, visual puns, and an ecstatic use of line and color, the members of the Hairy Who created work that has influenced subsequent generations of artists. The Hairy Who was composed of graduates of the School of the Art Institute of Chicago: Jim Falconer, Art Green, Gladys Nilsson, Jim Nutt, Suellen Rocca, and Karl Wirsum. These six artists banded together to exhibit their work and establish their own context, which was marked by a departure from the more prominent sensibilities of Pop and Minimalism.

In addition to figurative paintings, the Hairy Who produced publications, posters, buttons, and other ephemera, creating immersive multimedia environments that were unequalled at the time. Five official Hairy Who exhibitions were mounted between 1966 and 1969 at the Hyde Park Art Center in south Chicago, the San Francisco Art Institute, and the Corcoran Gallery of Art in Washington, D.C.

Your Work

Translation

1. The shift from the idea of art as a selection of attractive visual objects to art as a vehicle for ideas forced artists and aestheticians to reexamine and modify their thinking about the very concept of art, as well as its practice.

2. Dada first established its presence in Europe, and was ultimately more successful there, perhaps owing in part to its incompatibility with the progressive and pragmatic sentiments of American culture.

3. Apart from its underlying message of aesthetic anarchy, Dada warrants serious attention for highlighting certain concepts that have further enriched the field of aesthetics, such as the social role of art, the principle of contradiction, and the principle of chance.

Definitions
Dadaism

_____

_____

_____

_____

Fill in the Blank

_____ represents an aesthetic of action grounded in conflicting anarchist sentiments extending from _____ to _____. It exhibits a nonconformist human spirit with respect to societal and artistic conventions and traditions. Dada first established its presence in _____, and was ultimately more successful there, perhaps owing in part to its incompatibility with the progressive and pragmatic sentiments of _____. It refers to the artistic practices and ideas of gifted émigré writers and artists in Zurich who founded Cabaret Voltaire in 1916 and launched a movement that appeared more or less coincidentally with related happenings in New York and Paris.

Reading Material
Duchamp

Henri-Robert-Marcel Duchamp (28 July 1887—2 October 1968) was a French, naturalized American painter, sculptor, chess player and writer whose work is associated with Cubism, conceptual art and Dada, although he was careful about his use of the term Dada and was not directly associated with Dada groups. Duchamp is commonly regarded, along with Pablo Picasso and Henri Matisse, as one of the three artists who helped to define the revolutionary developments in the plastic arts in the opening decades of the twentieth century, responsible for significant developments in painting and sculpture. Duchamp has had an immense impact on twentieth-century and twenty first-century art.

By World War I, he had rejected the work of many of his fellow artists (like Henri Matisse) as "retinal" art, intended only to please the eye. Instead, Duchamp wanted to put art back in the service of the mind.

Dada or Dadaism was an art movement of the European avant-garde in the early twentieth century. It began in Zurich, Switzerland in 1916, spreading to Berlin shortly thereafter. To quote Dona Budd's The Language of Art Knowledge.

Dada was born out of negative reaction to the horrors of World War I. This international movement was begun by a group of artists and poets associated with the Cabaret Voltaire in Zurich. Dada rejected reason and logic, prizing nonsense, irrationality and intuition. The origin of the name Dada is unclear; some believe that it is a nonsensical word. Others maintain that it originates from the Romanian artists Tristan Tzara and Marcel Janco's frequent use of the words da, da, meaning yes, yes in the Romanian language. Another theory says that the name "Dada" came during a meeting of the group when a paper knife stuck into a French-German dictionary happened to point to "dada", a French word for "hobbyhorse".

The movement primarily involved visual arts, literature, poetry, art manifestoes, art theory, theatre, and graphic design, and concentrated its anti-war politics through a rejection of the prevailing standards in art through anti-art cultural works. In addition to being anti-war, Dada was also anti-bourgeois and had political affinities with the radical left.

The work (See figure 3-2), an oil painting on canvas with dimensions of 147 cm × 89.2 cm (57.9 in × 35.1 in) in portrait, seemingly depicts a figure demonstrating an abstract movement in its ochres and browns. The discernible "body parts" of the figure are composed of nested, conical and cylindrical abstract elements, assembled together in such a way as to suggest rhythm and convey the movement of the figure merging into itself. Dark outlines limit the contours of the body while serving as motion lines that emphasize the dynamics of the moving figure, while the accented arcs of the dotted lines seem to suggest a thrusting pelvic motion. The movement seems to be rotated counterclockwise from the upper left to the lower right corner, where the gradient of the apparently frozen sequence corresponding to the bottom right to top left dark, respectively, becomes more transparent,

Figure 3-2 Nude descending a staircase, No. 2

the fading of which is apparently intended to simulate the "older" section. At the edges of the picture, the steps are indicated in darker colors. The center of the image is an amalgam of light and dark, that becomes more piqued approaching the edges. The overall warm, monochrome bright palette ranges from yellow ochre to dark, almost black tones. The colors are translucent. At the bottom left Duchamp placed the title "NU DESCENDANT UN ESCALIER" in block letters, which may or may not be related to the work. The question of whether the figure represents a human body remains unanswered; the figure provides no clues to its age, individuality, character, or sex.

From: https://en.wikipedia.org/wiki/Marcel_Duchamp

UNIT 4

Pop Art

COMPETENCIES

After you have read this unit, you should be able to:
1. Discuss your comprehension about Pop Art.
2. Find the other representative figure and their magnum opus.

Text A

Pop Art Pioneer Richard Hamilton Dies at the Age of 89

British artist Richard Hamilton (See figure 4-1), regarded as a pioneer in the field of Pop art, has died at the age of 89 following a short illness.

The London-born artist's best known work was a 1956 collage featuring a body builder and a tin of ham, which earned him the title "Father of Pop".

The Gagosian Gallery, which announced his death, said the art world had "lost one of its leading lights".

He was working on a major retrospective just day before he died.

The exhibition is due to be seen in London, Los Angeles, Philadelphia and Madrid next year.

Larry Gagosian, who owns several galleries around the world, said: "This is a very sad day for all of us and our thoughts are with Richard's family, particularly his wife Rita and son Rod."

Figure 4-1　Richard Hamilton

Tate director Sir Nicholas Serota said Hamilton died as he "would have wished", working on his art.

In an interview with the BBC last year, Hamilton said: "I've always done exactly I wanted to do and I've always had the good fortune to do that."

The artist was born in London in 1922, trained as an engineering draftsman and worked at EMI during World War II.

He studied at London's Royal Academy but was expelled after defying the teacher's instructions.

Hamilton went on to study at the Slade School of Fine Art, leaving in 1951.

A year later, Hamilton founded the Independent Group at the Institute of Contemporary Arts (ICA) in London, with Eduardo Paolozzi, Lawrence Alloway and several other architects.

This group helped to develop English Pop Art.

In the late 1950s and early 1960s, he also taught at the Central School of Arts and Crafts and the Royal College of Art, where he was an early supporter of David Hockney.

Aside from his famous collages, Hamilton also designed the cover of the Beatles' White Album and poster in 1968.

Hamilton's design is the only Beatles' album cover that does not show the four band members.

The artist told how Sir Paul McCartney called him to ask him to design the new cover.

Hamilton said: "Peter Blake's album sleeve (for Sgt Pepper) was crowded with people and very colourful. I thought it would be appropriate to present an album that was just white."

Vulgar American imagery

During his career, Hamilton exhibited at some of the world's most famous art galleries, including the Tate in London and the Guggenheim Museum in New York.

His later work focused on political images, which often parodied post-war consumerism.

Serota said: "This fascination with the consumer society was highly critical, a moral position that was also evident in his distrust of the political establishment ranging from Mrs Thatcher to Tony Blair and Hugh Gaitskell."

Shock and Awe (2007—2008) featured Tony Blair wearing a cowboy shirt, with guns and holsters.

Hamilton said he produced the image after he saw Blair "looking smug" following a conference with George Bush.

In 2010, London's Serpentine Gallery exhibited Hamilton's Modern Moral Matters, which focused on his political and protest works.

Asked recently about being called the father of Pop art, Hamilton said it was not a term he aligned himself with.

"While I was interested in the pop phenomenon, I never associated myself with the term, which I used to describe Elvis Presley and rather vulgar American imagery of ice cream cones or hamburgers," he said.

"However, significant things were happening in the 1950s and it seemed not only to be a cool moment but a momentous moment for humanity."

From: http://www.bbc.com/news

New Words

Pop Art n. 流行艺术;波普艺术
Pioneer n. 先驱者;拓荒者;开发者;创始者;vt. 开拓,开发;做(……的)先锋;提倡
Gallery n. 画廊,走廊
Phenomenon n. 现象,事件;奇迹;非凡的人
Imagery n. 意象;比喻;形象化的描述;〈集合词〉像,肖像,画像,雕像;塑像术

Exercises

Translation

1. The London-born artist's best known work was a 1956 collage featuring a body builder and a tin of ham, which earned him the title "Father of Pop".

2. "While I was interested in the pop phenomenon, I never associated myself with the term, which I used to describe Elvis Presley and rather vulgar American imagery of ice cream cones or hamburgers," he said.

Definitions

Pop Art
_____
_____
_____
_____

Richard Hamilton
_____
_____
_____
_____

Reading the article and writing down your comprehension of Richard Hamilton and his work.

Richard Hamilton's Just what is it that makes today's homes so different, so appealing? is one of the most celebrated images in twentieth-century British art. It was created for the catalogue and used for one of the posters for the exhibition *This is Tomorrow* held at the Whitechapel Art Gallery, London, during August and September

1956. Collaged with images drawn chiefly from American illustrated magazines, it has become an emblem of the Age of Boom, the post-War consumer culture of the late 1950s. It has also become a manifesto for a movement. In one of the first accounts of British Pop art, published in 1963, it was presented as a catalytic work, and the next year was decreed "the first genuine work of Pop". More recently it has been compared with the *Demoiselles d'Avignon*, has been hailed as "the starting point of planetary Pop Art" and as the "perfect Pop work". John Russell's description over thirty years ago of the endless "pockets of meaning" that can be found in "this little picture" remains true today. Above all, it was a startling prognosis of the use of comic books, tinned food and burlesque nudes that formed the iconography of Pop art, and of the widespread use by artists of the metonymic language of advertising. Such a mythic status is all the more remarkable for an object not originally intended for display but as a design for lithographic reproduction. Despite this fame, however, the immediate origins of Hamilton's collage have remained obscure. The new archival and source material presented in this article sheds light on these origins, addressing problems surrounding the authorship of the work. Newly identified sources for various parts of the collage allow for a revised interpretation of its contents.

by John-Paul Stonard

Text B

Restless Genius: Pablo Picasso

Pablo Picasso's Garcon a la Pipe has become the world's most expensive painting, selling at auction in New York for $104m (£58m). BBC News Online looks back at the artist's life.

Born in Malaga, Spain on 25 October, 1881, Pablo Picasso was to dominate Western art in the twentieth century.

The son of an academic painter, Picasso began to draw at an early age.

In 1895, his family moved to Barcelona (See figure 4-2) where Picasso studied at the city's academy of fine arts.

His association with fellow artists and intellectuals at the city's landmark cafe Els Quatre Gats saw Picasso's early artistic style flourish. His first exhibition was held in

Figure 4-2 Picasso is credited with founding the cubist movement

Barcelona in 1900, and the city remained his home until 1904.

Cubist Movement

In April 1904, Picasso moved to Paris where his circle of friends included Gertrude and Leo Stein. Early collectors of Picasso's work, the Steins also counted the artists Matisse and Cezanne among their proteges.

From his initial experiments with Impressionism, Picasso's style evolved, giving rise to the Blue Period (1901—1904) and the Rose Period (1905) (See figure 4-3).

Figure 4-3 Garcon a la pipe is an example of Picasso's Rose Period

However, it was his pivotal work Les Demoiselles d'Avignon in 1907, that was to ensure Picasso's place in art history, as founder of the Cubist movement.

Through Cubism, Picasso sought to recreate compositional form in terms of planes and angles, fragmenting his subject matter to create "an assemblage of geometric forms".

In Cubism, Picasso and co-founder Georges Braque created an austere, often depersonalised pictorial style. Strikingly modern and dauntingly ambiguous, it was to become the most influential art movement of the modern age.

Civil War

From 1912, Picasso began to experiment with new techniques including papier colle—pasting overlapping paper detritus to canvas—to create the style better known today as collage.

Turning his back on Cubism in his late 30s, Picasso's work began to take on more colour and saw a return to the use of classical forms. It was a style he would revert to for decades to come while toying with more controversial ideas.

During the 1920s, the artist also contributed to the Surrealist movement, spearheaded by Salvador Dali and Andre Breton, before turning his attention to sculpture.

Picasso was hugely affected by the outbreak of civil war in Spain, and in 1936 began one of his most significant works Guernica—depicting the horror and turmoil of war.

The potent image, focusing on the bombing of a Spanish villa by Franco's German allies, was displayed at the World Fair in Paris—and at a series of international exhibitions.

Global Attention

Protected by his increasing fame, Picasso remained in France throughout World War II, despite the German occupation and the Nazis' low opinion of his "degenerate art".

In 1944, the artist joined the French Communist Party and became a loud supporter of Joseph Stalin, a position which saw him rejected for French citizenship, it was recently revealed.

Never one to shun the public eye, Picasso continued to work prolifically in painting, drawing and ceramics, as well as flirting with creative writing.

A notorious womaniser, who once said women were either "goddesses or doormats", the artist died in 1973 in France at the age of 92 (See figure 4-4), leaving four children (by three different mistresses) and his second wife, Jacqueline Roque.

Figure 4-4　Picasso stood by his communist ideals until his death in 1973

His forceful personality, coupled with his frequent changes of artistic style, ensured that few artists have ever been as famous in their lifetime as Picasso.

http://news.bbc.co.uk/2/hi/entertainment

New Words

Genius *n.* 天才;天赋;天才人物;(特别的)才能
Pablo Picasso [名]巴勃罗·毕加索
Cubist *n.* 立体派艺术家;*adj.* 立体派的
Controversial *adj.* 有争议的,引起争议的,被争论的;好争论的
Sculpture *n.* 雕刻(术),塑像;雕刻品;刻纹;*vt.* 雕塑;以雕刻装饰;侵蚀;*vi.* 雕刻

Exercise

Translation

1. Born in Malaga, Spain on 25 October, 1881, Pablo Picasso was to dominate Western art in the twentieth Century.

2. In Cubism, Picasso and co-founder Georges Braque created an austere, often depersonalised pictorial style. Strikingly modern and dauntingly ambiguous, it was to become the most influential art movement of the modern age.

3. Turning his back on Cubism in his late 30s, Picasso's work began to take on more colour and saw a return to the use of classical forms. It was a style he would revert to for decades to come while toying with more controversial ideas.

4. His forceful personality, coupled with his frequent changes of artistic style, ensured that few artists have ever been as famous in their lifetime as Picasso.

Find Pablo Picasso's collage works, and write your opinion.

_____
_____
_____
_____
_____

Text C
Andy Warhol and the Can That Sold the World by Gary Indiana

Americans, who expect to live in paradise, are always asking why they have been expelled from the happy garden. Lately the inquest has become urgent. David Thomson's new book on Psycho surveys the country's current moral squalor and blames its venality and violence on Hitchcock's sadistic film; now Gary Indiana returns to the same problem of disillusionment and despair, bemoans his image-crazed, commercially obsessed society, and fingers Andy Warhol as the joking demon who was responsible for its corruption. For

Indiana, Warhol is consumer capitalism in person, the embodiment of a "corporate monoculture" that equates high and low, art and kitsch, celebrity and nonentity. Hiring lookalikes to represent him at parties and on lecture tours, he put an end to the illusion of human individuality, and transformed himself into a content less image, the perfection of "boredom, apathy, emotional emptiness, partial autism, and ugliness".

It is a heavy rap to lay on some brightly banal paintings of Campbell's soup cans, and Indiana—whose little book contains no illustrations, since its real concern is Warhol's persona not his art—has trouble making sense of the thesis proclaimed in his title. Warhol's Soup Cans certainly sold (See figure 4-5). When the blotchy canvases were exhibited in 1962, they didn't cost a lot more than the mass-produced supermarket items they so reverently imitated; recently, one of them was auctioned for $11m. Inflation as insane as that in the Weimar republic, I agree, but does this mean that Warhol had sold the world on a vacuous idea, or persuaded the world to sell its soul for a mess of industrialised pottage?

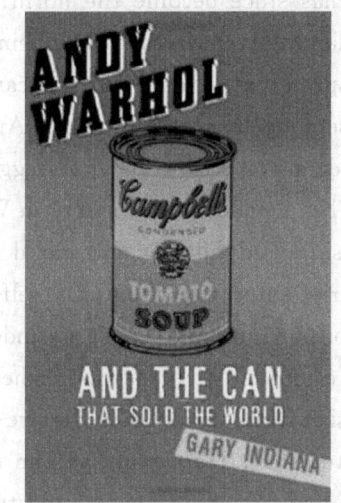

Figure 4-5 Andy Warhol and the Can

The abstract expressionist painters, who scoffed at Warhol's swishiness and disparaged him as a department store window-dresser, extolled a rugged cowboy individualism that turned their hurling of paint at canvas into a kind of gestural politics. In the Eisenhower era, Jackson Pollock and Jasper Johns were pressed into service as advertisements for American freedom; the Rockefellers began hanging abstract art in branches of their Chase Manhattan Bank, as an ideological riposte to socialist realism. Warhol bided his time, and spent the 1950s sketching shoe advertisements. Then, at the start of the next decade, he unveiled his alternative to the "polemics and agonic practices" of the macho AbEx brigade.

Pop art, as Indiana says, was "the negation of subjectivity", a style that corresponded to the neutered emotional blankness of Warhol himself. Rather than vistas of infinity— present in the earliest American landscape paintings of the Hudson river and its gorges or the Grand Canyon, and still discernible in Pollock's jungles of dribbled pigment—his work displayed the spectacle of man-made glut, symbolised by those stockpiled cans. Warhol detested Campbell's soup, having been force-fed it by his mother during his childhood in Pittsburgh, so the images stimulated hunger but could not satisfy it; they took insolent pride in "the absence of substance". Consumers in any case were expected to remain ravenous, feeding their stomachs in order to make up for spiritual famine.

At this point Indiana takes a risky intuitive leap from art to the psychoanalysis of society. He calls Soup Cans "a window into the abyss", through which we can see the hole in which we're all still living. The cans demonstrate that image matters more than reality; this, he argues, is "symptomatic of an affectlessness invariably found in sociopaths", and is also "the prevailing character of American life today". It's a breathtakingly bold assertion, and it's probably right. Indiana's evidence is the moronic or robotic role Warhol played—a whispering ninny in a skewed silver wig. At the time this was a mad affectation, but it has since become the norm: "In American society, having an image was steadily becoming more rewarding than being a person. People have problems, whereas images just have spectators… Neuroticism became a lively asset rather than a liability." Of course the malaise is no longer confined to America: look at Gazza, Pete, Amy, Naomi and all the other damaged creatures who stagger through our national life.

The so-called "superstars" in Warhol's gang of groupies were at least endearingly zany and—since redundancy and rapid turnover were imperative at the Factory, as in any industrial enterprise-obligingly self-destructive. Nowadays we can't rely on celebrities to overdose or jump out of high windows. They have become an economic necessity, a rare and precious proof of economic health: as Indiana says, "capitalism in its current, all-pervasive form exacerbates the pre-extant desire for fame and money and ratifies egregious opportunism". Here you have an explanation of the vile-bodied and empty-headed Katie Price, who appears to be as indestructible as a plastic bag discarded in the gutter. Warhol (See figure 4-6) was over-generous when he allowed every human being 15 minutes of fame: he surely never expected that his prophecy would come true! Luckily his shorter-tempered successor is Simon Cowell, who like an overworked executioner ensures that the hordes of self-deluded wannabes will enjoy at most three minutes of exposure, followed by humiliation and a merciful return to invisibility.

Figure 4-6　Andy Warhol

The zeitgeist occasionally arranges creepy coincidences. Thomson's recent study of Psycho and Indiana's diatribe about the poisonous soup cans both home in on the assassination of JFK in 1963. Thomson sees the event as part of the nihilistic crime wave that began at the Bates motel, while Indiana, a little more plausibly, notes that the president's death exemplified Warhol's theory of democratised celebrity: "world's most important person killed by world's most insignificant person". Murder—either the random slaughter of passersby or the targeting of someone great and famous—rewards rancorous nobodies with immortality, or at least infamy. I'm alarmed by the way both Thomson and Indiana brood about that awful day in Dallas. Americans, who not so long ago believed they had found a saviour, appear to be bracing for another shock. It would be bad magic to say more. Anyway, you know what I mean.

From: http://www.theguardian.com/artanddesign

Author: Peter Conrad

New Words

Disillusionment n. 幻灭；醒悟
Illustration n. 插图；说明；例证；图解
Persona n. 人物角色；伪装的外表
Proclaim vt. 表明；宣告，公布；赞扬，称颂
Blotchy adj. 有斑点的，有污渍的；斑污
Canvas n. 帆布；油画；vt. 用帆布覆盖；adj. 帆布制的
Realism n. 实在论；(文艺的)现实主义；现实主义的态度和行为；<哲>唯实论
Negation n. 否定；否认；反面；对立面
Subjectivity n. 主观性，主观
Correspond vi. 相应；通信；符合，一致
Intuitive adj. 直观的；直觉的；凭直觉获知的
Demonstrate vt. 论证；证明，证实；显示，展示；演示，说明
Coincidence n. 巧合；一致；同时存在；并存

Exercises

Translation

1. It is a heavy rap to lay on some brightly banal paintings of Campbell's soup cans, and Indiana—whose little book contains no illustrations, since its real concern is Warhol's persona not his art—has trouble making sense of the thesis proclaimed in his title. Warhol's Soup Cans certainly sold.

2. Pop art, as Indiana says, was "the negation of subjectivity", a style that corresponded to the neutered emotional blankness of Warhol himself.

3. Thomson sees the event as part of the nihilistic crime wave that began at the Bates motel, while Indiana, a little more plausibly, notes that the president's death exemplified Warhol's theory of democratised celebrity: "world's most important person killed by world's most insignificant person".

Definitions
Andy Warhol

Reading Material
"My Mind Split Open": Andy Warhol's Exploding Plastic Inevitable

In 1968 a fledgling critic by the name of Wayne McGuire sent an unsolicited article to Crawdaddy! magazine proclaiming the Velvet Underground to be "prophets of a new age, of breakthrough on an electronic: intermedia: total scale." Describing them as "the only true intermedia group in the country," McGuire situated them within the context of Andy Warhol's Exploding Plastic Inevitable, or EPI, an overwhelming expanded cinema production collaboratively orchestrated from 1966 to 1967. At the height of its development, the Exploding Plastic Inevitable included three to five film projectors, often showing different reels of the same film simultaneously; a similar number of slide projectors, movable by hand so that their images swept the auditorium; four variable-speed strobe lights; three moving spots with an assortment of colored gels; several pistol lights; a mirror ball hung from the ceiling and another on the floor; as many as three loudspeakers blaring different pop records at once; one to two sets by the Velvet Underground and Nico; and the dancing of Gerard Malanga and Mary Woronov or Ingrid Superstar, complete with props and lights that projected their shadows high onto the wall. Advertisements for the EPI emphasized the variety of included effects, touting in addition to Warhol and the music:

Superstars Gerard Malanga And Mary Woronov On Film On Stage On Vinyl: Live music, dancing, ultra sounds, visions, lightworks by Daniel Williams; color slides by Jackie Cassen, discotheque, refreshments, Ingrid Superstar, food, celebrities, and movies, including: Vinyl, Sleep, Eat, Kiss, Empire, Whips, Faces, Harlot, Hedy, Couch, Banana, Blow Job, etc., etc., etc. all in the same place at the same time.

The cumulative effect was one of disruptive multiplicity and layering, as the Velvet Underground, Nico, and other of Warhol's superstars appeared amidst the barrage of sounds, lights, images, and performance. Critics who saw the shows consistently labeled the effect "decadence" or "perversion". While noting the showing of such anodyne films as Eat (1964), they more consistently pointed to such scenes as Malanga's sadomasochistic reprogramming in Vinyl (1965); Mario Montez's drag in films like Harlot (1964), Mario Banana (1964), and More Milk, Yvette (1965); the slyly allusive activity of Blow Job (1964); or the explicitly pornographic engagements in Couch (1964)—all accompanied by the Velvet Underground's lengthy, atonal improvisations and dark, provocative songs like "Heroin", "Venus in Furs", and "Sister Ray".

"It is no accident", noted McGuire, *that the Velvet Underground was an organic element in Andy Warhol's Exploding Plastic Inevitable. The now defunct Inevitable remains as the strongest and most developed example of intermedia art. Although productions ... have since achieved greater technical dexterity on a visual plane, no one has yet managed to communicate a guiding spirit through the complex form as well as Warhol and the Underground.*

Elaborating on this guiding spirit, McGuire related Warhol to William S. Burroughs—as the "two oracles" of the time—and proceeded to explain that:

Put in a nutshell, the real question is: how can we control and humanize an increasingly uncontrollable and proliferating technology, an overpoweringly dehumanizing technology, when the value foundation for that attempted humanization is rapidly disintegrating and when the attempt by humans to control such power (who would be the master programmer?) would most certainly be corrupting in the extreme?

McGuire was not alone in setting the EPI at the forefront of the development of intermedia artforms. In 1966 Jonas Mekas credited "The Plastic Inevitables" with being "the loudest and most dynamic exploration platform" for the new "intermedia shows and groups". Nor was McGuire the only writer to relate the Exploding Plastic Inevitable to such social and technological developments. A few months later, Bob Stark of the Detroit underground paper *The Fifth Estate* published a more concise, but no less intriguing, review of the Velvet Underground and *Nico* album. Neglecting the conventional format of the record review or any attempt at qualitative evaluation, Stark was prompted instead to ask, "Have you ... ever considered what your role in society will be after the impending Cybernetic revolution?" Like McGuire, he then proceeded to relate Warhol and the Velvet Underground to Burroughs's "Nova Police," to the displacement of a traditional humanist subjectivity, and to the then unimaginable possibility of a future in which "everybody can have one computer or machine which he or she can sit and watch all day." "What will you (yes, YOU) do," he asked.

When machines do all the manual labor and computers run all the machines?

On a much larger scale, how will you as a part of society be able to maintain your ego role as The Superior Being on Earth when machines have replaced you and all your work functions and can do a better job? And who will program the computers? You, maybe? Or maybe your elected representatives? Or maybe the computers themselves? Then what will you do?

... I can only suggest places to look which brings us to the subject of the article ... The one group working in the context of Rock that presents a system which represents anything more than their own personal temporary answers to any of these questions is the Velvet Underground.

If I am drawn to the testimony of Stark and McGuire to begin an analysis of the Exploding Plastic Inevitable, it is not on account of their conclusions; far from it. For neither one does, ultimately, arrive at satisfactory answers to the provocative questions that they pose.10 Rather, it is for the manner in which their invocations of cybernetics, automation, the dissolution of humanist subjectivity, and Burroughsian visions of social control foreground, with particular concision, a constellation of ideas that hovered insistently about Warhol's late-sixties production—his relationship to what a reviewer of a, Warhol's tape-recorded novel from the same period, called "a bizarre new class, untermenschen prefigurations of the technological millennium". But I am also drawn to the fact that certain individuals, like Stark and McGuire, saw in the apparent darkness and chaos of the EPI a possibility of transformation, if not liberation, a possibility that was both within and somehow at odds with the general ethos of the sixties, one that was, in McGuire's words, "bathed in a strange light, a demon light electric."

From: *"My Mind Split Open": Andy Warhol's Exploding Plastic Inevitable*
Author: Branden W. Joseph

UNIT 5

Montage

COMPETENCIES

After you have read this unit, you should be able to:
1. Discuss what is montage.
2. Find some movies use montage and make notes.

Text A

Montage (filmmaking)

For the use of montage in the 1920s Soviet Union, see Soviet montage theory. For other uses of the word montage, see Montage (See figure 5-1).

Figure 5-1 Space-time video montage

Montage is a technique in film editing in which a series of short shots are edited into a sequence to condense space, time, and information. The term has been used in various contexts. It was introduced to cinema primarily by Sergei Eisenstein, and early Soviet directors used it as a synonym for creative editing. In France the word "montage" simply denotes cutting. The term "montage sequence" has been used primarily by British and American studios, which refers to the common technique as outlined in this article.

The montage sequence is usually used to suggest the passage of time, rather than to create symbolic meaning as it does in Soviet montage theory.

From the 1930s to the 1950s, montage sequences often combined numerous short shots with special optical effects (fades, dissolves, split screens, double and triple exposures) dance and music. They were usually assembled by someone other than the director or the editor of the movie.

Development

The word montage came to identify … specifically the rapid, shock cutting that Eisenstein employed in his films. Its use survives to this day in the specially created "montage sequences" inserted into Hollywood films to suggest, in a blur of double exposures, the rise to fame of an opera singer or, in brief model shots, the destruction of an airplane, a city or a planet.

Two common montage sequence devices of the period are a newspaper one and a railroad one. In the newspaper one, there are multiple shots of newspapers being printed (multiple layered shots of papers moving between rollers, papers coming off the end of the press, a pressman looking at a paper) and headlines zooming on to the screen telling whatever needs to be told. There are two montages like this in *It Happened One Night*. In a typical railroad montage, the shots include engines racing toward the camera, giant engine wheels moving across the screen, and long trains racing past the camera as destination signs zoom into the screen.

"Scroll montage" is a form of multiple-screen montage developed specifically for the moving image in an internet browser. It plays with Italian theatre director Eugenio Barba's "space river" montage in which the spectators' attention is said to "[sail] on a tide of actions which their gaze [can never] fully encompass." "Scroll montage" is usually used in online audio-visual works in which sound and the moving image are separated and can exist autonomously: audio in these works is usually streamed on internet radio and video is posted on a separate site.

Noted Directors

Film critic Ezra Goodman discusses the contributions of Slavko Vorkapić, who worked at MGM and was the best-known montage specialist of the 1930s:

He devised vivid montages for numerous pictures, mainly to get a point across economically or to bridge a time lapse. In a matter of moments, with images cascading across the screen, he was able to show Jeanette MacDonald's rise to fame as an opera star in Maytime (1937), the outbreak of the revolution in Viva Villa (1934), the famine and exodus in the Good Earth (1937), and the plague in Romeo and Juliet (1936).

From 1933 to 1942, Don Siegel, later a noted feature film director, was the head of the montage department at Warner Brothers. He did montage sequences for hundreds of features, including Confessions of a Nazi Spy; Knute Rockne, All American; Blues in the Night; Yankee Doodle Dandy; Casablanca; Action in the North Atlantic; Gentleman Jim;

and They Drive By Night.

Siegel told Peter Bogdanovich how his montages differed from the usual ones:

Montages were done then as they're done now, oddly enough—very sloppily. The director casually shoots a few shots that he presumes will be used in the montage and the cutter grabs a few stock shots and walks down with them to the man who's operating the optical printer and tells him to make some sort of mishmash out of it. He does, and that's what's labeled montage.

In contrast, Siegel would read the motion picture's script to find out the story and action, then take the script's one line description of the montage and write his own five page script. The directors and the studio bosses left him alone because no one could figure out what he was doing. Left alone with his own crew, he constantly experimented to find out what he could do. He also tried to make the montage match the director's style, dull for a dull director, exciting for an exciting director.

Of course, it was a most marvelous way to learn about films, because I made endless mistakes just experimenting with no supervision. The result was that a great many of the montages were enormously effective.

Siegel selected the montages he did for Yankee Doodle Dandy (1942), The Adventures of Mark Twain (1944), and Confessions of a Nazi Spy, as especially good ones. "I thought the montages were absolutely extraordinary in 'The Adventures of Mark Twain'-not a particularly good picture, by the way."

Analysis of Two Typical Examples

The two montage sequences in Holiday Inn (1942) show the two basic montage styles. The focus of the movie is an inn that presents elaborate nightclub shows only on the holidays. The film was in production when the United States entered World War II.

The first montage occurs during the Independence Day show, as Bing Crosby sings "Song of Freedom". The 50 second montage combines several single screen sequences of workers in an aircraft factory and various military units in motion (troops marching, planes flying, tanks driving) with multiple split screens, with up to six images in one shot. The penultimate shot shows a center screen head shot of General Douglas MacArthur in a large star with military images in the four corners.

The second montage occurs near the end of the film, showing the passage of time. Unlike the clarity of the "Song of Freedom" montage, this one layers multiple images in an indistinct and dream-like fashion. In the film, the character played by Fred Astaire has taken Crosby's partner, Marjorie Reynolds, to star in a motion picture based on the idea of the inn. The 60 second montage covers the time from Independence Day to Thanksgiving. It opens with a split screen showing three shots of Hollywood buildings and a zoom title, Hollywood. Then comes a zoom into a camera lens where Astaire and Reynolds are seen dancing to a medley of tunes already introduced in the film. The rest of the sequence continues to show them dancing, with multiple images of motion picture cameras, cameramen, a director, musical instruments, single musical notes, sheet music and dancers' legs circle around them. Several times six images of themselves also circle the dancers. Only the opening shot uses a clearly defined split screen and only the second shot is a single shot.

Both of these styles of montage have fallen out of favor in the last 50 years. Today's montages avoid the use of multiple images in one shot, either through splits screens as in the first example or layering multiple images as in the second. Most recent examples use a simpler sequence of individual short, rapidly paced shots combined with a specially created background song to enhance the mood or reinforce the message being conveyed.

From: Wikipedia, the free encyclopedia

New Words

Montage *n.* 蒙太奇;(电影、电视的)镜头组接;合成画;叠化剪辑
Soviet *n.* 苏联;苏维埃;代表会议;劳工代表会议; *adj.* 苏联的,苏维埃的
Edit *vt.* 编辑;剪辑;(影片、录音)校订;主编; *n.* 编辑
Sequence *n.* 顺序; *vt.* 使按顺序排列,安排顺序
Hollywood *n.* 好莱坞
Multiple *adj.* 多重的;多个的;复杂的;多功能的
Revolution *n.* 革命;旋转;彻底改变;运行,公转
Sloppily *adv.* 马虎地,草率地

Exercises

Translation

1. Montage is a technique in film editing in which a series of short shots are edited into a sequence to condense space, time, and information.

2. "Scroll montage" is a form of multiple-screen montage developed specifically for the moving image in an internet browser.

3. Montages were done then as they're done now, oddly enough—very sloppily.

4. The first montage occurs during the Independence Day show, as Bing Crosby sings "Song of Freedom".

5. The second montage occurs near the end of the film, showing the passage of time. Unlike the clarity of the "Song of Freedom" montage, this one layers multiple images in an indistinct and dream-like fashion.

Definitions

Montage

Reading Material

Taxi Driver (1976)

Are you talking to me? Well, I'm the only one here. —Travis Bickle in "Taxi Driver" (See figure 5-2)

Figure 5-2   Taxi Driver (1976)

It is the last line, "Well, I'm the only one here," that never gets quoted. It is the truest line in the film. Travis Bickle exists in "Taxi Driver" as a character with a desperate need to make some kind of contact somehow—to share or mimic the effortless social interaction he sees all around him, but does not participate in.

The film can be seen as a series of his failed attempts to connect, every one of them hopelessly wrong. He asks a girl out on a date, and takes her to a porno movie. He sucks up to a political candidate, and ends by alarming him. He tries to make small talk with a Secret Service agent. He wants to befriend a child prostitute, but scares her away. He is so lonely that when he asks, "Who you talkin' to?" he is addressing himself in a mirror.

This utter aloneness is at the center of "Taxi Driver," one of the best and most powerful of all films, and perhaps it is why so many people connect with it even though Travis Bickle would seem to be the most alienating of movie heroes. We have all felt as alone as Travis. Most of us are better at dealing with it.

Martin Scorsese's 1976 film (re-released in theaters and on video in 1996 in a restored color print, with a stereophonic version of the Bernard Herrmann score) is a film that does not grow dated, or over-familiar. I have seen it dozens of times. Every time I see it, it works; I am drawn into Travis' underworld of alienation, loneliness, haplessness and anger.

It is a widely known item of cinematic lore that Paul Schrader's screenplay for "Taxi Driver" was inspired by "The Searchers," John Ford's 1956 film. In both films, the heroes grow obsessed with "rescuing" women who may not, in fact, want to be rescued.

They are like the proverbial Boy Scout who helps the little old lady across the street whether or not she wants to go.

"The Searchers" has Civil War veteran John Wayne devoting years of his life to the search for his young niece Debbie (Natalie Wood), who has been kidnapped by Commanches. The thought of Debbie in the arms of an Indian grinds away at him. When he finally finds her, she tells him the Indians are her people now, and runs away. Wayne then plans to kill the girl, for the crime of having become a "squaw." But at the end, finally capturing her, he lifts her up (in a famous shot) and says, "Let's go home, Debbie."

The dynamic here is that Wayne has forgiven his niece, after having participated in the killing of the people who, for 15 years or so, had been her family. As the movie ends, the niece is reunited with her surviving biological family, and the last shot shows Wayne silhouetted in a doorway, drawn once again to the wide open spaces. There is, significantly, no scene showing us how the niece feels about what has happened to her.

In "Taxi Driver," Travis Bickle also is a war veteran, horribly scarred in Vietnam. He encounters a 12-year-old prostitute named Iris (Jodie Foster), controlled by a pimp named Sport (Harvey Keitel). Sport wears an Indian headband. Travis determines to "rescue" Iris, and does so, in a bloodbath that is unsurpassed even in the films of Scorsese. A letter and clippings from the Steensmas, Iris' parents, thank him for saving their girl. But a crucial earlier scene between Iris and Sport suggests that she was content to be with him, and the reasons why she ran away from home are not explored.

The buried message of both films is that an alienated man, unable to establish normal relationships, becomes a loner and wanderer, and assigns himself to rescue an innocent young girl from a life that offends his prejudices. In "Taxi Driver," this central story is surrounded by many smaller ones, all building to the same theme. The story takes place during a political campaign, and Travis twice finds himself with the candidate, Palatine, in his cab. He goes through the motions of ingratiating flattery, but we, and Palatine, sense something wrong.

Shortly after that Travis tries to "free" one of Palatine's campaign workers, a blonde he has idealized (Cybill Shepherd), from the Palatine campaign. That goes wrong with the goofy idea of a date at a porno movie. And then, after the fearsome rehearsal in the mirror, he becomes a walking arsenal and goes to assassinate Palatine. The Palatine scenes are like dress rehearsals for the ending of the film. With both Betsy and Iris, he has a friendly conversation in a coffee shop, followed by an aborted "date," followed by attacks on the men he perceived as controlling them; he tries unsuccessfully to assassinate Palatine, and then goes gunning for Sport.

There are undercurrents in the film that you can sense without quite putting your finger on them. Travis' implied feelings about blacks, for example, which emerge in two long shots in a taxi driver's hangout, when he exchanges looks with a man who may be a drug dealer. His ambivalent feelings about sex (he lives in a world of pornography, but the sexual activity he observes in the city fills him with loathing). His hatred for the city, inhabited by "scum." His preference for working at night, and the way Scorsese's cinematographer, Michael Chapman, makes the yellow cab into a vessel by which Travis journeys the underworld, as steam escapes from vents in the streets, and the cab splashes through water from hydrants—a Stygian passage.

The film has a certain stylistic resonance with "Mean Streets" (1973), the first Scorsese film in which Keitel and De Niro worked together. In the earlier film Scorsese uses varying speeds of slow-motion to suggest a level of heightened observation on the part of his characters, and here that technique is developed even more dramatically; as the taxi drives through Manhattan's streets, we see it in ordinary time, but Travis' point-of-view shots are slowed down: He sees hookers and pimps on the sidewalks, and his heightened awareness is made acute through slow motion.

The technique of slow motion is familiar to audiences, who usually see it in romantic scenes, or scenes in which regret and melancholy are expressed—or sometimes in scenes where a catastrophe looms, and cannot be avoided. But Scorsese was finding a personal use for it, a way to suggest a subjective state in a POV shot. And in scenes in a cab driver's diner, he uses close-ups of observed details to show how Travis's attention is apart from the conversation, is zeroing in on a black who might be a pimp. One of the hardest things for a director to do is to suggest a character's interior state without using dialog; one of Scorsese's greatest achievements in "Taxi Driver" (See figure 5-3) is to take us inside Travis Bickle's point of view.

Figure 5-3 Taxi Driver (1976)

There are other links between "Mean Streets" and "Taxi Driver" that may go unnoticed. One is the "priest's-eye-view" often used in overhead shots, which Scorsese has said are intended to reflect the priest looking down at the implements of the Mass on the altar. We see, through Travis' eyes, the top of a taxi dispatcher's desk, candy on a movie counter, guns on a bed, and finally, with the camera apparently seeing through the ceiling, an overhead shot of the massacre in the red-light building. This is, if you will, the final sacrifice of the Mass. And it was in "Mean Streets" that Keitel repeatedly put his finger in the flame of a candle or a match, testing the fires of hell: here De Niro's taxi driver holds his fist above a gas flame.

There has been much discussion about the ending, in which we see newspaper clippings about Travis' "heroism," and then Betsy gets into his cab and seems to give him admiration instead of her earlier disgust. Is this a fantasy scene? Did Travis survive the shoot-out? Are we experiencing his dying thoughts? Can the sequence be accepted as literally true?

I am not sure there can be an answer to these questions. The end sequence plays like music, not drama: It completes the story on an emotional, not a literal, level. We end not on carnage but on redemption, which is the goal of so many of Scorsese's characters. They despise themselves, they live in sin, they occupy mean streets, but they want to be forgiven and admired. Whether Travis gains that status in reality or only in his mind is not the point; throughout the film, his mental state has shaped his reality, and at last, in some way, it has brought him a kind of peace.

From: http://www.rogerebert.com
Author: Roger Ebert

Reading Material
Avatar 3D Film Employs Cutting Edge Visual Effects

The special effects created by artists for Avatar

"People ask things like 'will Avatar change cinema?' In many ways it already has and that has happened in production behind the camera," said James Dyer, editor in chief of Empire Digital.

Avatar is the new movie by Hollywood director James Cameron (See figure 5-4)—the 3D film is nearly 60% computer generated and is rumoured to have cost $300m (£187m).

Much of the budget was spent on cutting-edge visual effects, and inventing entirely new technologies to produce what is a live action film set in a CG world.

"We have a brand spanking new stereoscopic 3D camera for the live action portion of the shoot which is separate from the virtual camera and the performance capture techniques," said Mr. Cameron. Performance capture was used to record real actors' movements which were then translated into animated CG aliens called Na'vi.

Figure 5-4　James Cameron

This action was recorded on a sound stage dubbed "the volume" which has already been used by directors Peter Jackson and Steven Spielberg.

"It's a motion capture stage where the sensors in the ceiling pick up absolutely everything that the actors do on the stage," said Mr. Dyer.

"The selling point is it renders the action in real time so as a director… you get on your monitor a rough rendering of what the finished film would look like," he added.

3D challenge

Filming and special effects work for the film spanned three continents, including countries such as the US, New Zealand, and England.

Visual effects company Framestore in London was hired to do some of the movie's CG work.

"So what we got from the production was literally an actor in a green background, and we were required to put everything else, including set material props and people," said Jonathan Fawkner from Framestore.

Mr. Cameron maintained artistic control by giving Framestore a meticulous pre-visualisation video of how the finished shot should look.

He also created an additional challenge for the CG artists working on the project because all the images must work in a 3D format.

"On Avatar (See figure 5-5) we had an optical stereo image to deal with—that's two images, one for each eye… that's double the workload," said Mr. Fawkner.

Figure 5-5   Avatar

Ocula software developed by visual effects firm The Foundry was used to complete the 3D work.

"So the live action sequences of Avatar have been shot with two cameras so you've got a left image and a right image to get the 3D effect," explained Dr Bill Collis, chief executive of The Foundry.

"Occula allows you to manipulate these images—for example, if the two cameras shooting the scene aren't quite aligned… will you feel possibly nauseous or a strain on your eyes," he said.

Push boundaries

An abundance of cutting edge tech has been used to bring Avatar's alien world to life on the screen.

But the story itself sticks to a fairly traditional formula—alien creatures who live on the distant world of Pandora are threatened by humans.

The blue-skinned and 10 feet tall Na'vi have to battle an exploitative human firm which is after a precious mineral.

Paraplegic ex-marine Jake Sully is hired to remotely control an Avatar to get to know the locals but it ends up falling in love with a local tribal princess.

Film reviews have been mostly positive, but Mr. Dyer believes the film was written to push technological boundaries rather than for the storyline.

James Dyer said Avatar was produced to push technological boundaries (See figure 5-6 and figure 5-7)

Figure 5-6 Avatar

Figure 5-7 Avatar

"Cameron wrote it fairly unapologetically as vehicle for his effects company Digital Domain," he said.

"He wrote this to push digital boundaries so much so that when he went to people at Digital Domain and said I want to make this film they said it can't be done we can't convincingly bring this to the screen."

"The story in itself is not a bad one. It's an archetype Dances With Wolves, it's Pocahontas, it's that kind of thing," he added.

Director Cameron said he decided to go ahead with the film rather than wait for the rest of the film industry to catch up.

"We took the bull by the horns and just got on with it ourselves. Through some time and energy, we came up with a tool set and a process that allowed us to create these alien creatures," Mr. Cameron said.

The director took both a technological and financial gamble, but Avatar's success now rest with audiences worldwide.

"It's a big financial investment and there's a lot riding on it but it's not the first time Cameron's been in this position. Terminator 2 was the most expensive film ever made, Titanic was the most expensive film ever made, this is what he does," said Mr. Dyer.

"When he goes to a studio and say look I want X amount of hundred million to make a ground breaking 3D film about cat people in space, they believe him."

From: http://news.bbc.co.uk

Chapter 3

Technical Elements

Chapter 3

Technical Elements

UNIT 6

Overview Of Computer

COMPETENCIES

After you have read this unit, you should be able to:
1. Discuss computer and computer revolution.
2. Describe computer hardware and software.
3. Describe computer network and Internet.
4. Name several network applications.

Text A

Evolution of Computer

The word "computer" has been part of the English language since 1646, but if you look in a dictionary printed before 1940, you might be surprised to find a computer defined as a person who performs calculations! Prior to 1940, machines designed to perform calculations were referred to as calculators and tabulators, not computers. Modern definition and use of the term "computer" emerged in the 1940s, when the first electronic computing devices were developed.

The "computer revolution" which started in the 1950s is an ongoing change in the way we do things. It has already had two distinct phases and is just entering its third phase.

The first phase concentrated on calculations. Computers were originally conceived of as tools for performing large, repetitive sets of numerical calculations quickly and correctly. The programs developed during this phase simplified the work of engineers and scientists. The kinds of problems they solved involved "number-crunching." In some cases, number-crunching programs made it possible to do things that would have been impossible without the aid of computers. For example, putting a satellite into orbit from an (orbiting) space shuttle(See figure 6-1) requires extremely fast computations that rely on up-to-the-minute information about position, speed, etc. No human could process the information quickly enough to accomplish these tasks satisfactorily and no group of humans could coordinate their answers to sub-problems fast enough. This sort of "**real-time**" calculation is only possible with the aid of computers.

Figure 6-1 Space Shuttle in orbit

The second phase of the revolution uses computers as "**information processors**." By the 1960s, it had become obvious that computers could store and examine **non-numerical data** as well as get answers from numerical data. This led to automating the general process of record-keeping. This phase is most closely associated with organization. Programs are intended to simplify the work of librarians, administrators, and ordinary individuals. Many programs involve managing "databases," large collections of information whose individual items have to be readily available. Other programs make it easy to prepare tables and reports; these automate the tasks of formatting and editing.

These first two phases both involve algorithmic activities. We can instruct the computer on precisely what to do under any set of conditions that arises. We know how to solve the problems correctly, and computers are useful because they can solve them faster and/or because they do some of the work for us.

The third phase, which we are just entering, involves solving problems that don't have well-defined solutions. These problems involve either a lot of interrelated factors that we can't disentangle or questions that we simply don't have the answers to yet. As humans, we can frequently "solve" them through "hunches," "educated guesses," or "common sense"—by using information that we have but may not be able to explain. Medical diagnosis is one such problem, and parsing of ungrammatical sentences is another.

Computer and Internet Basics

Computers and the Internet are the cornerstones of a technology revolution that is dramatically transforming the way we live, work, play, and think. Whether you realize it or not, you already know a lot about computers. Here we provide an overview of computer, give you a basic understanding of how computers work and get you up to speed with a basic computer vocabulary.

A **computer** (See figure 6-2) is an electronic device that accepts input, processes data, and produces output, all according to a series of stored instructions. Computer **input** is whatever is typed, submitted, or transmitted to a computer system. Input can be supplied by a person, by the environment, or by another computer. An input device, such as a keyboard or mouse, gathers input and transforms it into a series of electronic signals for the computer to store and manipulate.

Figure 6-2　Microcomputer

In the context of computing, **data** refers to the symbols that represent facts, objects, and ideas. Data is used to describe facts about something. When stored electronically in files, data can be used directly as input for computers. Four common types of files are:

- **Document files**, created by word processors to save documents such as memos, term papers, and letters.
- **Worksheet files**, created by electronic spreadsheets to analyze things like budgets and to predict sales.
- **Database files**, typically created by database management programs to contain hily structured and organized data.
- **Presentation files**, created by presentation graphics programs to save presentation materials. For example, a file might contain audience handouts, speaker notes and electronic slides.

Computers manipulate data in many ways, and this manipulation is called **processing**. The series of instructions that tell a computer how to carry out processing tasks is referred to as **computer program**, or simply a "program." These programs form the **software** that sets up a computer to do a specific task. There are two major kinds of software—**system software** and **application software**. The most important system software program is the **operating system**.

In a computer, most processing takes place in a component called the **central processing unit** (**CPU**), which is sometimes described as the computer's "brain." A computer stores data so that it will be available for processing. Most computers have more than one location for storing data, depending on how the data is being used. **Memory**, also known as primary storage, is an area of a computer that temporarily holds data waiting to be processed, stored, or output. **Secondary storage** is the area where data can be left on a permanent basis when it is not immediately needed for processing. **Output** is the result produced by a computer. An output device displays, prints, or transmits the results of processing. Computers produce output on output devices such as monitors and printers. In the subsequent units of this book, we will discuss hardware and software in detail.

When you think of computer, perhaps you think of just the equipment itself. But the way to think about a computer is as part of an information system. An information system has the five parts: people, procedure, software, hardware and data.

Almost all of today's computer systems add an additional part to the information system. This part is connectivity, which allows computers to connect and to share information. **Connectivity** is the capability of your microcomputer to share information with other computers. Data and information can be sent over telephone lines or cable and through the air. Thus, your microcomputer can be connected to other computers. It can connect you to the Internet and other sources of information that lie well beyond your desk.

Connectivity and the wireless revolution expand the use of computer severalfold. Central to the concept of connectivity is the **computer network**. The **Internet** is the largest network in the world (See figure 6-3). It is a collection of local, regional, national, and international computer networks that are linked together. It has changed society dramatically. **E-mail** and **instant messaging** have caused a major shift in the way people communicate. **Online stores** have changed our shopping habits. The ability to easily download music has stirred up controversy about intellectual property. The possibility of unauthorized access to online databases has made us more aware of our privacy and safety. The second half of the book will focus on network, the Internet and other related subjects.

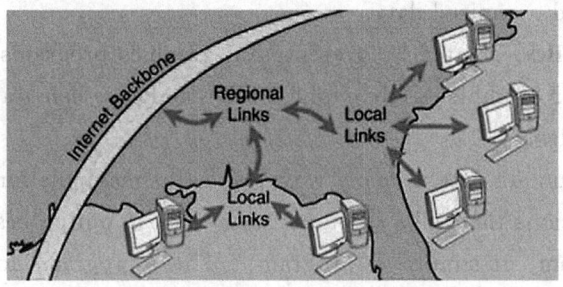

Figure 6-3 Internet

New Words

Cornerstone *n.* thing on which something is built; foundation, 基础

e.g. Hard work was the cornerstone of his success. 努力奋斗是他成功的基础

Prior to *prep.* Before, 在……之前

Refer to…as… 称……为……

Tabulator *n.* thing that arrange (facts or figures) in a table or list. 制表机

Number-crunching *v.* 数字密集运算,大量数值数据的运算

Up-to-the-minute *adj.* having or including the most recent information possible. 包含最新信息的

Algorithmic *adj.* 算法的

Disentangle *v.* make (rope, hair, etc) straight and free of knots. 将(绳子、毛发等)理直并解开其结子,理顺

Hunch *n.* an idea based on intuition or instinct and not on evidence. 基于直觉的想法

Educated guess (习语) guess based on experience (and therefore probably correct), 根据经验做出的猜测(因此可能是正确的)

Common sense practical good sense gained from experience of life, not by special study. 常识;情理

Diagnosis *n.* 诊断;确定毛病;判断问题

Parse *v.* 对……做语法分析

Ungrammatical *adj.* contrary to the rules of grammar. 不符合语法的;违反语法规则的

-Fold suff 后缀……倍;severalfold,几倍

Controversy *n.* public discussion or argument, often rather angry, about something which many people disagree with. 公开辩论;论战

stir something **up** cause (trouble, etc) 惹起(麻烦等)

Intellectual property 知识产权

Privacy *n.* state of being alone or undisturbed. 独处或不受干扰的状态;隐私

Context *n.* circumstances in which sth happens or in which sth is to be considered. 环境,背景

Permanent *adj.* lasting or expected to last for a long time or for ever. 永久的;永恒的;长久的;长期的

Authorize *v.* give authority to (somebody). 授权;委任;委托 unauthorized *adj.* 未授权

Exercises

Multiple Choice

Circle the letter or fill in the correct answer.

1. A(n) _____ is an electronic device that accepts input, processes data, and produces output.
   A. input   B. input device   C. output device   D. computer

2. _____ is whatever is typed, submitted, or transmitted to a computer system.
   A. Input   B. Output   C. Computer   D. Printer

3. An _____ gathers input and transforms it into a series of electronic signals for the computer to store and manipulate.
   A. output device B. input device   C. memory   D. data

4. The most important system software program is the _____.
   A. application software   B. system software
   C. utility   D. operating system

5. In a computer, most processing takes place in a component called the _____.
   A. memory   B. central processing unit
   C. bus   D. system unit

6. _____ is the area where data can be left on a permanent basis when it is not immediately needed for processing.

 A. Secondary storage   B. CMOS

 C. CPU   D. Primary storage

7. _____ is the result produced by a computer.

 A. medium   B. Output   C. Monitor   D. repeater

8. _____ and the wireless revolution expand the use of computer severalfold.

 A. WWW   B. router   C. EM   D. Connectivity

9. _____ is a collection of local, regional, national, and international computer networks that are linked together.

 A. World Wide Web   B. Network

 C. Internet   D. WWW

10. _____ instructs a computer to do a specific task.

 A. Program   B. Instruction   C. Keyboard   D. Mouse

Matching

Match each numbered item with the most closely related lettered item. Write your answers in the spaces provided.

a. primary storage   1. A component of computer that most processing takes place in.

b. Internet   2. A device that displays, prints, or transmits the results of processing.

c. data   3. An area of a computer that temporarily holds data waiting

d. central processing unit   to be processed, stored, or output.

e. output device   4. Symbols that represent facts, objects, and ideas.

f. document files   5. The largest network in the world.

g. database files   6. Typically created by database management programs.

            7. Created by word processor to save documents.

Reading

Microsoft Opens up Windows

Software company Microsoft has agreed to help its competitors access information about Windows as part of an anti-trust settlement with the United States Government.

Microsoft (See figure 6-4) will make it cheaper and easier for other software companies to access key pieces of computer code that their software needs to work well with Windows.

The announcement comes after months of negotiations between Microsoft and the U. S. Justice Department, which is overseeing an anti-trust settlement involving Microsoft.

That followed a long-running case in which Microsoft was found guilty of abusing its monopoly in personal computer operating systems.

As part of the settlement, Microsoft agreed to make it cheaper and easier for rivals to

Figure 6-4 Licensing Microsoft technology will now become easier

license key parts of its operating system.

Substantial Revision

"These changes are designed to make it easier for companies to license our technology," said Brad Smith, Microsoft's senior vice president for law and corporate affairs.

The changes could be helpful to companies such as Sun Microsystems that are battling Microsoft in the market for software that runs servers, the powerful machines that manage computer networks.

The Justice Department said the changes would "substantially" revise the licensing terms for the Microsoft software.

Earlier this month, Microsoft also agreed to make changes requested by the government to its Windows operating system as part of the anti-trust settlement.

That will make it easier for consumers to use software from rival companies to browse Web pages, listen to music and send instant messages.

From: http://news.bbc.co.uk/2/hi/technology

After reading this article, can you talk about what do you think about Microsoft opens up Windows?

Reading Material
Who Invented the Computer?

The question "Who invented the computer?" doesn't have a simple answer, because the modern digital computer evolved from a series of prototypes developed by various groups of people. A prototype is an experimental device that typically must be further developed and perfected before going into production and becoming widely available.

Between 1937 and 1942, an Iowa State University professor, John V. Atanasoff, and a graduate student, Clifford E. Berry, worked on a prototype for an electronic computer. The **Atanasoff-Berry Computer** (ABC) was the first to use vacuum tubes instead of mechanical swtiches. Its design also incorporated the idea of basing calculations on the binary number system. The ABC is often considered the first electronic digital computer.

While Atanasoff worked on the ABC, a German engineer named Konrad Zuse developed a computer called the Z3, which, like the ABC, was designed to work with binary numbers. Built in Nazi Germany during World War II, the Z3 was cloaked in secrecy, even though Hitler believed that computers had no strategic use in the war effort. Information on Zuse's invention did not surface until long after the war ended. So although Zuse was on the trail of modern computer architecture, his work had little effect on the development of computers.

Even with the work of Atanasoff and Zuse, it was not clear that computers were destined to be binary electronic devices. IBM had an entirely different computer architecture in mind. In 1939, IBM sponsored an engineer named Howard Aiken, who embarked on an audacious plan to integrate 73 IBM Automatic Accounting Machines into a single unified computing unit. What emerged was a mechanical computer officially named the IBM Automatic Sequence Controlled Calculator(ASCC), but now usually referred to as the **Harvard Mark I** because it was moved to Harvard University shortly after completion.

Although the Harvard Mark I was one of the first working computers, as a prototype, it strayed considerably from the path of development leading to modern computers. The Harvard Mark I was digital but used decimal rather than binary representation, which is used by today's computers. In contrast, the ABC, with its electronic vacuum tubes and binary representation, was a much closer prototype of generations of computers to come. Some computer prototypes were pressed into service barely before they were completed.

In 1943, a team headed by John W. Mauchly and J. Presper Eckert started work on ENIAC, a gigantic, general-purpose electronic computer. ENIAC (Electronic Numerical

Integrator and Computer)(See figure 6-5) was designed to calculate trajectory tables for the U.S. Army, but wasn't finished until November 1945, three months after the end of World War II. ENIAC was over 100 feet long and 10 feet high and weighed 30 tons. This gigantic machine contained over 18,000 vacuum tubes and consumed 174,000 watts of power. It could perform 5,000 additions per second and was programmed by manually connecting cables and setting 6,000 switches-a process that generally took two days to complete.

Figure 6-5 ENIAC

ENIAC was formally dedicated at the Moore School of Electrical Engineering of the University of Pennsylvania on February 15, 1946, and immediately pressed into service making atomic energy calculations and computing trajectories for new missile technologies. ENIAC received several upgrades and remained in service until 1955.

Generations of Computers

A computer called the UNIVAC is considered by most historians to be the first commercially successful digital computer. First generation computers can be characterized by their use of vacuum tubes, as those in figure 6-6, to store individual bits of data. A vacuum tube is an electronic device that controls the flow of electrons in a vacuum. Each tube can be set to one of two states. One state is assigned a value of 0 and the other a value of 1.

In addition to vacuum tube technology, first-generation computers can be characterized by custom application programs, made to order for the specific task the computer was to perform. Programming first-generation computers was difficult. As the computer

Figure 6-6 Vacuum Tube

era dawned, programmers were forced to think in 1s and 0s to write instructions in machine language. First-generation computers didn't have operating systems, as we know them today. Instead, each software application included the instructions necessary for every aspect of the computing job, including input, output, and processing activities, Programmers were quick to realize that this style of programming was terribly inefficient, they began to look for a more efficient method to standardize such routines and consolidate the into programs that any application software could access. These routines were gathered tighter into operating systems, which became a characteristic of second-generation computers.

Second-generation computers used transistors (See figure 6-7) instead of vacuum tubes. First demonstrated in 1947 by AT&T's Bell Laboratories, transistors regulate current of voltage flow and act as a switch for electronic signals. Transistors performed functions similar to vacuum tubes, but they were much smaller, cheaper, less power hungry, and more reliable. By the late 1950s, transistors, had replaced vacuum tubes as the processing and memory technology for most computers.

Figure 6-7 Transistors

Several successful transistorized computers were manufactured by companies such as IBM, Burroughs, Control Data, Honeywell, and Sperry Rand (which was the new name given to Remington Rand after its merger with Sperry Corp). In addition to the important hardware breakthrough provided by transistors, an equally important development in software differentiated second-generation computers from their first-generation ancestors.

In addition to operating systems, second-generation computers also ran programming language compilers that allowed programmers to write instructions using English-like commands rather than the binary numbers of machine language. High-level language, such as COBOL (Business-Oriented Language) and FORTRAN (Formula Translator), were available for use on second-generation computers and remain in use today. The availability of high-level computer programming languages made it possible for third parties to develop software, and that capability was instrumental in the birth of the software industry.

Third-generation computers became possible in 1958, when Jack Kilby at Texas Instruments and Robert Noyce at Fairchild Semiconductor independently developed integrated circuits (See figure 6-8). Integrated circuit tubes or transistors onto a single miniature chip, greatly reducing the physical size, weight, and power requirements for devices such as computers.

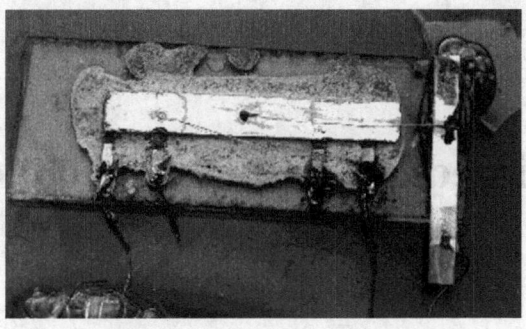

Figure 6-8   Integrated Circuit

The technology for fourth-generation computers appeared in 1971, when Ted Hoff developed the first general-purpose microprocessor. Called the Intel 4004, this microprocessor dramatically changed the computer industry, resulting in fourth-generation microprocessor-based computer systems that were faster, smaller, and even less expensive than third-generation computers.

Microprocessor manufactures soon flourished. Early industry leaders included Intel, Zilog, Motorola, and Texas Instruments. Intel's 4004 microprocessor (See figure 6-9) was smaller than a corn flake but matched the computing power of ENIAC. The 4004 packed the equivalent of 2300 transistors or vacuum tubes on a single chip and was able to perform 60,000 instructions per second. The 4004 was followed by the 8008, the first commercial 8-bit microprocessor, and then the 8080.

Today, microprocessors are key components of computers—ranging from PDAs to supercomputers. Intel reigns as the world's leading microprocessor manufacturer, although microprocessors are also produced by companies such as Hitachi, Texas Instruments, Sun Microsystems, AMD, Toshiba, and Motorola.

Figure 6-9   Intel 4004 microprocessor

UNIT 7

Multimedia Computer Technology

COMPETENCIES

After you have read this unit, you should be able to:
1. Discuss multimedia computer technology in your life.
2. Find multimedia computer technologies and learn how to use them.

Text A
Windows Media Player 12

Designed by media lovers, for media lovers. Windows Media Player 12—available as part of Windows 7, Windows 8.1, and Windows 10—plays more music and video than ever, including Flip Video and unprotected songs from your iTunes library! Organize your digital media collection, sync digital media files to a portable device, shop online for digital media content, and more—with Windows Media Player 12 (See figure 7-1).

Figure 7-1 Windows Media Player 12

Streamlined Playback Modes

The Now Playing mode is a study in minimalism: It shows only the controls you need, so nothing comes between you and your music or video. A new taskbar thumbnail with playback controls makes previewing easier and fun.

Plays More Media in More Places

Windows Media Player 12 has built-in support for many popular audio and video formats. Sync music, videos, and photos or stream media to your devices so you can enjoy your library anywhere, at home or on the road.

Skins for Windows Media Player

With skins (See figure 7-2), you can change the look of Windows Media Player in a couple of clicks, as often as you like. Some skins just change the appearance of the Player with graphics and animations, while some also add new features. Skins are easy to download and install—and you can freely switch between different skins in the Player using the Skin chooser feature.

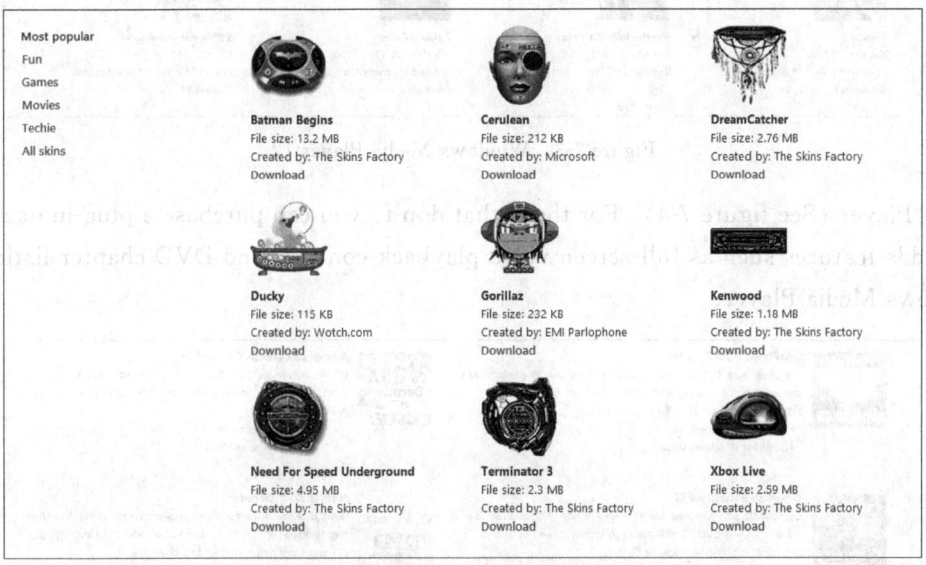

Figure 7-2 Windows Media Player 12

Note: Some skins are optimized for Windows Vista and Windows XP and might not have the same appearance when used in Windows 7, Windows 8.1, and Windows 10.

Visualizations for Windows Media Player

Visualizations (See figure 7-3) are colors, shapes, and patterns that move to the music in Windows Media Player Now Playing mode. The Player comes with a number of visualizations, and you can download more on this page.

Plug-ins and Add-ons for Windows Media Player

Plug-ins or add-ons add functionality—such as audio effects or DVD capability—to Windows Media Player. You can download plug-ins or add-ons for your version of the Player using the links below.

DVD Playback Plug-ins and Add-ons

Some editions of Windows include full-featured DVD playback capability in Windows

Figure 7-3　Windows Media Player 12

Media Player (See figure 7-4). For those that don't, you can purchase a plug-in or add-on that adds features such as full-screen video playback controls and DVD chapter listings to Windows Media Player.

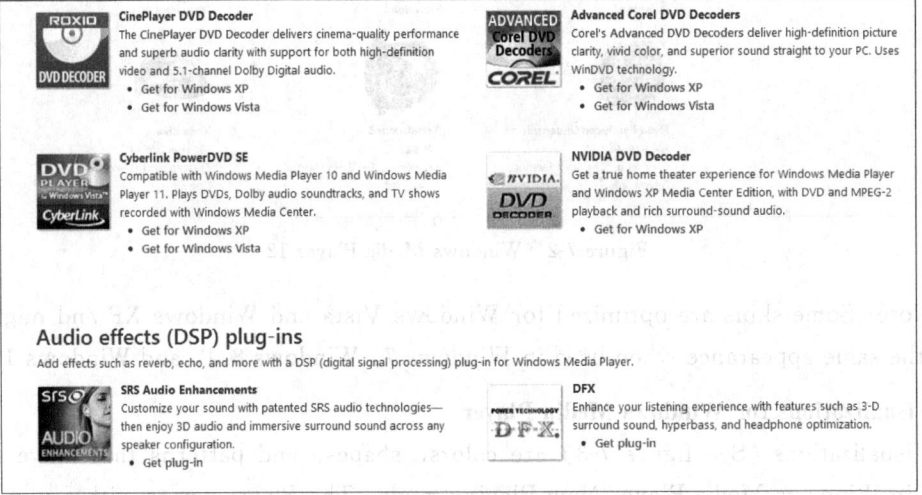

Figure 7-4　Windows Media Player 12

- **For Windows** 10. The Windows DVD Player App is available free for a limited time for people upgrading to Windows 10 from Windows 7 Home Premium, Windows 7 Professional, Windows 7 Ultimate, Windows 8, or Windows 8.1 with Windows Media Center.
- **For Windows** 8.1. If you're running Windows 8.1 or Windows 8.1 Pro, you can search for a DVD player App in the Windows Store (learn more about the

Windows Store).

- **For Windows** 7. Windows 7 Home Premium, Ultimate, and Enterprise come with DVD playback capability built in. Full DVD capability is not available on Windows 7 Home Basic or Starter.
- **For Windows XP or Windows Vista**. If you're running Windows XP, Windows Vista Home Basic, Windows Vista Business, or Windows Vista Enterprise, you can enhance your DVD playback experience by purchasing one of the DVD decoder packs listed below.

From: http://windows.microsoft.com/en-us/windows

New Words

Multimedia *n.* 多媒体；*adj.* 多媒体的
Media *n.* 媒体；介质
Mode *n.* 方式；状况；时尚，风尚；调式
Download *v.* 将(程序、资料等)从大计算机系统输入小计算机系统，下载
Install *vt.* 安装；安顿，安置；任命；使……正式就职
Visualization *n.* 形象(化)，形象化；想象；目测
Edition *n.* 版次，版本；(报纸、杂志的)一份；(广播、电视节目的)一期；(书、报、杂志等的)一版印刷总数
Upgrade *vt.* 提升；使(机器、计算机系统等)升级

Exercises

Translation

1. Windows Media Player 12—available as part of Windows 7, Windows 8.1, and Windows 10—plays more music and video than ever, including Flip Video and unprotected songs from your iTunes library!

2. Some skins just change the appearance of the Player with graphics and animations, while some also add new features. Skins are easy to download and install—and you can freely switch between different skins in the Player using the Skin chooser feature.

3. Visualizations are colors, shapes, and patterns that move to the music in Windows Media Player Now Playing mode.

Find other Media Players, can you compare their difference?

Reading the following interview, if you are interested in this software (See figure 7-5), you can learn how to use it.

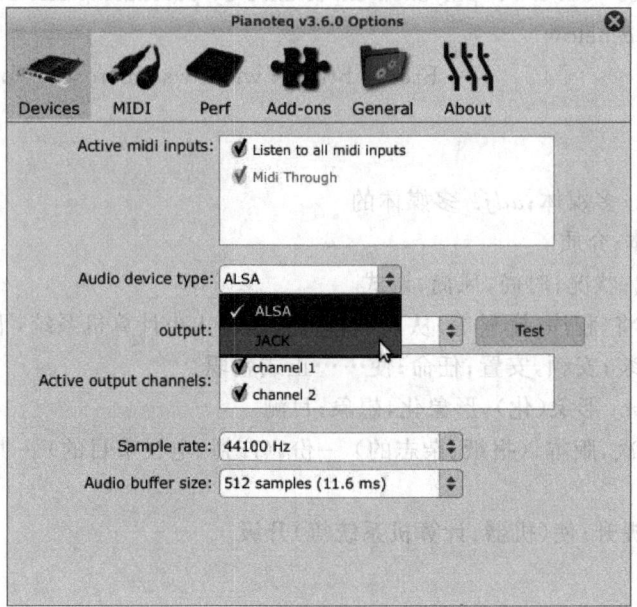

Figure 7-5 Pianoteq

In Use

Initially, having so much power over sound could be overwhelming—looking at the number of parameters you can adjust in the real-time mathematical model. Aside from the presets (which themselves sound pretty terrific), how would you suggest someone go about beginning to explore the options? Is there a workflow that makes sense for approaching adjusting the sound?

Answer from Pianoteq:

Ed.: So I should have read the manual! Here's their advice:

If you need to adapt the piano sound you could for example try adjusting the hammer hardness to achieve a different brightness of the hammer strokes. Increasing unison width makes it a bit out of tune (resembling certain acoustic pianos). The new powerful sound recording feature lets you place up to 5 virtual microphones anywhere around the piano to achieve ultimate ambience and tone colour. The dynamics and velocity curve will most likely need to be adjusted to the keyboard used in a MIDI file performance.

Indeed, this commentary makes sense. Hammer hardness is something that could be adjusted in the maintenance of an actual piano. Since you listen to a software piano model as though it is amplified, adjusting mic placement (as on a number of piano software emulations) is a no-brainer. And dynamics and velocity curve are essential not only for MIDI files, but if your keyboard controller lacks these controls onboard.

From: createdigitalmusic.com

Author: Peter Kirn *Makers of Pianoteq Talk Piano Modeling, Developing for Linux*

Text B

Adobe Fast Facts

Adobe is changing the world through digital experiences. Our creative, marketing and document solutions empower everyone—from emerging artists to global brands—to bring digital creations to life and deliver them to the right person at the right moment for the best results.

A Culture of Exploration

We love to explore, tinker and mix things up to make things work better. You can see the results everywhere—in our award-winning research and hundreds of patents; our "innovation-in-a-box" program that's spawned new product offerings; and the employee check-ins that have inspired our people to do their best work (See figure 7-6).

Figure 7-6 A culture of exploration

Igniting Creativity in Young People

How are we enhancing education around the world? Through Project 1324, where youth create digital media to tell powerful stories for social change. Through programs that teach underrepresented youth how to code. And through a $300 million commitment to Title 1 secondary schools in the U.S. (See figure 7-7).

Accelerating Innovation Velocity

Adobe Kickbox is a proven, open source process that helps innovators define, refine, validate and evolve their ideas. "You can't really just pay people to innovate," says Mark

Figure 7-7 Igniting creativity in young people

Randall, vice president of innovation. "They have to get excited about solving a problem for a customer, and the company has to get behind that. (See figure 7-8)"

Figure 7-8 Accelerating innovation velocity

Driving Greater Diversity and Inclusion.

We're taking action to make Adobe an even better place to work (See figure 7-9).

Figure 7-9 Driving greater diversity and inclusion

Our Solutions

Document Cloud

Adobe Document Cloud enables people to manage critical documents at work, at home

and across mobile devices with an integrated set of services for creating, reviewing, approving, signing and tracking documents from anywhere. At the heart of Document Cloud is Adobe Acrobat DC, the world's best PDF solution, which offers a stunning, touch-enabled interface, powerful companion mobile Apps and e-signing capabilities.
- Over 150 million agreements have been processed with Adobe Document Cloud eSign Services.
- In 2015, over 50 billion PDFs were opened in Adobe products alone.
- There are up to 300,000 installs per day of Acrobat Reader, just from the three major App stores.
- A document signed, shared and stored in Document Cloud has a 91% smaller environmental footprint than it would printed on paper—and it costs 90% less.
- Acrobat, together with Reader, is one of the most widely distributed pieces of software, used on over a billion desktops and mobile devices worldwide.

Creative Cloud

Creative Cloud delivers the world's leading creative desktop tools, mobile Apps, and services like Adobe Stock images. It connects them seamlessly together with Adobe CreativeSync technology and CC Libraries, enabling users to work effortlessly across desktop and mobile devices for connected creative workflows. Featuring Apps such as Adobe Photoshop, InDesign and Illustrator, Creative Cloud helps people produce their best work—and the value of membership increases all the time through exclusive product and service offerings and feature updates.
- Over 90% of the world's creative professionals use Adobe Photoshop.
- Adobe has shipped thousands of new and enhanced features to members since Creative Cloud was introduced in 2012.
- Behance, Adobe's online creative community, has over 6 million members. Creatives worldwide use Behance to showcase work and find inspiration.

Marketing Cloud

Adobe Marketing Cloud empowers companies to use big data to effectively reach and engage customers with highly personalized marketing content across all digital touch points. Eight tightly integrated solutions offer marketers a complete set of technologies for analytics, web and App experience management, testing and targeting, advertising, video, audience management, social engagement and campaign orchestration.
- More than two-thirds of Fortune 50 companies use Marketing Cloud today, including 8 of the top 10 Internet retailers, all of the top 10 commercial banks and all of the top 10 media companies and top 10 auto manufacturers.
- 8 of the 10 largest agencies and 8 of the top 12 systems integrators have built their digital marketing practices around Marketing Cloud.
- In 2015, Marketing Cloud processed over 40 trillion transactions, including 1.5

- In 2015, Adobe predicted total online sales for Thanksgiving, Black Friday and Cyber Monday 2015 within 97% accuracy.

From: http://www.adobe.com

New Words

Adobe *n.* 奥多比公司
Digital *adj.* 数字的；数据的；手指的；指状的
Innovation *n.* 改革，创新；新观念；新发明；新设施
Accelerate *vt.* 促进；（使）加快
Engage *vi.* 从事；与…建立密切关系；衔接；紧密结合
Orchestration *n.* 管弦乐编曲，管弦乐作曲法
Manufacturer *n.* 制造商，制造厂；厂主

Exercises

Translation

1. Adobe is changing the world through digital experiences. Our creative, marketing and document solutions empower everyone—from emerging artists to global brands—to bring digital creations to life and deliver them to the right person at the right moment for the best results.

2. They have to get excited about solving a problem for a customer, and the company has to get behind that.

3. Adobe Document Cloud enables people to manage critical documents at work, at home and across mobile devices with an integrated set of services for creating, reviewing, approving, signing and tracking documents from anywhere.

4. Creative Cloud delivers the world's leading creative desktop tools, mobile Apps, and services like Adobe Stock images.

5. Adobe Marketing Cloud empowers companies to use big data to effectively reach and engage customers with highly personalized marketing content across all digital touch points.

Text C

Adobe Character Animator

Adobe Character Animator gives life to characters you create in Adobe Illustrator or Adobe Photoshop when you act out their movements in front of a webcam. Installed with Adobe After Effects CC 2015, Character Animator tracks your facial movements, lets you record dialogue or a voice performance, and enables you to trigger actions with your keyboard.

Step 1 of 6

Create multi-layered artwork for your character (See figure 7-10)

Figure 7-10　Step 1 of 6

In Photoshop, open freda.psd and take a look at the Layers panel. Each component of the character artwork is placed on a separate layer. If you name the layers to indicate which body part they correspond to (chest, head, eyes, mouth), you can immediately control the character in Adobe Character Animator.

Note: If you'd like to use your own artwork, draw or copy your artwork into the corresponding layers of the freda.psd file, and save.

Step 2 of 6

Create a puppet from your artwork (See figure 7-11)

Figure 7-11　Step 2 of 6

In Adobe Character Animator, choose File > Import and select freda.psd to create a puppet. Select freda in the Project panel and click the Add to New Scene button. The puppet is automatically opened in the Scene panel and selected in the Timeline panel.

Step 3 of 6

Get to know your puppet (See figure 7-12)

Figure 7-12   Step 3 of 6

Character Animator captures your facial expressions from your webcam and animates the puppet based on your performance. Position your face in the circular area of the Camera & Microphone panel. Look directly at your puppet while keeping your facial expression neutral;then click Set Rest Pose. Red tracking dots will appear around your face. Try moving your head around and talk into your microphone. Use your mouse to drag near the character's limbs to manipulate them.

Step 4 of 6

Record and playback your puppet's performance (See figure 7-13)

Figure 7-13   Step 4 of 6

Click the Record button in the Scene panel and perform your character's movements. Click again to end the take. Toggle the various behaviors in the Properties panel off to record them separately from one another. This is useful if you prefer to record Face behaviors separately from Mouse Tracker or Lip Sync behaviors.

Play the animation by pressing the Spacebar.

Further refine to your puppet's behaviors; try changing the scale and other puppet properties, or add another puppet to the scene.

Step 5 of 6

Export your puppet sequence (See figure 7-14)

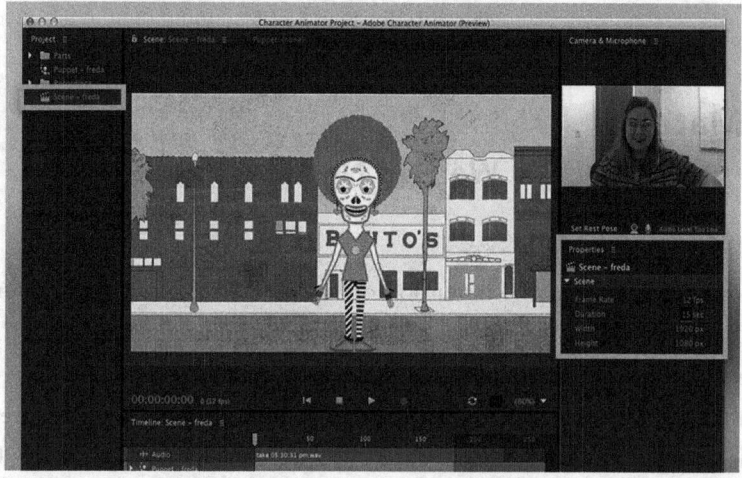

Figure 7-14 Step 5 of 6

When you are done with your animation, select the scene in the Project Panel and adjust the scene's duration in the Properties panel. Choose File > Export > Scene, and specify a name and location. Export the video as a PNG sequence and the audio as a WAV file to use in After Effects.

Launch Adobe After Effects and create a new composition. Choose File > Scripts and select New Comp from Character Animator Recording.jsx. Preview the composition to see the results. You can use the puppet in a composite. To do so, import a background from Adobe Stock or from a shared Creative Cloud Library.

Step 6 of 6

Make your final video (See figure 7-15)

Once you're ready for final output, open Adobe Media Encoder, add a source to the queue, select the output format, and render the final file.

From: http://www.adobe.com

Figure 7-15　Step 6 of 6

Reading Material

We Had No Idea

Abstract

Steve Sassons talks about the invention of the world's first digital camera.

Editor's Note: Steve Sasson, the inventor of the digital camera, will be inducted today into the Consumer Electronics Hall of Fame in San Diego, CA.

In December of 1975, after a year of piecing together a bunch of new technology in a back lab at the Elm grove Plant in Rochester, we were ready to try it. "It" being a rather odd-looking collection of digital circuits that we desperately tried to convince ourselves was a portable camera. It had a lens that we took from a used parts bin from the Super 8 movie camera production line downstairs from our little lab on the second floor in Bldg 4. On the side of our portable contraption, we shoehorned in a portable digital cassette instrumentation recorder. Add to that 16 nickel cadmium batteries, a highly temperamental new type of CCD imaging area array, an A/D converter implementation stolen from a digital voltmeter application, several dozen digital and analog circuits all wired together on approximately half a dozen circuit boards, and you have our interpretation of what a portable all electronic still camera (See figure 7-16) might look like.

It was a camera that didn't use any film to capture still images—a camera that would capture images using a CCD imager and digitize the captured scene and store the digital info on a standard cassette. It took 23 seconds to record the digitized image to the cassette. The image was viewed by removing the cassette from the camera and placing it in a custom playback device. This playback device incorporated a cassette reader and a specially built frame store. This custom frame store received the data from the tape, interpolated the 100 captured lines to 400 lines, and generated a standard NTSC video signal, which was then sent to a television set.

Chapter 3 Technical Elements

Figure 7-16 Vintage 1975 portable all electronic still camera

There you have it. No film required to capture and no printing required to view your snapshots. That's what we demonstrated to many internal Kodak audiences throughout 1976. In what has got to be one of the most insensitive choices of demonstration titles ever, we called it "Film-less Photography". Talk about warming up your audience!

After taking a few pictures of the attendees at the meeting and displaying them on the TV set in the room, the questions started coming. Why would anyone ever want to view his or her pictures on a TV? How would you store these images? What does an electronic photo album look like? When would this type of approach be available to the consumer? Although we attempted to address the last question by applying Moore's law to our architecture (15 to 20 years to reach the consumer), we had no idea how to answer these or the many other challenges that were suggested by this approach. An internal report was written and a patent was granted on this concept in 1978 (U.S. 4,131,919). I kept the prototype camera with me as I moved throughout the company over the last 30 years, mostly as a personal reminder of this most fun project. Outside of the patent, there was no public disclosure of our work until 2001.

The "we" in this narrative was largely the people of the Kodak Apparatus Division Research Laboratory in the mid 1970s and, in particular, several enormously talented technicians—Rick Osiecki, Bob DeYager and Jim Schueckler. All were key to building the camera and playback system (See figure 7-17). I especially remember working with Jim for many hours in the lab bringing this concept to life. Finally, I remember my visionary supervisor, the late Gareth Lloyd, who supported this concept and helped enormously in its presentation to our internal world at Kodak. In thinking back on it, one could not have had a better environment in which to "be crazy."

Many developments have happened between this early work and today. Personal computers, the Internet, wide bandwidth connections and personal desktop photographic printing are just a few of these. It is funny now to look back on this project and realize that we were not really thinking of this as the world's first digital camera. We were looking at

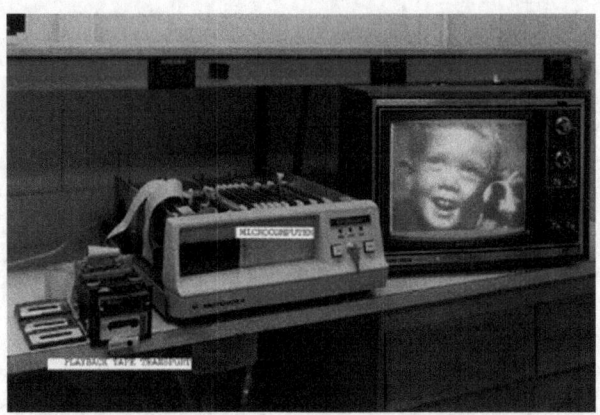

Figure 7-17　The playback device and TV

it as a distant possibility. Maybe a line from the technical report written at the time sums it up best:

"The camera described in this report represents a first attempt demonstrating a photographic system which may, with improvements in technology, substantially impact the way pictures will be taken in the future."

But in reality, we had no idea…

From: pluggedin.kodak.com
Author: Steve Sasson

UNIT 8

Computer Graphics

COMPETENCIES

After you have read this unit, you should be able to:
1. Discuss what is Computer graphics.
2. Discuss what is fractal.
3. Learn other fractal graphics.

Text A

Apple's First Macintosh Turns 25

MSN UK's technology editor Jane Douglas, who also turned 25 this year, pits her PC against an early Mac.

The Macintosh—the first Apple computer to bear the name—turns 25 on 24 January.

The machine debuted in 1984 and kicked off a product line that were Apple's flagship computers for many years.

The Macintosh (See figure 8-1) helped popularise the combination of graphical interface and mouse that is ubiquitous today.

The machine was unveiled using a hugely expensive TV advert, directed by film maker Ridley Scott and shown during the U.S. Super bowl on 22 January 1984.

Desktop Pioneer

The project to create the Macintosh was started by legendary computer maker Jef Raskin and the original machine had a 9in screen in an upright beige case, 128KB of RAM, internal floppy drive, and came with keyboard and single-button mouse.

Figure 8-1 Macintosh

Apple had previously produced computers using a graphical user interface (GUI), such as the Apple Lisa. But those machines cost far more than the original Macintosh.

Although Microsoft had launched its operating system—MS DOS—in 1981 it was not until 1985, a year after the Macintosh made its debut, that it introduced its own GUI, Microsoft Windows. However, this did not enjoy significant popularity until the advent of Windows 3.x (See figure 8-2) in 1990.

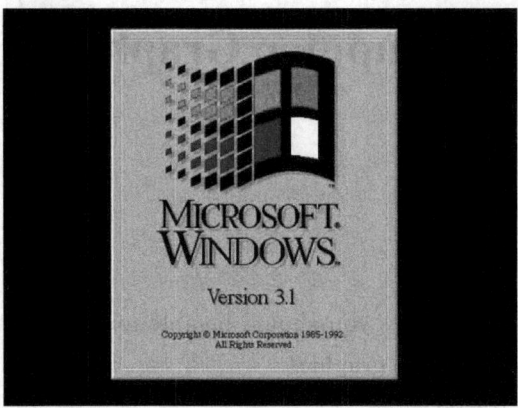

Figure 8-2　Windows 3.x

The Macintosh's relatively low price tag of £1,840 ($2,495) made it very affordable, said Mark Hattersley, editor in chief of Macworld UK.

"It was a hugely popular machine," said Mr. Hattersley.

"It took desktop computing away from IBM and back to Apple for a good number of years," he said. "It brought the notion of the desktop graphical interface to the mass market."

The "Macintosh" moniker was reportedly taken from the name of Mr. Raskin's favourite Apple-the McIntosh.

However, this form of the name had to be altered to avoid legal wrangles with another company already trading under that name.

Once successors to the first Macintosh were introduced by Apple, the original machine was re-badged as the 128KB version.

The initial production run of the first Macintosh have the signatures of the design team burned in to the inside of the case.

In the UK, science-fiction author Douglas Adams was the first to buy one of the original Macintosh machines. Second in line was Stephen Fry.

Sadly, he said, he no longer possesses the early machine.

He told the BBC: "Oh I wish I still had it. I remember giving it away in 1986 to a primary school in a village in Norfolk."

Apple has retained the Macintosh name for many of its products—in particular the shortened form re-emerged in 1998 (See figure 8-3) with the launch of the iMac.

Jason Fitzpatrick, from the Centre for Computing History in Haverhill, said that it was now hard to find a working 25-year old Macintosh.

Many, he said, have suffered what is known as "bit rot" in which the memory chips

Figure 8-3 The Macintosh name re-appeared with the iMac in 1998

inside the machine decay, leading to a gradual loss of functionality.

Kevin Murrell, director of the National Museum of Computing at Bletchley Park, said it had many working Apple machines even older than the 25-year-old Mac.

Swap Shop

Even new, he said, the Macintoshes had their quirks. The external hard drive available for later versions of the Macintosh had to be placed on the left side of the machine to avoid interference with its power supply.

The lack of hard drive meant that anyone working with the machine had save everything on a floppy disk, leading to an awful lot of disk swapping.

But despite this, he said, many people had very fond memories of the time they spent with an original Macintosh.

From: http://news.bbc.co.uk/2/hi/technology

New Words

Graphics *n*. [测] 制图学；制图法；图表算法
Macintosh *n*. 麦金塔计算机
Windows 3.x 微软公司的 Windows 系列操作平台
Flagship *n*. 旗舰
Graphical *adj*. 绘成图画似的，绘画的
GUI (Graphical User Interface) 图形用户界面
Interface *n*. 界面；<计>接口；交界面
Moniker *n*. 名字，绰号

Exercise

Translation

1. The project to create the Macintosh was started by legendary computer maker Jef Raskin and the original machine had a 9in screen in an upright beige case, 128KB of RAM, internal floppy drive, and came with keyboard and single-button mouse.

2. Although Microsoft had launched its operating system—MS DOS—in 1981 it was

not until 1985, a year after the Macintosh made its debut, that it introduced its own GUI, Microsoft Windows.

3. Apple has retained the Macintosh name for many of its products—in particular the shortened form re-emerged in 1998 with the launch of the iMac.

Text B
How Mandelbrot's Fractals Changed the World

What are fractals?
- Geometrical objects that are self-similar when the distance at which they are viewed is changed.
- Concept is helpful in allowing order to be perceived in apparent disorder.
- E. g., in the case of a river and its tributaries, every tributary has its own tributaries…
- …so that it has the same structure organisation as the entire river except that it covers a smaller area.

Source: *McGraw-Hill Concise Encyclopedia of Science and Technology*.

What is a Mandelbrot set?

The most famous computer-generated fractal is called the Mandelbrot set (See figure 8-4) —a swirling, feathery, seemingly organic landscape that is reminiscent of the natural world, but is nonetheless completely virtual. It is infinitely complex, but it is built from an extremely simple equation repeated endlessly. In the same way, natural fractal forms really are built up by simple rules—ultimately, the interactions between atoms.

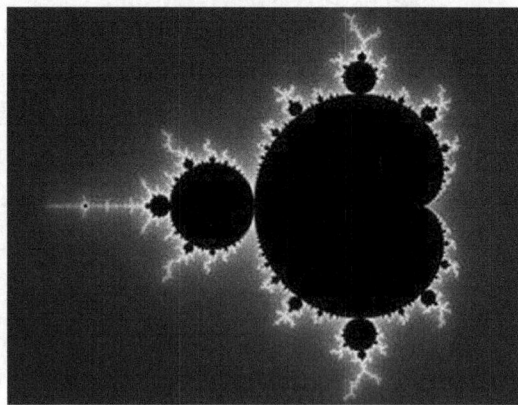

Figure 8-4   Mandelbrot set

In 1975, a new word came into use, when a maverick mathematician made an important discovery. So what are fractals? And why are they important?

During the 1980s, people became familiar with fractals through those weird, colourful patterns made by computers.

But few realise how the idea of fractals has revolutionised our understanding of the world, and how many fractal-based systems we depend upon.

On 14 October 2010, the genius who coined the word—Polish—born mathematician Benoit Mandelbrot (See figure 8-5)—died, aged 85, from cancer.

Unfortunately, there is no definition of fractals that is both simple and accurate. Like so many things in modern science and mathematics, discussions of "fractal geometry" can quickly go over the heads of the non-mathematically-minded. This is a real shame, because there is profound beauty and power in the idea of fractals (See figure 8-6).

Figure 8-5　Benoit B. Mandelbrot　　　　Figure 8-6　The fractal geometry of nature

The best way to get a feeling for what fractals are is to consider some examples. Clouds, mountains, coastlines, cauliflowers and ferns are all natural fractals. These shapes have something in common—something intuitive, accessible and aesthetic.

They are all complicated and irregular: the sort of shape that mathematicians used to shy away from in favour of regular ones, like spheres, which they could tame with equations.

Mandelbrot famously wrote: "Clouds are not spheres, mountains are not cones, coastlines are not circles, and bark is not smooth, nor does lightning travel in a straight line."

The chaos and irregularity of the world—Mandelbrot referred to it as "roughness"—is something to be celebrated. It would be a shame if clouds really were spheres, and mountains cones.

Look closely at a fractal, and you will find that the complexity is still present at a smaller scale. A small cloud is strikingly similar to the whole thing. A pine tree is composed of branches that are composed of branches—which in turn are composed of branches.

A tiny sand dune or a puddle in a mountain track have the same shapes as a huge sand dune and a lake in a mountain gully. This "self-similarity" at different scales is a defining characteristic of fractals.

The fractal mathematics Mandelbrot pioneered, together with the related field of chaos theory, lifts the veil on the hidden beauty of the world. It inspired scientists in many disciplines—including cosmology, medicine, engineering and genetics—and artists and musicians, too.

The whole universe is fractal, and so there is something joyfully quintessential about Mandelbrot's insights.

Fractal mathematics has many practical uses, too—for example, in producing stunning and realistic computer graphics, in computer file compression systems, in the architecture of the networks that make up the Internet and even in diagnosing some diseases.

Fractal geometry can also provide a way to understand complexity in "systems" as well as just in shapes. The timing and sizes of earthquakes and the variation in a person's heartbeat and the prevalence of diseases are just three cases in which fractal geometry can describe the unpredictable.

Another is in the financial markets, where Mandelbrot first gained insight into the mathematics of complexity while working as a researcher for IBM during the 1960s.

Mandelbrot tried using fractal mathematics to describe the market—in terms of profits and losses traders made over time, and found it worked well.

In 2005, Mandelbrot turned again to the mathematics of the financial market, warning in his book The (Mis)Behaviour of Markets against the huge risks being taken by traders—who, he claimed, tend to act as if the market is inherently predictable, and immune to large swings.

Fractal mathematics cannot be used to predict the big events in chaotic systems—but it can tell us that such events will happen.

As such, it reminds us that the world is complex—and delightfully unpredictable.

From: http://www.bbc.com/news
Author: Jack Challoner, 18 October 2010

New Words

Mandelbrot [名] 曼德尔布罗特：他创造了"分形"这个名词，并且描述了曼德布洛特集合

Mandelbrot set 曼德布洛特集合

Fractal *n.* （经典几何学中没有表示的）不规则碎片形；分形

Geometrical *adj*. 几何的，几何学的；几何图案的；呈几何级数增加的
Geometry *n*. 几何学；几何形状；几何图形；几何学著作
Irregular *adj*. 不规则的，不对称的；无规律的
Chaos *n*. 混乱，紊乱

Exercise

Translation

1. The most famous computer-generated fractal is called the Mandelbrot set—a swirling, feathery, seemingly organic landscape that is reminiscent of the natural world, but is nonetheless completely virtual.

2. Clouds, mountains, coastlines, cauliflowers and ferns are all natural fractals. These shapes have something in common—something intuitive, accessible and aesthetic.

3. Mandelbrot famously wrote: "Clouds are not spheres, mountains are not cones, coastlines are not circles, and bark is not smooth, nor does lightning travel in a straight line."

4. He fractal mathematics Mandelbrot pioneered, together with the related field of chaos theory, lifts the veil on the hidden beauty of the world.

5. Fractal mathematics cannot be used to predict the big events in chaotic systems—but it can tell us that such events will happen.

Definitions

Fractal

_____
_____
_____
_____

Mandelbrot set

_____
_____
_____
_____

Reading Material
Listening to Geometry

A British composer has produced what has been called the "theme tune of the Universe"—a piece of music composed by mother nature herself. Our science editor Dr David Whitehouse reports:

There is something instantly recognisable in Phil Thompson's music, which is surprising as it has come straight from mathematics.

He has taken images of fractals and translated them into music.

Fractals are geometric shapes that look the same under any level of magnification. A small section of a fractal image is a copy of the whole image.

"When I first heard it, I was slightly scared," said Mr. Thompson. "What was coming out of the loudspeakers was not noise, it was recognisable music."

Mathematical experts are impressed. Ian Stewart, Professor of Mathematics at Warwick University, said: "What amazes me with this kind of music is that it sounds much better than you would expect."

"Music has a certain structure, which our minds seem to like. You need theme and variation. By coincidence, or perhaps not, the mathematics of fractals is just like that."

With his work on fractals in the 1970s, mathematician Benoit Mandelbrot created a new branch of science and a new scientific icon for our age.

The strangely psychedelic images of fractals, one version of which bears his name, have become a symbol of the profound mystery of numbers and the strangeness of order emerging from chaos.

Fractals are everywhere. Most of the objects we encounter in our daily lives are fractal.

A mountain and its rocks are fractal, each rock when magnified looks like a tiny mountain. Such structures within structure are the hallmark of fractals.

Clouds are not spheres but fractals, coastlines are not smooth but fractal.

They are to be found in the timing of our heartbeats and the falling of a snowflake. Even the distribution of galaxies throughout space is fractal.

The Mandelbrot set does not just produce beautiful pictures, it has also produced a new branch of music. A number of composers have shown interest in the musical application of fractals.

Phil Thompson has turned the Mandelbrot set into a composition he has called "A Season in Hell".

There has always been some mathematics in music. Bach in his Toccata and Fugue in E Minor moves a trio of notes up and down on the staff in such a symmetrical way that you could take one trio of notes and lay it perfectly over another.

But fractal music is different, some say it touches something deeper within us than note symmetries on the page.

Throughout our evolution we have been surrounded by fractals in the form of the noise of a waterfall, the rustle of undergrowth and the sounds of our own bodies.

Because of this, some scientists say we react to them at a deep level. Perhaps that explains the sense of recognition we feel when we listen to fractal music?

From: http://news.bbc.co.uk/2/hi/science/nature

Reading Material
The Backbone of Fractals: Feedback and the Iterator

The scientist does not study nature because it is useful; he studies it because he delights in it, and he delights in it because it is beautiful. If nature were not beautiful, it would not be worth knowing, and if nature were not worth knowing, life would not be worth living.

Henri Poincaré

Fractals and Dynamic Processes

When we think about fractals as images, forms or structures we usually perceive them as static objects. This is a legitimate initial standpoint in many cases, as for example if we deal with natural structures like the ones in figures 8-7 and 8-8.

Figure 8-7   California oak tree photograph by Michael McGuire

Figure 8-8   Fern this fern is from K. Rasbach, Die Farnpflanzen Zentraleuropas, Verlag Gustav Fischer, Stuttgart, 1968

But this point of view tells us little about the evolution or generation of a given structure. Often, as for example in botany, we like to discuss more than just the complexity of a ripe plant. In fact, any geometric model of a plant which does not also incorporate its dynamic growth plan for the plant will not lead very far.

The same is true for mountains, whose geometry is a result of past tectonic activity as well as erosion processes which still and will forever shape what we see as a mountain. We can also say the same for the deposit of zinc in an electrolytic experiment.

In other words, to talk about fractals while ignoring the dynamic processes which created them would be inadequate. But in accepting this point of view we seem to enter very difficult waters. What are these processes and what is the common mathematical thread in them? Aren't we proposing that the complexity of forms which we see in nature is a result of equally complicated processes? This is true in many cases, but at the same time the long-standing paradigm "Complexity of structure is a result of complicated interwoven processes" is far from being true in general. Rather, it seems—and this is one of the major surprising impacts of fractal geometry and chaos theory—that in the presence of a complex pattern there is a good chance that a very simple process is responsible for it. In other words, the simplicity of a process should not mislead us into concluding that it will be easy to understand its consequences.

From: *Chaos and Fractals* (See figure 8-9)

Author: Heinz-Otto Peitgen, Hartmut Jürgens and Dietmar Saupe

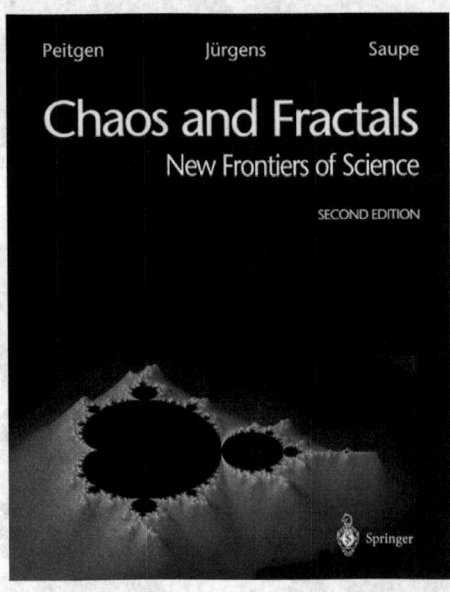

Figure 8-9　Chaos and Fractals

Chapter 4

Professional Outlook

UNIT 9

Virtual Reality

COMPETENCIES

After you have read this unit, you should be able to:
1. Discuss what is Virtual Reality.
2. Find the Virtual Reality in your life.

Text A

Building a Digital Museum

Building a digital museum (See figure 9-1).

Figure 9-1 Building a digital museum

Buried in dark vaults, cellars, and musty store rooms all over the UK are thousands, perhaps millions of historical and cultural gems.

Ancient documents and books, archaeological records and finds, old photographs and drawings; all of them consigned to years in storage because there simply isn't anywhere to show them to the public.

Combined, they represent the heritage and culture of the nation, and are of incalculable value.

Efforts have now started to take some of this heritage—fragments of fascinating data—and digitise them for posting on the Internet.

On the Internet, there is no need to limit the exhibition space (See figure 9-2). Putting the nation's cultural heritage on the web means that the information it contains will suddenly be made available to millions of people.

Years of Work

The New Opportunities Fund (NOF) is one of the bodies set up to dish out Lottery money to worthy causes.

Its NOF-Digitise is one such cause, designed to open up access to millions of historically important documents which would otherwise be rarely seen by human eyes.

It's an ambitious project which will take several years to complete, although the first batch of digitised information should be ready before the end of this year.

Digitised information will be categorised into three broad content areas (See figure 9-3):

Figure 9-2   Space is at a premium in museums

Figure 9-3   Computers themselves are becoming museum pieces

- Cultural enrichment: information that reflects the heritage of a community, region or country, including fine or performing arts, design or media.
- Citizenship in a modern state: information that helps people to access services, including information on their rights and obligations in society.
- Re-skilling the nation: helping people to enhance basic literacy skills, and understanding of other information such as science, health and IT.

"The intention was to build a library of freely-available learning materials across our three themes," says Chris Anderson, NOF's head of programmers.

"Our primary function is to provide access to material that people would otherwise rarely see, not to preserve it."

"But it's true that one outcome of the project will be to preserve, in digital format, some delicate documents that might not otherwise survive in the long term."

"The project materials are intended for use on the Internet but that does not mean that they won't be used elsewhere, such as on CD-ROMs or in-situ digital displays in museums."

In total, the organisers expect to generate more than a million different content items, such as texts or images. There will also be 400 specially-designed "learning journeys" to help people find their way through all the information (See figure 9-4).

Searchable Feature

To make sense of it all, NOF will build an Internet portal, much like many of the existing web search engines. It will offer searchable access to all the digitised documents.

The portal will not be ready for some time yet, but it is already possible to search the NOF-Digitise site to find out more about the organisations taking part.

Putting the entire project on the net should provide some protection from the perils of advancing technology.

It emerged recently that all the information gathered for the 15-year-old BBC Domes day Project was no longer accessible, because the technology for reading the 12-inch video discs (See figure 9-5) it was stored on had become obsolete.

Figure 9-4   Space is not a problem with computers

Figure 9-5   Laser disc technology is now outdated

Plans have already been drawn up to try to prevent a repetition of that problem.

Setting Standards

"We were aware of the Domes day video disc saga when we were planning the project", says Mr. Anderson.

"In order to future-proof the material as far as possible, we have established a set of technical standards based on advice from experts."

The standards focus on two main areas.

"We will use open standards so that nothing we produce will be dependent on specific technology, or installed proprietary software or plug-ins."

"Also, we'll ensure that the standards used offer maximum potential for migrating all the digital material to new and developing Internet technologies as they emerge."

While the web pages themselves may get out-dated, the original digital archives—the millions of photos, scans and e-texts—will be digitised to a high standard to make sure they can be re-used, or presented with new web technologies, in the future.

From: http://news.bbc.co.uk/2/hi/uk_news

New Words

Virtual Reality *n.* 虚拟现实
Archaeological *adj.* 考古学的，考古学上的
Digitise *v.* 将资料数字化
Incalculable *adj.* 不可估量的；数不清的；极大的；不可预料的
Internet *n.* 互联网
Categorise *vt.* 把…归类，把…分门别类
CD-ROMs *n.* 只读存储器，只读光盘（CD-ROM 的名词复数）
Maximum *adj.* 最大值的，最大量的；*n.* 最大的量、体积、强度等

Exercises

Translation

1. On the Internet, there is no need to limit the exhibition space. Putting the nation's cultural heritage on the web means that the information it contains will suddenly be made available to millions of people.

2. Citizenship in a modern state: information that helps people to access services, including information on their rights and obligations in society.

3. We will use open standards so that nothing we produce will be dependent on specific technology, or installed proprietary software or plug-ins.

Have you ever visited the museum on the Internet? Talk about your experience.

_____
_____
_____
_____
_____

Text B
5 Ways Virtual Reality Will Change Education

Education and technology are interconnected. This synergy is able to transform the world we live in. The contradictory phenomenon is that while being an early adopter of technology, education is also one of the last sectors to be fully transformed by it, due to institutional inertia and a number of other reasons.

Education hasn't changed for years in terms of teaching approaches and techniques applied. Although we are seeing some innovative variability in this area. Today millennial feel pretty comfortable with online education, doing research on the Internet, resorting to instructional videos on YouTube and distance learning powered by video technology. Obviously, virtual reality is next.

Some virtual reality projects used both in schools and higher educational institutions are already under way (See figure 9-6).

Figure 9-6 5 Ways virtual reality will change education

We've covered before a story about the students in Ireland who recreated a historic place in OpenSim and explored it with an Oculus Rift headset. The project was made possible with the help of MissionV—a platform, that provides Irish schools' students with tools to build virtual learning environments.

"We are getting ready to take the next step by supporting schools that will invest in head-mounted displays like the Oculus Rift", James Corbett, the managing director of MissionV, told Hypergrid Business. "We are in no doubt now that virtual reality will become an ever more important part of education."

The Medical Virtual Reality group at the University of Southern California Institute for Creative Technologies studies use cases of virtual reality simulation technology for clinical purposes.

Virtual reality is also used for training purposes in the military, which includes flight and battlefield simulations, medical training under battlefield conditions, virtual boot camp and more.

If the future for education is going to involve virtual space, how exactly can virtual reality technology make an impact on the learning process?

1. Collaboration in Virtual Reality Classroom Fosters Social Integration of Learners

Dr. Conor Galvin at the University College Dublin School of Education and Lifelong Learning evaluated the MissionV Schools Pilot Programme, which involved 20 primary schools. In his report Dr. Conor Galvin gives examples of how the virtual reality technology managed to tackle students' social issues.

He says, the students struggling to become part of the class group, were able to become accepted by their peers because of their technology skills. Owing to MissionV, shy students "come out of their shells" and the kids, previously lacking in confidence in their math skills, became self-assured technology experts.

"Additional evidence which wasn't published to the site, pointed to especially positive outcomes for individual children from ethnic minorities, or with learning difficulties, or experiencing problems at home", said MissionV's Corbett. "In fact, we heard some particularly heartwarming stories in that regard."

Virtual reality technology is apt to students with different needs and learning styles, according to the teachers at pilot schools. Also it gives a lot of opportunities for group work and peer teaching.

2. Not Possible in Reality Is Possible in Virtual Reality

"The pedagogies of constructivism and game-based learning show that children learn best by doing or by being", said Corbett. "So they shouldn't just read about history—they should 'be' historians. They shouldn't just study archaeology—they should 'be' archaeologists."

The ability to introduce practical knowledge to the classroom without actually leaving it, makes educational experience invaluable. Rather than listening to lectures, students can put words underneath a headset and get a real experience but in a virtual wrapper.

"My current project involves safety on a building site", said virtual education expert Inge Knudsen.

"I have created a virtual building site with many safety issues", she added. "Students can walk around in the virtual environment and take pictures of places that are not safe. This is a case that is not possible in real life and therefore highly suited for virtual worlds."

Virtual immersive environment lets students experience any sphere of professional and life application yet at the learning stage.

3. Virtual Game-based Experience Increases Students' Motivation

"Motivation and engagement are key factors of game-based learning, and virtual reality takes those to the next level", said MissionV's Corbett.

Thinking about the very purpose of education, it is basically a key to self-knowledge, a tool to get a job and also an experience that should better be positive and engaging, given the years people spend on it.

"In my own experience game-based learning is motivating because it is fun", Jane Wilde, an instructor at Marlboro College and an expert in using games and simulations for learning, told Hypergrid Business.

Educators use games as a matter of daily practice. Even though virtual reality games are not the only source of fun and engagement in class, they can make a substantial difference.

"Conducting game-based learning experiences in a virtual environment is enhanced by the following factors", said Wilde. "The player is immersed in the game world—an 'authentic context' for the activities. The playing field is leveled—a player's gender, weight, race don't have to interfere with their acceptance by other players. You are judged by your actions. A lot can be accomplished in a virtual environment that would not be possible in real life. Also it is memorable-the visual and kinesthetic experiences in virtual worlds contribute to our ability to learn."

"There are many educational games that lack the motivational features I have listed", added Wilde.

Students need inspiration and encouragement to keep exploring the potential of education for their own capabilities. Engagement that virtual reality can produce will eventually veer students' desire for exploration more toward intellect and away from play.

4. Virtual Reality Introduces New Approach to Rewards

Assessment of academic achievements and students' progress reports has been used in education for centuries. However, virtual reality is going to transform the traditional concept of incentives in the learning process.

"Success is acknowledged", said Wilde. "There are rewards for achievements. Failures are generally ignored. This is the opposite of much education—where success is neutral and failure is punished."

This kind of rewards engages the brain and keep learners questing for more. Emotional reward cannot be ignored either. It makes a huge impact on students' desire to study. Though there is always a risk of discouragement, let alone competition.

"It isn't easy", told Wilde. "There are challenges that can't be accomplished on the first try. There is increasing complexity. Taking risks and trying other ways are good strategies."

Students' rewards for the challenges virtual reality provides, are both individual and collective.

"Players need to work together and benefit for different skills, specializations of their team members. Everyone on the team is important", said Wilde.

5. Virtual Platforms and Headsets Are the New Tools For Inspiring Creative Learning

Virtual reality technology creates the world of imagination, which is capable of breaking the boundaries in traditional education. However, its adoption requires not only time and effort, but thoroughly elaborated methods to adjust the technology for the learning purposes.

"I'm actually slightly cynical about using virtual reality in education, in that I think people often get too excited at gadgets instead of thinking fully about what a great educational experience looks like", Tom Chatfield, an author of a number of books on digital culture and a gaming theorist, whose appearances include TED Global, told Hypergrid Business. "For me, perhaps the most exciting thing that could come of this type of technology is students themselves getting excited about, and using it to create things—and learn via the act of creating."

OpenSim virtual platform and the secure working environment it helps create seems to be a perfect choice to empower students' creativity. Educators are already using OpenSim to build historic recreations. But there are other options on the virtual bookshelf as well.

"One of the greatest tech tools for inspiring creative learning in recent years has been the game Minecraft, which is extraordinarily basic in its graphical appearance", said Chatfield. "What it offers as a tool for creating worlds and experimenting with some of the ideas underpinning logic and programming that make it exciting—together with the incredible community of users and their creations."

"I would love to see this kind of creativity combined with new tech like headsets, and people in education systems building and collaborating through them," added Chatfield.

Minecraft doesn't officially support Oculus Rift yet, but attempts to build a Minecraft virtual reality mod, called Minecrift. The beta version is already available for experiencing, though can only be run on an Oculus Rift Development Kit 1.

"I think the Oculus Rift has tremendous potential in any 3D platform that is built to accept it," said Wilde of Marlboro College. "I anticipate that it, or something like it, will become as ubiquitous as a mouse or game controller. I see both questing platforms like World of Warcraft and constructive platforms like Second Life and Minecraft being enhanced by the Oculus Rift."

"The world of reality has its limits; the world of imagination is boundless," said Jean-Jacques Rousseau, speaking in the 18th century.

Now, as we have the device for letting imagination into the real world called Oculus Rift, let's hope it will open new endless possibilities in our century.

From: http://www.hypergridbusiness.com
Author: Kate Abrosimova

New Words

Clinical *adj.* 临床的;诊所的;冷静的;简陋的
Integration *n.* 整合;一体化;结合
Pedagogy *n.* 教育学,教学法
Constructivism *n.* 构成主义,构成派
Archaeology *n.* 考古学;古物;古迹
Motivation *n.* 动机;动力;诱因
Strategy *n.* 策略,战略;战略学
3D (three dimensional) 三维

Exercises

Translation

1. Virtual reality is also used for training purposes in the military, which includes

flight and battlefield simulations, medical training under battlefield conditions, virtual boot camp and more.

2. Virtual reality technology is apt to students with different needs and learning styles, according to the teachers at pilot schools. Also it gives a lot of opportunities for group work and peer teaching.

3. The ability to introduce practical knowledge to the classroom without actually leaving it, makes educational experience invaluable. Rather than listening to lectures, students can put words underneath a headset and get a real experience but in a virtual wrapper.

4. A lot can be accomplished in a virtual environment that would not be possible in real life. Also it is memorable—the visual and kinesthetic experiences in virtual worlds contribute to our ability to learn.

5. Virtual reality technology creates the world of imagination, which is capable of breaking the boundaries in traditional education. However, its adoption requires not only time and effort, but thoroughly elaborated methods to adjust the technology for the learning purposes.

Can you talk about virtual reality changes your education?

_____

_____

_____

_____

Text C
Don't Compare Virtual Reality to the Smartphone

"Over the next 10 years, virtual reality will become ubiquitous, affordable, and transformative."

This was the justification for Facebook's massive purchase of Oculus, makers of the Rift virtual reality headset. While Facebook is still working diligently on mobile applications, CEO Mark Zuckerberg went so far as to hint that the acquisition places the company on the cutting edge for the next pervasive platform: virtual reality.

Unfortunately, Zuckerberg's "platform" reference has elicited many comparisons of Oculus to Google's purchase of Android, the company that would provide Google with its own Smartphone operating system. While Virtual Reality may one day be pervasive, the disruption of VR is nothing like disruption of mobility. And the strategists everywhere, who invest corporate capital in acquisitions, would do well to know why.

Disruption is an explanation of how small nimble companies unseat industry giants—but it is simultaneously a story of market expansion and the provision of ever cheaper and more accessible goods and services. The theory of disruption explains why incumbent businesses—with high fixed cost infrastructures and embedded beliefs about what the market wants—fail to adopt business models that lower the cost of their services and drive product accessibility to entirely new sets of users. For instance, when Henry Ford disrupted the automotive world by building a company that used process assembly at scale to drive down cost, he abandoned the industry held belief that variety was important. Others, with expectations that people needed variety, refused to play Ford's scale game (or failed trying). When Legalzoom decided to attack the overpriced industry of law, they used software systems to automate the provisioning of legal documents. The company offered far less variety than actual lawyers, but was able to drive prices to a point that more people could consume those services.

While the Rift may prove transformative to the gaming or entertainment industries, its reach is narrower than Android. Virtual reality is not a disruption to the computing market, instead it stands poised to disrupt content consumption. That stands in contrast with Android and mobility which, by its very nature, made computing cheaper and more accessible to people everywhere. Smartphones offered the opportunity to extend the same disruptions related to process automation and software aided intelligence that was brought on by the PC revolution to billions of computing endpoints around the world. Mobility offered a chance to recreate the entire information technology industry, an industry far more expansive than entertainment and media—an industry that is foundational to every company's value chain across the globe.

Virtual reality is a way of experiencing the content within a computing platform. It's a new type of user interface that immerses its user fully in a software environment. VR may require similar dedicated visual hardware, but it is not synonymous with augmented reality (e.g., Google Glass) which overlays digital information on the physical world around us. Augmented reality further extends the reaches of the Internet, tagging physical objects with optical recognition. VR is insular. It relies on the computing power we already have to transport users to a digital world that is stored in the computing devices we already own. It doesn't push the reach of the microprocessor.

Certainly, if Oculus is successful, Facebook could end up owning the VR platform that everyone loves. It could find itself offering the platform that makes the experience of courtside basketball, front row theater, and summiting Everest available to users who couldn't have imagined consuming those experiences before. It has the potential to begin disrupting the travel and entertainment markets and become a pillar of the high-end gaming industry. Facebook could have a very lucrative investment in its hands.

But by its nature, Oculus depends upon the computing infrastructure that is already in the world. It is not a platform that makes the consumption of all types of information cheaper and more accessible. Its system is more expensive and higher performing than a Smartphone. VR might very well become a major platform for consuming content, but until we all decide to plug into the Matrix, the disruption of VR can't be equated to the disruption of mobile computing.

From: https://hbr.org
Author: Maxwell Wessel

New Words

Smartphone *n.* 智能手机
Justification *n.* 辩解；正当的理由；无过失
Diligently *adv.* 用心；孜孜不倦；勤勉地，勤奋地
Application 在 IT 术语中，application 表示某种技术、系统或者产品的应用。application 还是应用程序(application program)的缩写
Mobility *n.* 移动性；流动性；机动性
Infrastructure *n.* 基础设施；基础建设
Entertainment *n.* 娱乐节目；娱乐，消遣；招待，款待
Disrupt *vt.* 破坏；使中断；*adj.* 混乱的；瓦解的

Exercises

Translation

1. Virtual reality is not a disruption to the computing market, instead it stands poised to disrupt content consumption. That stands in contrast with Android and mobility which, by its very nature, made computing cheaper and more accessible to people everywhere.

2. Virtual reality is a way of experiencing the content within a computing platform. It's a new type of user interface that immerses its user fully in a software environment. VR may require similar dedicated visual hardware, but it is not synonymous with augmented reality (e.g., Google Glass) which overlays digital information on the physical world around us.

3. VR might very well become a major platform for consuming content, but until we all decide to plug into the Matrix, the disruption of VR can't be equated to the disruption of mobile computing.

Definitions

Virtual Reality

Reading Material
"China's Google" Baidu is Making Smart Glasses

Baidu (See figure 9-7) says its glasses feature facial recognition capabilities.

Figure 9-7   Baidu

A spokesman for the Chinese firm said the glasses would be able to search by using facial recognition.

Kaiser Kuo told Reuters that Baidu had not yet decided whether the glasses would be made commercially available.

"We experiment with every kind of technology that is related to search," Mr. Kuo said.

Like Google Glass, the Baidu glasses—reportedly known internally as Baidu Eye—consist of a small LCD screen attached to a slim headset.

A leaked image taken at Baidu's offices show a person wearing a headset matching the description—but Baidu would not confirm if it was Baidu Eye.

Some early reports had suggested that news of the technology was in fact an April Fool's joke—but while some reports on 1 April were embellished, there was truth behind the rumours.

Mr. Kuo said that the technology makes the most of Baidu's considerable expertise in facial recognition.

"What you are doing with your camera, for example, taking a picture of a celebrity and then checking on our database to see if we have a facial image match, you could do the same thing with a wearable visual device."

Google Glass is eagerly awaited by technology enthusiasts.

Such words are likely to alarm those worried about the capabilities of this type of technology.

Campaign group "Stop the Cyborgs" has called for limits on when the headsets can be used.

"We want people to actively set social and physical bounds around the use of technologies and not just fatalistically accept the direction technology is heading in," a campaigner told the BBC last month.

Meanwhile, in San Francisco—home of Google—a cafe has said it will ban customers from using Google Glass on its premises.

In response to worries, Google has said: "We are putting a lot of thought into how we design Glass because new technology always raises important new issues for society."

From: bbc.co.uk

UNIT 10

Augmented Reality

COMPETENCIES

After you have read this unit, you should be able to:
1. Discuss what is Augmented Reality.
2. Describe the Augmented Reality in your life.

Text A
7 Ways Augmented Reality Will Improve Your Life

You might think augmented reality is the way of the future, but really, it has its roots in the 20th century. Morton Heilig, the "Father of Virtual Reality," patented the Sensorama Stimulator, which he called an "experience theater," on August 28, 1962. Over time, the idea of using technology to create a layer over the real world has been honed and refined and put in our palms, thanks to the proliferation of smartphones.

Confused about what augmented reality is? In short, it's a way to use technology to redefine space, and it places a virtual layer over the world with geographic specificity ensuring a good fit. Check out the video below—in real life, the woman is holding what appears to be a simple box of LEGOs. But when seen through an AR viewer, the box comes to life, serving as a platform for a beautiful carousel. It's not that you're imagining things—AR (See figure 10-1) uses computer animation to bring objects to life.

Figure 10-1　Augmented Reality

While mainstream examples of AR have been, to date, on the fluffy side, the technology has promise as an urban utility. Trak Lord of Metaio, an AR company based in Germany, says his company is researching how augmented reality can be used in urban environments. Cities present a challenge to the technology, since buildings and shops are so close together and GPS isn't yet accurate enough to distinguish among them. But Metaio developed a proprietary algorithm that works with GPS, Continuous Visual Search (CVS) and Simultaneous Localization and Mapping (SLAM) to "snap" AR layers into place with impressive accuracy.

"It's not a futuristic, fringy thing," says Goldrun founder Vivian Rosenthal. "I think we're there."

Improvements to the technology mean more promise for AR—and 2.5 billion AR apps are expected to be downloaded by 2017. But if you're wondering how you'll actually use AR, we've outlined seven real ways in which you, city dwellers across the globe, might soon use this bleeding-edge technology. AR has great potential to transform our cities and the way we learn and discover within them.

1. **Urban Exploration**

In a new neighborhood or exploring another city? Ditch the Fodor's and grab an AR App that shows you what's nearby and where you should go. These AR Apps let you filter by category so you can find exactly what you're looking for, whether it's a coffee shop, restaurant or museum. And you won't need to worry about getting turned around by the map—the AR App will adapt based on what you're facing, so it'll tell you to turn right and get you to your destination, as opposed to just indicating that you should walk northeast (how are you supposed to know which way is northeast?). This kind of AR App already exists—checks out Nokia's City Lens, Wikitudeand Metaio's Junaio and there are more to come.

2. **Museum**

Visiting a museum (See figure 10-2)? Metaio did integration with the British Museum where there were AR hot spots that offered more information, and the Junaio AR browser basically "attaches" information to the art so you don't need to buy one of those audio tours. Especially in the case of modern art, says Lord, "You could walk up to nearly any painting in any museum and the [AR] recognition will work on it," using LLA (Longitude, Latitude, Altitude) to navigate indoors.

Metaio also experimented with 3D virtual "docents," who are placed throughout the museum—but only visible through the browser—and can tell you more about the art in nearby exhibits. Lord explains that this is a helpful tool, especially when you're in a large museum, like the Louvre or New York's Metropolitan Museum of Art, where maps don't always help you find what you're looking for.

Figure 10-2   Museum

3. Shopping

Augmented reality lets you browse a virtual catalog of clothes from your favorite brands, shop directly within your Esquire magazine (below), or head to a virtual pop-up store and avoid the lines (See figure 10-3).

Figure 10-3   Shopping

Augmented reality is going to radically change the shape of commerce, says Rosenthal of Goldrun, who created an AR pop-up shop for Airwalk in a New York City park. AR could turn places as mundane as parks and airports into shopping destinations, which would be a great way to kill time (and a smart way for businesses to save money on commercial real estate). If there's no UNIQLO or Crate & Barrel in your city, AR could change that, and you could browse the stores virtually, using your phone. Think of it as v-commerce, as opposed to ecommerce.

4. Travel and History

If you're looking for budget "travel" options or a quick "getaway," you could find a solution in augmented reality (See figure 10-4). Just plop the Eiffel Tower or the Leaning Tower of Pisa right in your backyard and unlock monuments during a sort of virtual vacation, and you could learn tidbits about each one as you go. It's being a great way to teach your kids, too—"You could have your kid pose with each monument and basically take a 'trip around the world,'" says Rosenthal.

Figure 10-4　Travel and history

Using AR in this way would be great at home and in classrooms, where history teachers could take students on a "class trip" to the Great Wall of China and even pose for a picture, making education deeply personal and thus, more memorable. This, of course, is different from the AR uses mentioned in #1, since you wouldn't need to be physically in front of the monuments to see them with AR.

5. Customer Service

No one likes having to call customer service—you'll be put on hold and stuck listening to a script recited by a rep. But in the future, if you're having trouble setting up Apple TV, or your cable cuts off, you can have customer service come to you.

Metaio's AR software can access the user's camera (Lord assures us it's not as creepy as it sounds), so if you're setting up technology at home and having problems, the support team can access the camera and in real-time, overlay instructions through the camera. So instead of hearing generic instructions, like "Unplug the red cord" and "double-check the port," someone could walk you through the process and see the things you're seeing, enabling the customer service rep to point things out in more detailed, visual way and helping problems get solved in a more efficient manner.

6. Safety and Rescue Operations

Chris Grayson, an AR expert, says, "The enterprise space and government employees could see the first real-world benefits" of AR. Emergencies are a fact of life, and first responders, police and firefighters often arrive at chaotic scenes and need to make sense of the environment and navigate a place they've never been. Wouldn't it be cool if they could see a virtual map of the site or have "X-ray vision" to see underground water and power lines?

7. Moving & Decorating Your Home

Maybe this is only a problem in Manhattan, where we live in shoeboxes, but AR has fun and useful applications when it comes to moving day. There's no worse feeling than buying furniture, paying the delivery fee, having someone schlep it up five flights of stairs, only to have it not fit through the doorway or look like a Gulliver-sized sofa in a Lilliputian living room. What if you searched through an App and pulled up the Macy's bed frame, IKEA dresser (IKEA has already experimented with AR, see below) and Jennifer Convertibles sofabed through an App and virtually positioned them in your home so you could see what they'd look like—and whether they would actually fit—before you head to the store and pay?

"Augmented reality (See figure 10-5) isn't the absolute solution to [moving problems], but it's a start, making that pain point a little bit easier," says Lord.

Figure 10-5 Augmented Reality

And once you're all moved in, you'd surely want to decorate. Is there a painting or sculpture you've been eyeing, but you're not sure if it would fit, dimensionally or aesthetically? You could preview it with an AR App. "Augmented reality brings a whole new way to think about the transportation of physical goods—you can preview them as social goods," says Rosenthal, who recently launched The Artwall to help people preview art before buying.

How would you like to use augmented reality? Are you excited by the technology? Tell us in the comments.

From: mashable.com
Author: Lauren Drell

New Words

Augmented Reality 增强现实

Mainstream *n.* (思想或行为的) 主流；主要倾向，主要趋势

GPS (Global Positioning System) 全球定位系统
Commerce *n.* 商务；商业；贸易
Dimensionally *adv.* 在尺寸上，在幅员上
Aesthetically *adv.* 审美地，美学观点上地

Exercises

Translation

1. Morton Heilig, the "Father of Virtual Reality," patented the Sensorama Stimulator, which he called an "experience theater," on Aug. 28, 1962. Over time, the idea of using technology to create a layer over the real world has been honed and refined and put in our palms, thanks to the proliferation of smartphones.

2. In short, it's a way to use technology to redefine space, and it places a virtual layer over the world with geographic specificity ensuring a good fit.

3. These AR Apps let you filter by category so you can find exactly what you're looking for, whether it's a coffee shop, restaurant or museum.

4. Augmented reality lets you browse a virtual catalog of clothes from your favorite brands, shop directly within your Esquire magazine (below), or head to a virtual pop-up store and avoid the lines.

5. "Augmented reality brings a whole new way to think about the transportation of physical goods—you can preview them as social goods," says Rosenthal, who recently launched The Artwall to help people preview art before buying.

Definitions
Augmented Reality

Text B
Can Augmented Reality Help Save the Print Publishing Industry?

There's a memorable scene in the movie Minority Report (See figure 10-6) where a man reads a futuristic newspaper with rich embedded multimedia updating live with breaking news. While we are a long way seeing anything like this in the hands of the general public, a German newspaper has taken a small step in that direction with the release of a special augmented reality (AR) edition of its Friday magazine.

Figure 10-6　Minority Report

Süddeutsche Zeitung (SZ), Germany's largest national newspaper, has partnered with Munich-based AR vendor metaio to provide subscribers with an immersive reading experience that hints at the future of publishing. The experience is similar to Esquire's augmented reality edition from November of 2009, but with advancements that have been made to smartphone AR technology, a desktop webcam is not needed to view the content.

The magazine, hitting newsstands this Friday, features several AR experiences littered throughout its pages that can be activated using metaio's junaio (See figure 10-7) iPhone and Android Apps. The cover of the magazine features a popular German TV personality who comes to life in an interactive video unlocked by holding a smartphone up to the magazine. Other augmented features in the magazine include an illustration that becomes 3D, an interview with additional exclusive quotes and a crossword puzzle whose answers appear when viewed through the smartphone.

The example I find the most compelling, however, is a photo essay about German farmers that are worried their country's bid to host the Olympics could spell trouble for their coveted farmland (See figure 10-8). In one photo, a farmer is shown standing before a large empty field. When a smartphone is held to this picture, a new image featuring a large parking lot superimposed onto the man's land is swapped into its place.

Figure 10-7　Junaio　　　　Figure 10-8　A photo essay about German farmers

Augmented reality can not only add fun and interactivity to a print publication, but, as shown here, it can also vastly improve a journalist's ability to tell a story in a compelling way. This falls directly in line with metaio co-founder and CTO Peter Meier's vision for the future of AR, where kids will view interactive content on the side of their cereal boxes each morning.

The crux of this vision is that smartphones now allow publishers to build this type of interactive experience right into their existing print content. No special markers, no desktop computer, no webcams: All a user needs to interact with augmented magazines, newspapers or cereal boxes is a smartphone.

Holding a smartphone up to a magazine is a far cry from the flashy interactive newspaper seen in Minority Report, but it is perhaps a hint at how augmented reality can help the dwindling print publishing industry.

From: http://readwrite.com
Author: Chris Cameron

New Words

Memorable *adj.* 值得纪念的；显著的，难忘的；重大的，著名的
Immersive *adj.* 拟真的
Superimpose *vt.* 添加；附加
Interactivity *n.* 互动性；交互性
Journalist *n.* 新闻工作者，新闻记者；记日志者
Dwindling *vi.* 减少，变小，缩小；衰落，变坏，退化

Exercises

Translation

1. There's a memorable scene in the movie Minority Report where a man reads a futuristic newspaper with rich embedded multimedia updating live with breaking news.

2. The experience is similar to Esquire's augmented reality edition from November of 2009, but with advancements that have been made to smartphone AR technology, a desktop webcam is not needed to view the content.

3. The cover of the magazine features a popular German TV personality who comes to life in an interactive video unlocked by holding a smartphone up to the magazine.

4. Other augmented features in the magazine include an illustration that becomes 3D, an interview with additional exclusive quotes and a crossword puzzle whose answers appear when viewed through the smartphone.

5. No special markers, no desktop computer, no webcams: All a user needs to interact with augmented magazines, newspapers or cereal boxes is a smartphone.

Reading

3D Projection at Liverpool Pier Head Buildings

The centenary of Liverpool's Royal Liver Building and the opening of the new Museum of Liverpool are being celebrated with a 3D projection event illuminating the city's waterfront (See figure 10-9).

Figure 10-9　3D projection at Liverpool Pier Head buildings

3D Son et Lumiere, by Czech company The Macula, will project Liverpool's 800 year history on to the Pier Head buildings over three nights from 22 July till 24 July.

The free event, which is expected to attract thousands of people to Liverpool's waterfront, will be accompanied by musical performances.

Blues singer Connie Lush will perform on the Friday evening, the Royal Liverpool Philharmonic Orchestra on the Saturday night and local group 6ix Toys on Sunday.

The event is the first in the UK by The Macula company which created a 600th anniversary show for Prague's Astronomical Clock.

Text C
(geolocation + augmented reality + QR codes) Libraries

While I was not officially at ALAMW in Boston, I did happen upon attending the Virtual Reference Discussion Group (VRDG) meeting on Saturday. Lisa Carlucci-Thomas started off the discussions with a presentation about mobile—a topic on which I will speak to later because I have very much to say—and the group got to discussing geolocation services (like foursquare) and augmented reality (like Layer). It's not something in the American mainstream yet, more and more of my tech/librarian Twitter are using it and talking about it. And while on a personal level it annoys me (takes up a lot of the twitter stream these days), I think there's a lot of value here for libraries.

Geolocation

Geolocation is the identification of real-world geographic location information of internet-based devices like your computer or cellphone. Prior to foursquare, we (at least in the VR realm) were talking geolocation so that customers could automatically be routed into their Ask service if they were already in the state. QandANJ did this when they reached capacity after a successful MTV advert.

But now the world has foursquare which, as they say on the site, "gives you & your friends new ways of exploring your city. Earn points & unlock badges for discovering new things." Why would you want people to know where you are? Well, maybe you don't. But as a library, you want people to know what you offer, where you are, and perhaps drum up some interest from folks who don't use the library but see their friends are there.

David Lee King explains it best with his top five reasons why foursquare has library value:

1. Add your library as a place, or edit the entry if someone else has already added it. You can enter your street address (Google map is included), phone number, and your library's Twitter name.

2. Add tags relevant to the library. For example, I have added the tags library, books, music, movies, and wifi to my library's Foursquare entry. If you are in the area (Foursquare is a location-based service, so it knows where you are) and search for wifi—guess who's at the top of the list? Yep—the library.

3. Add Tips and To Do lists. When you check in to a place, you have the option to add tips of things you can do there, and you can create To-Do lists of things you want to do there. For libraries, both are helpful—it's a way to broadcast your services to foursquare players. To Do lists are handy, because you can make the list and other players can add those To Do list items to their lists, too. When they do something on those lists, they gain points. Think of it as a fun way to get people doing stuff at your library! Just think—someone could gain points by getting a library card—how cool is that?

4. Add your big events. Then, you can have an event check-in with prizes for the first person who checks in, etc.

5. Shout outs. These are a type of status update, and can be sent to Twitter and Facebook. So do stuff, and then shout out that you've done them.

It's a fun, easy, and * cough * FREE way to get people involved at your library. And, since this isn't mainstream yet, it's another way the library can look high tech and forward thinking (you know, not that we're not already).

Augmented Reality

Talk about high-tech and forward thinking ... even though augmented reality (See figure 10-10) has been in the language since the 1990s, it's just now starting to come into the mainstream consciousness. It's the overlay of (computer-generated or cloud-generated) information, graphics, etc onto real-world scenes.

Why does this have library value? Imagine if you will, a library clean and crisp, bustling with activity. A customer holds her device up to the shelf of books she's looking

Figure 10-10 Augmented Reality

at and it tells her that the library has databases on her subject and that on Tuesday there is a guest lecture program she might be interested in. Or perhaps that the next in the series is due in the library next month and she can reserve it now! What a new world! No more messy signage or missed promotional opportunities.

And take open catalogs and websites to the next level and not only allow conversation to happen between customers via tagging or comments but lets customers add their own value to the virtual space around your library! Did sally like this book? Pete found the Tuesday tech talks to be invaluable! Rodger was looking for a book on X and preferred Title A to Title B. YES!

This is the point at which I admit I do not have a device that can handle any of the augmented reality apps that are already out there (truth be told, I'm waiting for the tablet or at least the iphone to come to vz) but Lauren Pressley gives some great examples about AR you're already seeing and what Apps you might want to check out (like Layar).

QR Codes

QR codes (See figure 10-11) are those funny looking bar codes you've no doubt started seeing recently. Although they've been in use in Japan for years, they're only just now infiltrating the mainstream American consciousness. I think I first heard about them back in 2007 in use in Japan for historical monuments. Public parks would have QR codes with additional information about the monument someone was looking at. And indeed when we were in England in September, we saw them on pretty much every drink bottle.

Figure 10-11 QR Codes

Where's the value for libraries? Like augmented reality, but perhaps something you can use now, imagine the same vision of customers getting extra information about the things they like, want, or need exactly where they are at that moment. You could cross reference your library and provide customers with more information about what services you provide, programs you have, and maybe even the expertise of and contact information for your librarians.

The world I live in values libraries as innovators and saviors of information access for all. With geolocation, QR codes and augmented reality, we have another opportunity to engage customers with the cool (the tech) and the necessary (the content). While this stuff might seem scary, unnecessary, or impossible to some but how will you know the value it might bring to you and your customers until you try? Sure, these might be ideas ahead of your library's times but it's something simple and easy you can do and has high wow-factor.

From: http://strangelibrarian.org

New Words

Geolocation *n.* 地理定位
Identification *n.* 认同；鉴定，识别；验证；身份证明
Automatically *adv.* 自动地；无意识地；不自觉地；机械地
Graphic *adj.* 图解的，用图表示的；用文字表示的；形象的，生动的
Website *n.* 网站
Code *n.* 代码，密码；信号；*vt.* 将……译成电码；编码，加密
Infiltrate *vt.* (使)渗入；(使)潜入；*n.* 渗透物

Exercises

Translation

1. Geolocation is the identification of real-world geographic location information of internet-based devices like your computer or cellphone.

2. A customer holds her device up to the shelf of books she's looking at and it tells her that the library has databases on her subject and that on Tuesday there is a guest lecture program she might be interested in.

Are you or any of your libraries using any of these techs? Please share your experiences or ideas in the comments!

Reading Material
GPS App Keeps Drivers' Eyes on the Road

An Android App navigates via camera images of the actual road—and any obstacles that might be there at the moment (See figure 10-12).

Many drivers use GPS to find their way, but shifting their attention to the maps on the device can distract them from actual driving. A new App, Wikitude Drive, aims to

Figure 10-12 GPS App keeps drivers' Eyes on the road

help drivers navigate without diverting their attention away from the road. Philipp Breuss-Schneeweis, founder of Wikitude GmbH, the Austrian company that developed the App, claims that "seeing the cars in front of you in the camera image can help you to avoid a crash. Many accidents actually happen when drivers look at the navigation system and the car ahead stops."

Wikitude Drive works by using an Android tablet or smart phone's camera to capture the roadway in front of the driver. The App then pulls information from a wide variety of sites, including Wikipedia, Yelp, Last.fm, Foursquare, and other online databases, to collect points of interest for the user, such as local businesses and concert locations. It uses the GPS and digital compass built into many phones and tablets to mark these sites directly on a live feed displayed on the device's screen—a technique known as augmented reality.

Wikitude Drive has only been officially supported on a handful of phones, but in practice it works on most Android devices.

Breuss-Schneeweis says that he's long wanted to use augmented reality for navigation. "The idea was to draw the driving instructions directly onto reality rather than an abstract map," he says. The company began developing the App in 2009, and released it in Europe in December of last year. Along the way, Breuss-Schneeweis says, the developers had to ensure that the App used GPS sensors accurately, matching driving directions to streets exactly. They also had to make the App work consistently despite a flurry of changes to the Android operating system and the wide variety of devices that use it.

Wikitude Drive's developers hope this approach will keep users more focused on the road. As pointed out on the Wikitude Drive site, when a driver takes his or her eyes off the road for one second to look at a map screen when driving at 100 kilometers (60 miles) per hour, "the driver is actually 'blind' for 28 meters (92 feet)."

However, Paul Green, a research professor at University of Michigan's Transportation Research Institute, is skeptical as to whether the App is addressing the biggest safety concerns. Drivers are most distracted by GPS devices and apps, he says, when they're programming a destination. Green believes the best way to improve GPS driving safety would be to "lock out destination entry while the [navigational] system is in use."

Green does say that the App could help solve very specific driving concerns, such as confusion while performing complex navigation maneuvers, or navigating through turns in an area with many roadways.

From: https://www.technologyreview.com
Author: Ian E. Muller

UNIT 11

New Media Advertisement

COMPETENCIES

After you have read this unit, you should be able to:
1. Discuss what is New Media Advertisement.
2. Find some new media advertisements, which style is your favorite.

Text A

Mobile Advertising Is Soaring While Newspapers Continue Their Inexorable Decline

The Interactive Advertising Bureau, a trade body, today released its full-year report on trends in the advertising industry compiled by PricewaterhouseCoopers. The headline finding is that advertising in various digital formats—through search, on mobile phones, videos and others—hit a record high of $36.6 billion in the U.S. last year, up 15% from 2011's $31.7 billion (See figure 11-1). Revenues crossed $10 billion in a single quarter for the first time in the final three months of 2012.

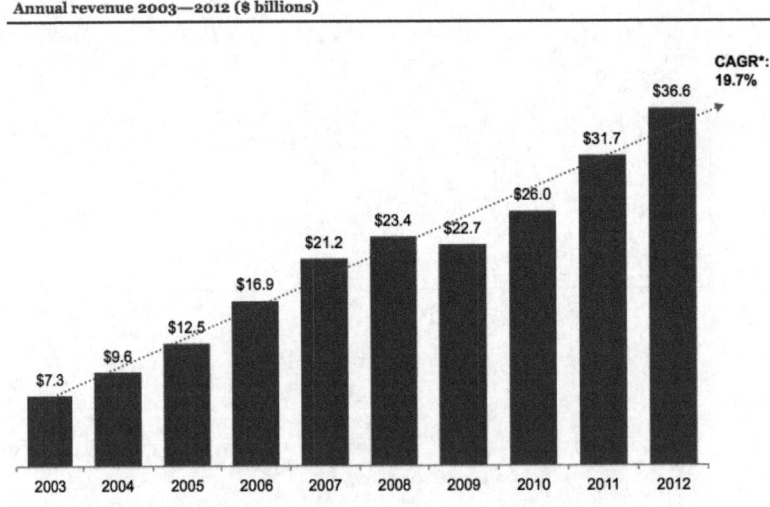

Figure 11-1　Annual revenue 2003—2012 ($billions)IAB/PwC

However, every online advertising format, except digital video which ticked up a bit, lost market share compared to the previous year. That includes search, which still accounts for nearly half on online ad spending. Why? Because all those dollars are being diverted to mobile, which more than doubled its share to $3.4 billion from $1.6 billion the previous year.

That's still a drop in the ocean—search was a shade under $17 billion. But mobile ad revenues have more than doubled in each of the past two years, before which IAB didn't even gather data on the category (See figure 11-2).

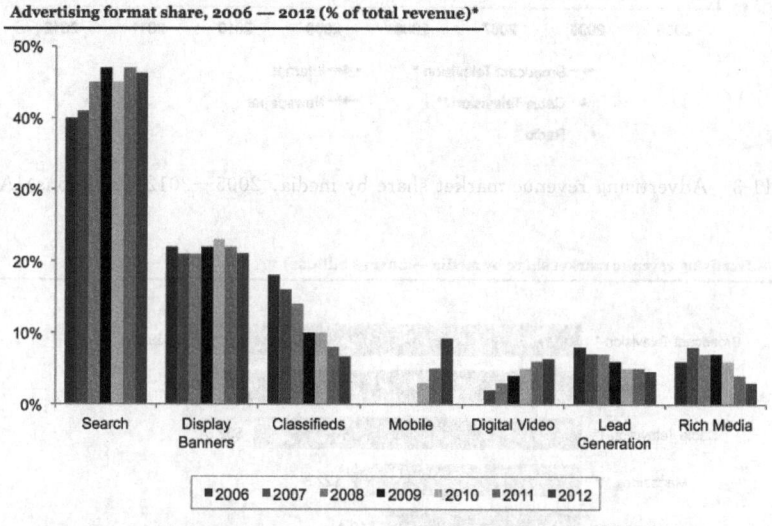

Figure 11-2   Advertising format share, 2006—2012, % of total revenue IAB/PwC

It's not just the increasing ubiquity of mobiles that's driving the growth. There are other factors too, including better speeds on 4G, more tablets and—ick, that word—phabletsthat can display more and bigger ads, and a lot of work from the likes of Google and Facebook trying to figure out how to stick ads onto your screens.

And where is all that growth coming from? This chart is going to be painful for some to look at:

No other category has fallen as sharply as newspaper advertising (See figure 11-3).

Online advertising is now the second biggest category after broadcast television (See figure 11-4). If you combine broadcast with cable, which is third, television is still light years ahead of the Internet.

But don't bet on it lasting. The people over at Aereo and Hopper, two services that are eating into the advertising and fee-based revenues of traditional TV networks, probably saw these charts too. And what they see is not an insurmountable gap but a wide-open opportunity measuring in the tens of billions of dollars.

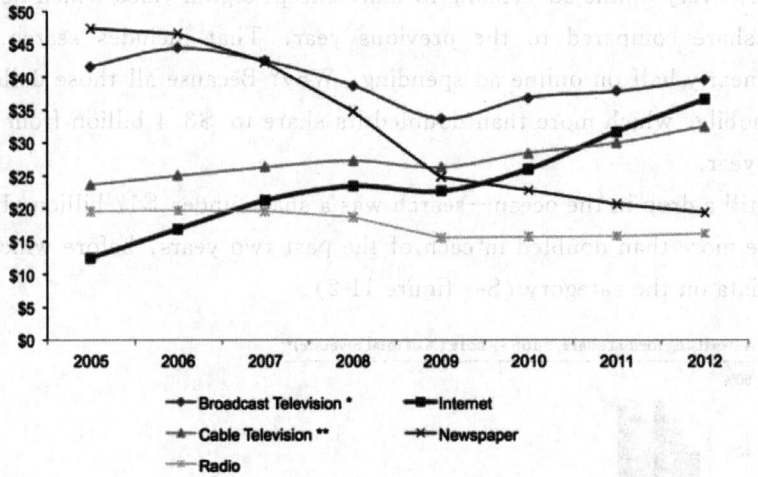

Figure 11-3   Advertising revenue market share by media, 2005—2012（$billions）IAB/PwC

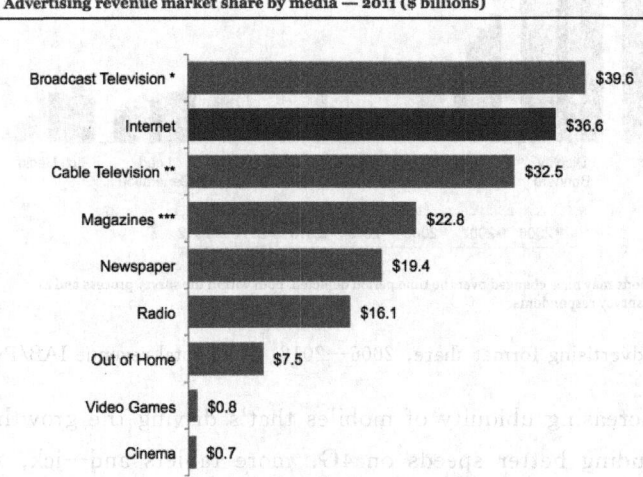

Figure 11-4   Mobile advertising is soaring while newspapers continue their inexorable decline

From: http://qz.com
Author: Leo Mirani

New Words

Advertisement *n*. 广告,宣传;公告;出公告,做广告
Data *n*. 资料
Category *n*. 类型,部门,种类,类别,类目
Insurmountable *adj*. 不可逾越的;不能克服的

Exercises

Translation

1. The Interactive Advertising Bureau, a trade body, today released its full-year report (pdf) on trends in the advertising industry compiled by PricewaterhouseCoopers.

2. However, every online advertising format, except digital video which ticked up a bit, lost market share compared to the previous year.

3. There are other factors too, including better speeds on 4G, more tablets and—ick, that word—phabletsthat can display more and bigger ads, and a lot of work from the likes of Google and Facebook trying to figure out how to stick ads onto your screens.

Definitions

New Media Advertisement

Text B
8 Reasons to Join the Digital Media and Advertising Industry

Graduating this summer, lost in the job search and confused about what you should look to go into?

Are you excited by tech, love marketing, enjoy talking to people? Have you considered a career within digital media and advertising?

If you haven't already then you definitely should look into it. There are many benefits to being in the digital advertising and media industry. If you haven't already heard of its reputation then we've listed some comments below to give you a better understanding. Not only is it one of the fastest growing industries, but digital advertising and digital media are also extremely well respected and despite the relaxed and fun environment these people work extremely hard and love what they do. Here's some of the reasons why.

Money

Basic salaries range from £20-25k (See figure 11-5) however get a year under your belt with experience in programmatic and you can be looking at achieving nearer the £30k mark a good wage to be on a year after uni.

Social

Why come out of the social hub of university to go into a stuffy office, no need. Digital is cool, young and fun with loads of socials, team nights out, summer balls and

Figure 11-5 Money

Christmas extravaganzas. Companies are usually located in the heart of the trendiest streets in London so I'm sure you'll find a cool local nearby (See figure 11-6).

Figure 11-6 Social

Innovative

Do you want to work in a sector that is always growing and developing new technology a world where it's ever evolving and finding new ways to engage in the right audience? This is a really dynamic and exciting industry that welcomes new technologies daily.

Benefits

Unlike industries such as finance and banking here you don't have to work 12 hour days, have no lunch break and commit yourself to a life of reading the financial times. Digital offers flexibility, sociable working hours and benefits such as beer and wine fridges, ping pong tables etc.

Progression

You don't need to work for a company for 5 years to become a senior member of staff, if you have the passion, charisma and knowledge you can move up as fast as you want. This is across the industry, Agency to Ad tech or within job role, from an Analyst to an Account Manager. It's all possible as the industry is known for its flexibility.

International

The Digital Media and Advertising industry is growing fast and it is hugely international, think about it France use the web, smart phones and tablets as much as us! Therefore there are many digital hubs around the world; the majority of companies we work with do have international offices (See figure 11-7).

Figure 11-7 International

Training

There are many graduate jobs within digital, from analytical, technical and commercial opportunities many people want to work in digital. If you work for one of these companies you will receive fantastic training, development, networking and career opportunities, not to mention making lots of friends along the way.

Names

Working within digital you will be working with some of the biggest brands in the world. Think about it, they all advertise and are all looking to market to the right people at the right time.

There are many benefits to working in the Digital Media and Advertising industries, if you are interested in a career with one of them please get in touch. We will meet with you, talk you through your options and give you advice, helping you start your career.

From: http://www.spherelondon.co.uk

New Words

Dynamic *adj.* 动态的;*n.* 动态

Flexibility *n.* 柔度;灵活性

Analytical *adj.* 分析的,分析法的;善于分析的

Commercial *adj.* 商业的;贸易的;赢利的;靠广告收入的;*n.*（电台或电视播放的）广告

Exercises

Translation

1. Not only is it one of the fastest growing industries, but digital advertising and digital media are also extremely well respected and despite the relaxed and fun environment these people work extremely hard and love what they do.

2. Digital is cool, young and fun with loads of socials, team nights out, summer balls and Christmas extravaganzas.

3. You don't need to work for a company for 5 years to become a senior member of staff, if you have the passion, charisma and knowledge you can move up as fast as you want.

4. The Digital Media and Advertising industry is growing fast and it is hugely international, think about it France use the web, smart phones and tablets as much as us!

Design

Can you design a new media advertisement for a digital media company?

_____
_____
_____
_____
_____

Reading Material

What is Digital Media?

What is common between a weather App on your phone, a racing game on your console and a state-of-the-art imaging tool in a hospital? All of these are digital media products, and to build them requires teams of digital media professionals.

Digital media is content that is stored in digital formats and usually distributed online. The world we live in today is populated by digital media products, and the shift from traditional media has taken place in many industries, including industries that aren't typically associated with digital media—such as health, government and education.

Digital media products can be found in:

eCommerce;

Games—console, online and mobile;

Websites and mobile applications (See figure 11-8);

Animation;

Social media;

Video;

Augmented reality;
Virtual reality;
Data visualization;
Location-based services;
Interactive Storytelling.

Digital media can include these industries:
Entertainment;
Technology;
eCommerce;
Non-Profit;
Health;
Education;
Marketing and advertising;
Government;
Sports;
Environment;
Television (See figure 11-9);
Publishing.

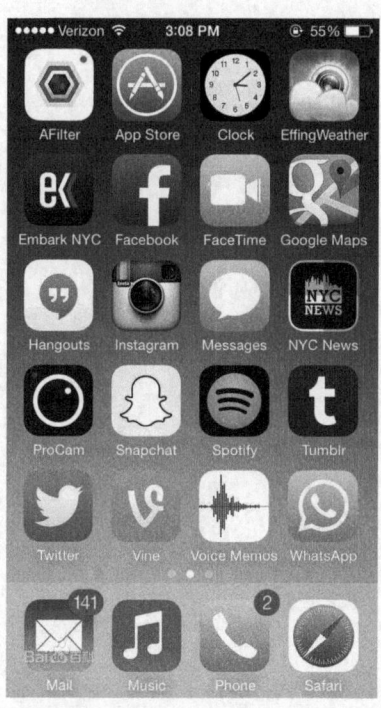

Figure 11-8   Mobile applications

Figure 11-9   Television

How does digital media relate to the master of digital media program?
Digital media industries are unique in two ways—they have multi-skilled teams and

their business processes are unique. For example, making a game requires a programmer, an artist, a project manager and an animator. The business processes required to manage these multi-skilled team members and the fast-paced nature of the industry make them different from traditional industries.

The Master of Digital Media program educates students on these two aspects—working in multi-skilled teams and engaging with business processes—while making digital media products. Additionally, they are also trained to develop six core competencies that will serve them well in their careers.

Students acquire these skills by classroom learning and working on multiple projects. Projects at the CDM run throughout the three semesters. These projects require students to collaborate with colleagues with different skill sets, and they also get to practise the business processes they learn. Projects in semesters two and three are industry projects for clients looking for digital media solutions.

The Master of Digital Media program caters well to students with an entrepreneurial vision. In addition to developing their business skills, they also hone their abilities to pitch, seek the right partners and investors, and manage resources.

From: http://thecdm.ca/program

UNIT 12

UI

COMPETENCIES

After you have read this unit, you should be able to:
1. Discuss what is UI.
2. Talk about what kind of interface is your favorite.

Text A

Realism in UI Design

The history of the visual design of user interfaces can be described as a gradual change towards more realism. As computers have become faster, designers have added increasingly realistic details such as color, 3D effects, shadows, translucency, and even simple physics. Some of these changes have helped usability. Shadows behind windows help us see which window is active. The physicality of the iPhone's user interface makes the device more natural to use.

In other areas, the improvements are questionable at best. Graphical user interfaces are typically full of symbols. Most graphical elements you see on your screen are meant to stand for ideas or concepts. The little house on your desktop isn't a little house, it's 《home》. The eye isn't an actual eye, it means "look at the selected element". The cog isn't a cog, it means «click me to see available commands». You are typically not trying to replicate physical objects, you are trying to communicate concepts.

Details and realism can distract from these concepts. To explain this, I'll take a page from Scott McCloud's 《Understanding Comics》, a book which should be required reading for all designers.

The image on the left is a face of a specific person. The image on the right is the concept "face"; it could be any person (See figure 12-1). When designing user interfaces, we rarely ever want to show a specific entity; typically, we want to convey an idea or a concept. Details can easily distract from that idea or concept.

At the same time, it's obvious that some details are required. Too few details and the user won't recognize the idea at all (See figure 12-2).

Figure 12-1 Realism in UI design

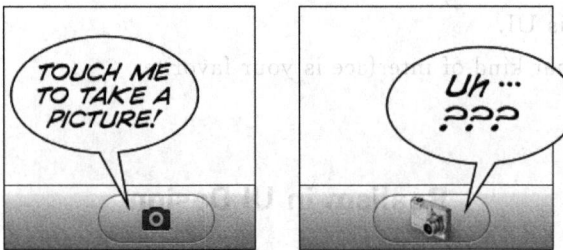

Figure 12-2 Realism in UI design

The circle on the left clearly shows a face. The circle on the right isn't recognizable as a face anymore (See figure 12-3).

Figure 12-3 Realism in UI design

Let's look at a symbol we actually see in user interfaces, the home button. Typically, this button uses a little house as its symbol.

The thing on the left is a house (See figure 12-4). The thing on the right means "home". Somewhere between the two, the meaning switches from "a specific house" to

Figure 12-4 Realism in UI design

"home as a concept". The more realistic something is, the harder it is to figure out the meaning. Again, if the image is simplified too much, it's not clearly and immediately recognizable anymore.

The thing on the left is a home button (See figure 12-5). The thing on the right might as well be an arrow pointing up; or perhaps it's the ⇧ key.

Figure 12-5   Realism in UI design

Let me explain this concept using an entirely unscientific graph (See figure 12-6):

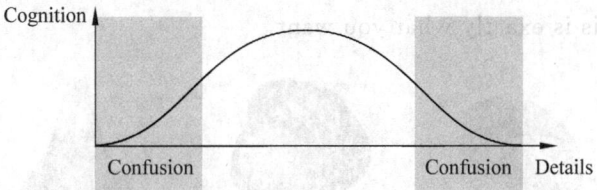

Figure 12-6   Realism in UI design

People are confused by symbols if they have too many or too few details. They will recognize UI elements which are somewhere in the middle.

The trick is to figure out which details help users identify the UI element, and which details distract from its intended meaning. Some details help users figure out what they're looking at and how they can interact with it; other details distract from the idea you're trying to convey. They turn your interface element from a concept into a specific thing. Thus, if an interface element is too distinct from its real-life counterpart, it becomes too hard to recognize. On the other hand, if it is too realistic, people are unable to figure out that you're trying to communicate an idea, and what idea that might be.

The button on the left is too realistic (See figure 12-7). The button on the right does not have enough details to be immediately recognizable as a button.

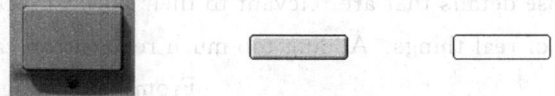

Figure 12-7   Realism in UI design

The same applies to these toggles (See figure 12-8). Shadows and gradients help the user figure out what he's looking at and how to interact with it. Adding too many details, however, ends up being confusing. The toggle switch is no longer just a toggle switch that is part of a user interface, it is clearly recognizable as a photograph of a specific toggle switch; it loses its meaning. It's no longer a symbol, it has become a specific thing.

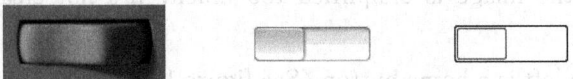

Figure 12-8 Realism in UI design

An Exception

There is at least one specific area where more details are good: Application icons. You want your icon to depict one specific idea: Your application.

Coda's leaf isn't a representation of the idea of a leaf; it's a very specific leaf, the Coda leaf (See figure 12-9). Acorn's acorn isn't just any acorn, it's the Acorn. Adding details moves these images from a generic concept towards a specific entity, and in the case of an application icon, this is exactly what you want.

Figure 12-9 Realism in UI design

Conclusion

Graphical user interfaces are full of symbols. Symbols need to be reduced to their essence. This helps avoid cluttering the user interface with meaningless distractions, and makes it easier for people to "read" the symbol and figure out the meaning of an interface element. Realistic details can get in the way of what you're trying to communicate to your users.

Unless you are creating a virtual version of an actual physical object, the goal is not to make your user interface as realistic as possible. The goal is to add those details which help users identify what an element is, and how to interact with it, and to add no more than those details. UI elements are abstractions which convey concepts and ideas; they should retain only those details that are relevant to their purpose. UI elements are almost never representations of real things. Adding too much realism can cause confusion.

From: http://ignorethecode.net/blog

Author: Lukas Mathis

New Words

UI (User Interface) 用户界面
Realism n. 现实主义
Element n. 要素

Designer *n.* 设计师;设计者;构思者
Essence *n.* 香精;本质,实质;精华,精髓
Abstraction *n.* 抽象;抽象化;抽象概念

Exercises

Translation

1. The history of the visual design of user interfaces can be described as a gradual change towards more realism. As computers have become faster, designers have added increasingly realistic details such as color, 3D effects, shadows, translucency, and even simple physics. Some of these changes have helped usability.

2. The trick is to figure out which details help users identify the UI element, and which details distract from its intended meaning.

3. There is at least one specific area where more details are good: Application icons. You want your icon to depict one specific idea: Your application.

4. Symbols need to be reduced to their essence. This helps avoid cluttering the user interface with meaningless distractions, and makes it easier for people to "read" the symbol and figure out the meaning of an interface element.

5. UI elements are abstractions which convey concepts and ideas; they should retain only those details that are relevant to their purpose. UI elements are almost never representations of real things.

Definitions
UI

Text B
Experience vs Function—a Beautiful UI is Not Always the Best UI

A good user interface (UI) is essential if you want your product to be usable, but you must always be careful to not fall into the trap of focusing too much on that interface.

A good UI should fade away, putting content in the front seat—it should be transparent. Sometimes there can be too much "UI"—controls and buttons that are too strong and distracting win over content in their battle for attention.

Remember that the visitor or user is there to do something—they're not there to appreciate the aesthetic of your buttons and marvel at the style of your navigation bar. If you let the UI take over, if it's no longer transparent and in the background, then it will dominate content and in turn would be too distracting to use.

Let's see an example. Here's a site called newspond (See figure 12-10). It collects news from around the Web and ranks it using a popularity algorithm:

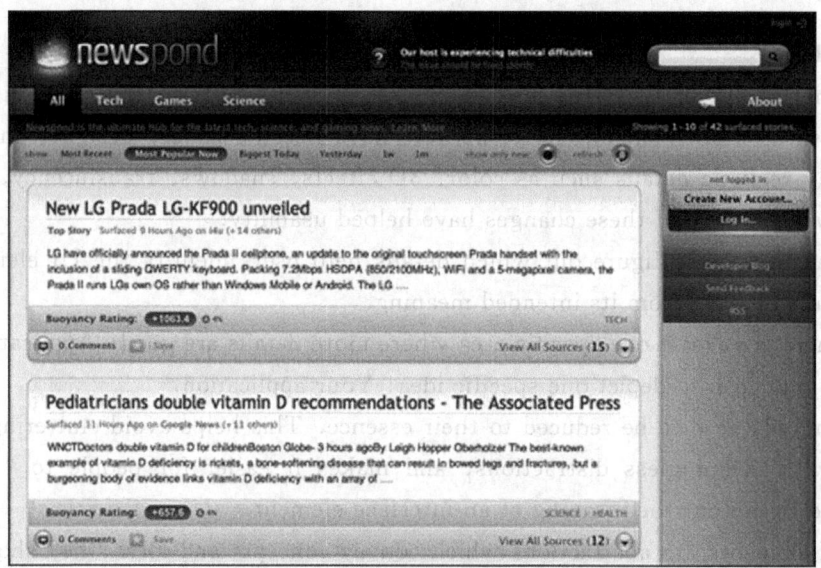

Figure 12-10 Newspond

It's a pretty nice system with a very beautiful interface. And that's the problem. The interface is too beautiful, there's too much of it—it's distracting because you cannot easily focus on the news stories. The beautifully crafted (and to some extent a fairly usable) UI is the downfall of this powerful service. The designer has fallen into the trap of focusing too much on the interface, and not enough on the content.

What would work instead? Let's see an example from a similar site. This is Hacker News (See figure 12-11) from YCombinator, a social news site for entrepreneurs and developers:

It's very basic. It's pretty much just content. While I can only see a couple of news stories on my screen on newspond, on Hacker News I can see about twenty. I get what I'm looking for: stories. I can get to them without having to block out the UI. It's simple, and it accomplishes its function beautifully.

Imagine if Google looked like newspond—would you still use it? I know I wouldn't. Part of a great user experience is to be able to get to information quickly—very quickly. If you have to block out UI in your mind to read the headlines then that UI has failed. There's not much "UI" in Google—it's just a list of links. And that's exactly why it works. It's just content.

Experience vs Function

Cutting back on UI style isn't always the right thing to do—it all depends on the

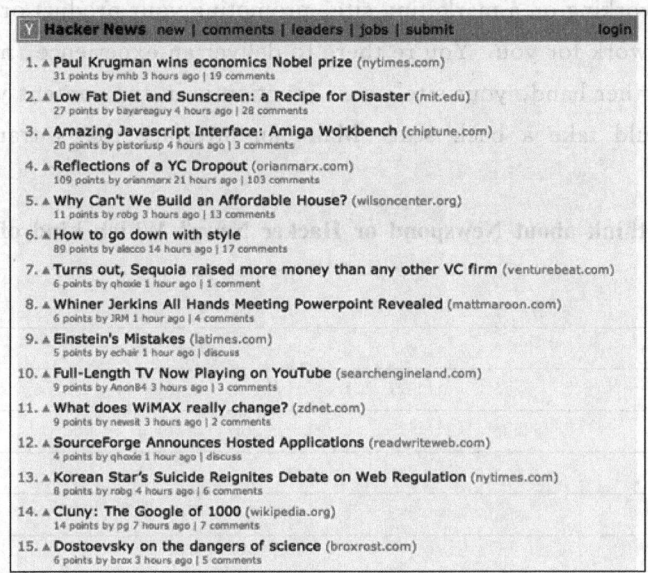

Figure 12-11　Hacker news

function of your website.

If you're working on a marketing site, promoting your product or company, then a beautiful UI may work for you. You're there to deliver an experience, not just content.

If on the other hand, your site's core function is in the content you publish, then the interface should take a back seat. Make an interface that's transparent and not distracting to use. Remember that the UI is not the content and not the focus of your site. Getting these priorities right will help you make a great user interface.

From: http://usabilitypost.com
Author: Dmitry Fadeyev

New Words

Function *n.* 功能，作用；函数

Transparent *adj.* 透明的；清澈的；易识破的；显而易见的

Aesthetic *adj.* 审美的；美学的；有关美的；具有审美趣味的；*n.* 审美观；美学标准，美感

Marvel *n.* 奇迹；令人惊奇的事物；漫威；*vt.* 惊奇，对……感到惊奇

Algorithm *n.* 演算法；运算法则；计算程序

Entrepreneur *n.* ＜法＞企业家；主办人；承包人

Core *n.* 中心，核心，精髓

Exercises

Translation

1. A good user interface (UI) is essential if you want your product to be usable, but you must always be careful to not fall into the trap of focusing too much on that interface.

2. If you're working on a marketing site, promoting your product or company, then a beautiful UI may work for you. You're there to deliver an experience, not just content.

3. If on the other hand, your site's core function is in the content you publish, then the interface should take a back seat. Make an interface that's transparent and not distracting to use.

What do you think about Newspond or Hacker News? Which kind of interface is your favorite?

_____
_____
_____
_____
_____
_____
_____
_____

Reading Material
Eye-Catching Mobile App Interfaces with Sleek Gradient Effect

With iOS 7 we took a fresh look at gradient effect that, to be honest, is one of the simplest embellishments in designers' toolkit. It has a numerous variations that can either liven up or, vice versa, ruin the design, crucially depending on opted colors and overall theme. Besides, like most decorative tools, it also undergoes changes depending on current trends.

A present-day's dominant trend is a smooth and gentle neon-like gradient that is usually paired with a light, almost luminous, text and simple, easy-to-understand glyphs that are regularly bolstered by low opacity layers. Such an exquisite combination naturally adds a note of refinement and subtlety to any UI.

Today we are going to talk not only about this type of gradient—that is, undoubtedly, quite popular—but also about another basic and wide-spread approach of applying gradient. The method involves the use of a gradient more as a differentiation tool, the principal purpose of which is supporting content in a visual manner.

At the beginning, let's inspect remarkable mobile App interfaces based on the hot trend gradients.

Gradient Effect in Mobile App

iOS 7 lockscreen by Michael Shanks (See figure 12-12) opens our collection with its magnificent sleek gradient-based interface. The minimalistic screen includes only essential information that is executed by means of elegant light type and highlighted with a help of subtle shadows and semi-transparent stripe.

Figure 12-12 iOS 7 lockscreen by Michael Shanks

Sense by Tommy Borgen (See figure 12-13). The designer also takes a minimal approach with its UI. The screen looks simple but truly delicate. The slightly blurred outline circle in the centre beautifully cooperates with narrow subtle typography in it and goes nicely with a flowing background.

Figure 12-13 Sense by Tommy Borgen

Personal Site Idea v1.1 by Ross Popoff-Walker (See figure 12-14). The designer makes use of marvelous splash of colors borrowed from a daybreak gradient. The background serves as a firm base for white graphics and letterings that favorably stands out from it. A lot of white-space as well as light grey solid color header and footer—that includes most of the navigation—beautifully complete the theme.

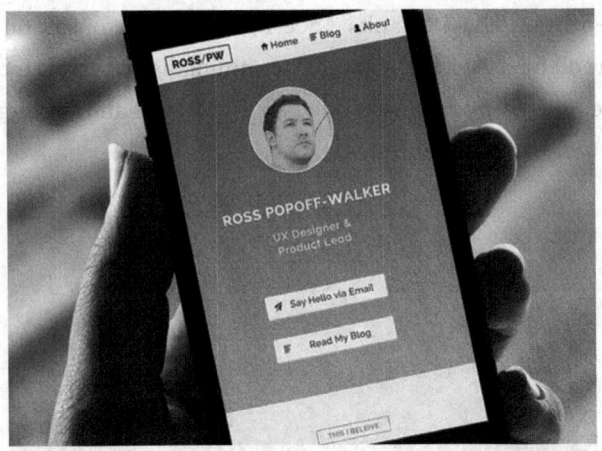

Figure 12-14　Personal Site Idea v1.1 by Ross Popoff-Walker

Screens by Yasser Achachi (See figure 12-15) look absolutely amazing and attention-grabbing. The prodigious kaleidoscope of colors that is implemented to background in cooperation with light font, regular pixel-perfect icons, translucent stripes and colorful boxes ably manages to craft truly breathtaking interfaces.

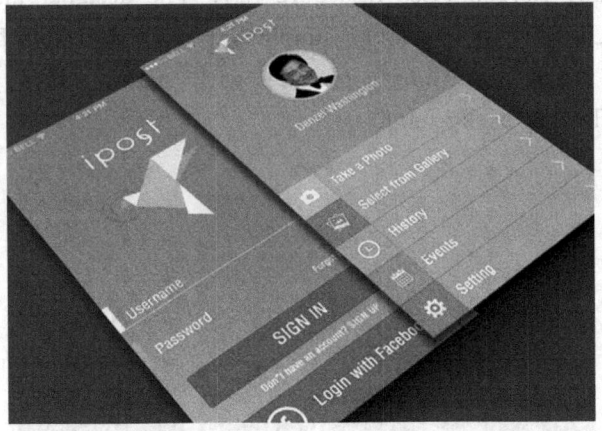

Figure 12-15　Screens by Yasser Achachi

Coloring Clock by Kyung Min Kim (See figure 12-16) features a hot flaming gradient canvas that is supported by matching block of bold text and a lot of free space. The delicate and organic color palette naturally sets the screen off. You can also specify your favorite gradient theme, giving the UI your own personal touch.

Instasave iPhone App by chirag dave (See figure 12-17)—uijunction demonstrates a wonderful radial gradient image that plays a role of a solid background for side menu. The designer uses a lighter part of the background for laying emphasis on a navigation, which is represented through tiny delicate glyphs and slim type.

Figure 12-16 Coloring Clock by Kyung Min Kim

Figure 12-17 Instasave iPhone App by chirag dave

  Beam Day (concept clock) by Vladimir (See figure 12-18). Here, the background is aimed to clearly highlight an exility of graphical components. Ultra-narrow outline circles and thin typography complement each other perfectly.

  Aero Weather by Alex Patrascu (See figure 12-19). Here, the clean bright gradient naturally brings the eye to the weather forecast that includes a whole deal of helpful information. The light casual font is perfectly coupled with a background, and makes the data look legible.

  iOS 7 Shortcuts Menu by Gaétan Pautler (See figure 12-20). Although the designer doesn't actually use traditional gradient, since a backdrop image is a heavily blurred picture with a lopsided touch, the background for shortcut menu, nonetheless, has a barely noticeable descending gradient from blue to pinkish creamy.

Figure 12-18　Beam Day (concept clock) by Vladimir

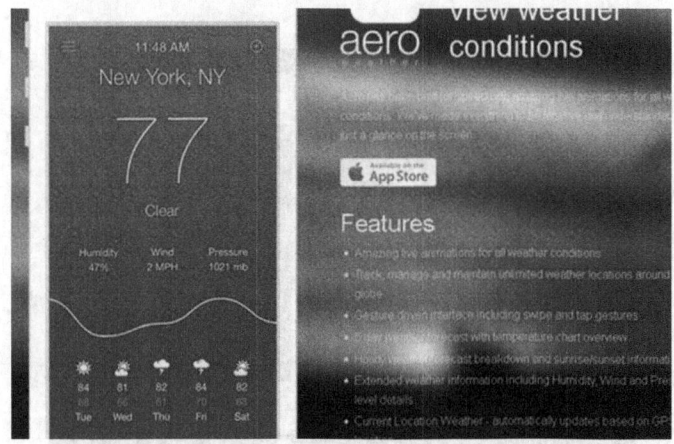

Figure 12-19　Aero Weather by Alex Patrascu

Figure 12-20　iOS 7 Shortcuts Menu by Gaétan Pautler

Gradient Effect as Reinforcement Medium

This part of the collection is dedicated to App interfaces that use gradient effect as reinforcement medium.

IndiaNIC App by Keyuri Bosmia (See figure 12-21) has a lovely rainbow touch. The designer skillfully colorizes menu in garish hues in order to clearly set each menu item apart. On the whole, concept looks vibrant and cheerful.

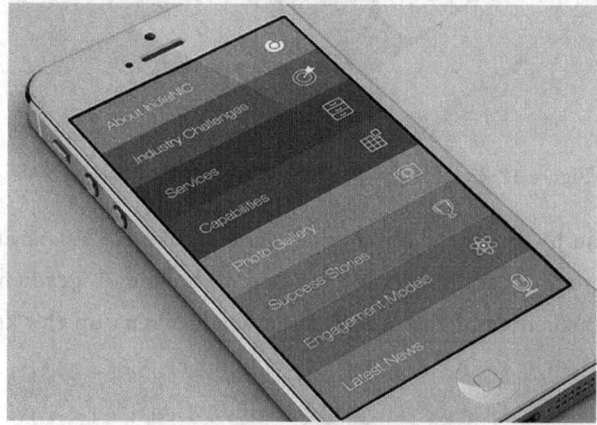

Figure 12-21   IndiaNIC App by Keyuri Bosmia

SunFun App by Andrus Valulis (See figure 12-22). This UI, on the contrary, is based on a more smooth and natural gradient effect. Since the App is dedicated to displaying sunset and sunrise data, it's not surprising that the designer employs warm colors to support the theme.

Figure 12-22   SunFun App by Andrus Valulis

Flat Style Color Wheel by Frantisek Krivda (See figure 12-23). Unlike the previous example, the UI utilizes a cold color scheme that eventually flows into neutral white. As a result, the interface looks more sharp, strong and serious. The curvy lines of vibrant functional circles add a note of sleekness.

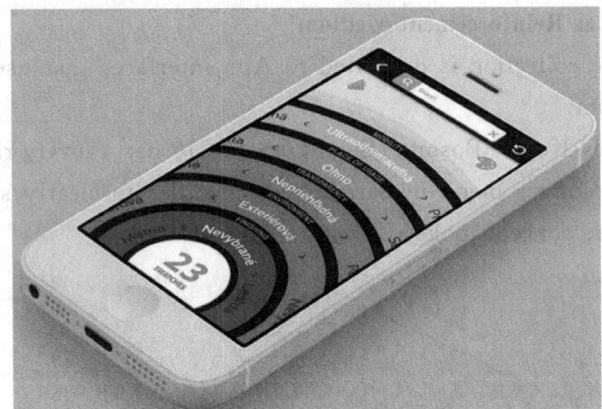

Figure 12-23 Flat Style Color Wheel by Frantisek Krivda

Haze Rays theme by Franz (Taptanium) (See figure 12-24) is another concept that strongly relies on a crisp, chilling color palette. The radial gradient naturally focuses users' attention on the center of the screen, and easily livens up the key data.

Figure 12-24 Haze Rays theme by Franz (Taptanium)

Waygo App V2 by Carrie Phillips (See figure 12-25). The designer employs a warm vivid gradient theme, made in fresh shades of orange, to brighten up the menu section. The color choice matches the main color scheme perfectly, and nicely reinforces the theme.

Bird App GIF by Rustem Ramadanov (See figure 12-26) features a well-organized and legible tile layout that capably pinpoints categories via sleek color differentiation. The designer makes use of well-tried and modest blue and white colors combo.

Brisk by Eddie Lobanovskiy (See figure 12-27). The interface exhibits a comprehensive gradient that features various shades from tropical orange to arctic blue. Here, the background plays more functional role rather than decorative, each color helps to graphically support temperature indicator.

Goo App by Nick Murphy (See figure 12-28) is based on a stunning pastel coloring. The soft gradient beautifully interacts with content, giving the UI a gentle and dulcet

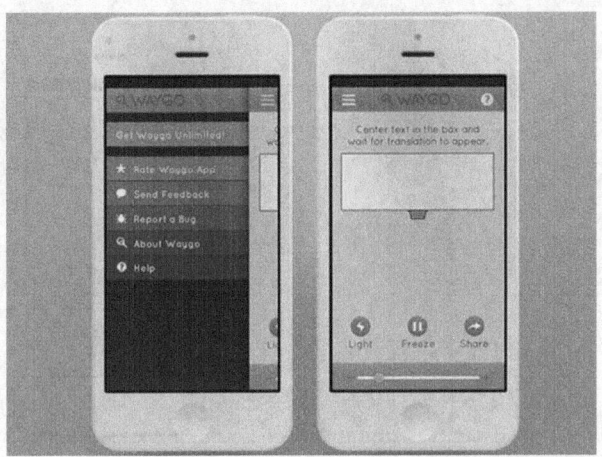

Figure 12-25　Waygo App V2 by Carrie Phillips

Figure 12-26　Bird App GIF by Rustem Ramadanov

Figure 12-27　Brisk by Eddie Lobanovskiy

appeal.

Figure 12-28　Goo App by Nick Murphy

Reflection

Designers wisely make use of various gradient effects starting from fluid polished canvases, which flow without interruptions, and ending with rough inconsistent backgrounds that are visually broken into stripes. They leverage this vibrant embellishment not only as a blunt decoration but also as a tool for reinforcing the chosen theme.

From: http://designmodo.com

Author: Nataly Birch

UNIT 13

Web Design

COMPETENCIES

After you have read this unit, you should be able to:
1. Discuss what is web design.
2. Describe your favorite website's web design.

Text A

Design Trend: Ghost Buttons in Website Design

The biggest trend of 2014 is something I'm not sure we saw coming. And it's all based on one of the smallest design components of almost any website—the button.

Ghost Buttons—those transparent, clickable items—are popping up everywhere. And taking the web design world by storm. Who ever thought something as simple as a button could change the way we look at web design?

What's a ghost button?

A ghost button (See figure 13-1) is created as a basic, flat shape—square, rectangle, circle, diamond—with no fill and a simple outline. It is completely (or almost completely transparent) asides from the outline and text. (Hence the name "ghost")

Figure 13-1 What's a ghost button?

These buttons are often somewhat larger than traditional clickable buttons on websites and are placed in prominent locations, such as the center of the screen.

Ghost buttons can be found on a number of different types of websites (and mobile applications) and in a variety of design styles but are most commonly associated with one-page sites and those with minimalist or almost-flat design schemes. This style of button is also quite popular on pages that use full-screen photography, because this simple style of button is thought to not intrude into the image as much as a more traditional button.

Did you ever take a close look at the round buttons on your iPhone (running iOS 7)? Every one of the UI elements is a ghost button. Here's what one Designmodo designer had to say about the emerging trend:

"The appearance of ghost buttons is somehow connected with the passion for making full screen backgrounds with 50 percent opacity, and making interfaces and forms over them. Here, an opportunity arises to distribute a person's attention between the background photo, the product's reflecting style, and at the same time the form with ghost elements, which doesn't shut out loud about its presence, but is still visible."

Elements of the Design

Ghost buttons typically have a common set of components (See figure 13-2). While this is not a complete set of rules for usage, many of these factors are in play when ghost buttons are used.

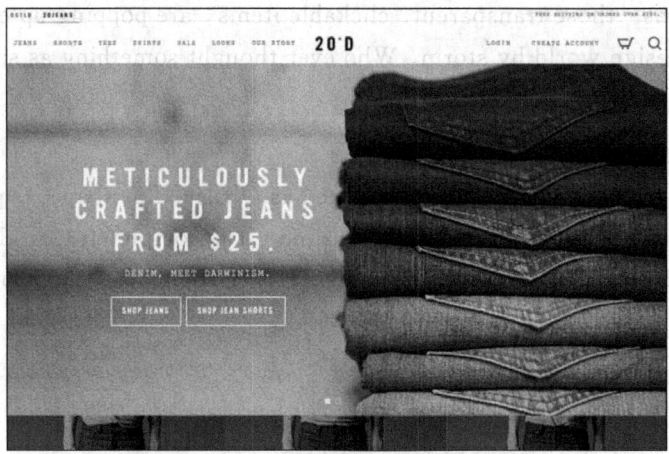

Figure 13-2 Elements of the design

- The button is hollow.
- It is surrounded by an outline, often only a couple of points thick.
- It contains simple text.
- The color is often white or black.
- Buttons are often larger than traditional buttons.
- Ghost buttons often are placed prominently on the page.
- Ghost buttons can be placed alone or in small groupings of buttons.

- The element is used with flat or almost-flat design schemes.
- Small, geometric icons can be used inside of ghost buttons, but sparingly.

Pros of Ghost Buttons
- So what makes a ghost button work? Is this design trend something that you should incorporate into your next project (See figure 13-3)?

Figure 13-3 Pros of ghost buttons

- Ghost buttons have a particularly clean look and feel. The simple nature of the button allows the primary design of the page to really stand out more. (It works especially nice on large images)
- Ghost buttons work with almost any design schema because they are transparent. This allows the button to essentially take on the properties of the surrounding design.
- Ghost buttons are continuing the evolution of the "trend of 2013—flat design." The only way for a design trend such as this one to really stay popular and in the now is to continue to change and be adapted with new concepts. This is a nice evolution of that process.
- Ghost buttons provide an element of visual surprise because the button is different than what a user may expect.
- Ghost buttons are easy to design and create. Remember to keep it simple. Ghost buttons are supposed to be subtle, no flashiness here.
- Ghost buttons create a focal point for calls-to-action without being obtrusive. In many site designs, ghost buttons are the only large element on the screen (this is often what makes the concept work so well). Because of this, it draws the eye and entices users to click or tap the button. And that's exactly what any good user interface element should do.
- Ghost buttons contribute to a design style that looks sophisticated. Simple is often classy when it comes to design.

Cons of Ghost Buttons

While ghost buttons come with a lot of design pros, there are some cons to consider as well. Before using any new trend, make sure to weight both pros and cons to determine if this concept will work in your project (See figure 13-4).

Figure 13-4 Cons of ghost buttons

Ghost buttons can fall too far into the background and frustrate users. Not all users may be design savvy; some may have trouble identifying an non-traditional button style and knowing how to use it.

Ghost buttons can be tricky to use over images with highly contrasting or varying colors. Typically these buttons are white or black. If you have an image with alternative black and white spaces, a ghost button can be near impossible to see or read.

Ghost buttons rely on size and placement for ease of use. Be cautious when placing the button so that it is easy to find and does not cover a key part of your image.

Ghost buttons can sometimes overpower the image they are paired with.

Ghost button text is more complicated than click here. The words used in these buttons needs to be clearly thought out, edited and placed in context with the rest of the design.

Ghost buttons are everywhere right now. Do you want to look like you are just latching on to a trend? Make sure this design style really works for your project before opting in to what's popular.

Gallery of the Ghost Button Trend

Remember, the key to any trend is to use it well. As a Designmodo said about the trend:

"I believe that each and any trend born in design could be thoughtfully used. The most important is not to be addicted to it, and choose the happy mean."

That is the key to using ghost buttons or any other trend for that matter (See figure

13-5).

Figure 13-5 Gallery of the ghost button trend

So we'll leave you with a gallery of ghost buttons that will hopefully inspire your creativity. This collection is pulled from a variety of published websites and working projects and portfolio elements on sites such as Dribbble and Behance.

From: http://designmodo.com
Author: Carrie Cousins

New Words

Web design 网页设计
Ghost button 幽灵按钮
Prominent *adj.* 著名的；突出的，杰出的；突起的
Background *n.* （画等的）背景；底色；背景资料；配乐
Component *n.* 成分；组分；*adj.* 成分的；组成的；合成的；构成的
Hollow *adj.* 空洞的；空的；*n.* 洞；山谷；*vt.* 挖空（某物）；挖出；（孔、洞）
Sophisticate *n.* 老于世故的人；见多识广的人

Exercises

Translation

1. A ghost button is created as a basic, flat shape—square, rectangle, circle, diamond—with no fill and a simple outline. It is completely (or almost completely transparent) asides from the outline and text. (Hence the name "ghost")

2. The appearance of ghost buttons is somehow connected with the passion for making full screen backgrounds with 50 percent opacity, and making interfaces and forms over them.

3. Ghost buttons have a particularly clean look and feel. The simple nature of the button allows the primary design of the page to really stand out more. (It works especially

nice on large images)

4. Ghost buttons can fall too far into the background and frustrate users. Not all users may be design savvy; some may have trouble identifying an non-traditional button style and knowing how to use it.

5. I believe that each and any trend born in design could be thoughtfully used. The most important is not to be addicted to it, and choose the happy mean.

Definitions

Ghost button

_____
_____
_____
_____

Web design

_____
_____
_____
_____

Text B

How To Create a Web Design Style Guide

Creating websites is getting more and more complex and is usually not a one person job. It is important to ensure that design is consistent and optimized to meet business objectives and create enjoyable experiences for users.

One of the ways to ensure that team is on the same page when designing separate parts of the website or saving designs from developers is to create design documentation or a web design style guide.

It is beneficial to have a style guide in order to create a cohesive experience among different pages. Also it helps to ensure that future development or third-party production will follow brand guidelines and will be perceived as part of the overall brand.

Luke Clum has touched the surface of using style guides as your first step in web design last year and I would like to take a more in-depth look on how to create a usable web design style guide for your projects.

What is a Style Guide?

A style guide is a collection of pre-designed elements, graphics and rules designers or developers should follow to ensure that separate website pieces will be consistent and will create a cohesive experience at the end (See figure 13-6).

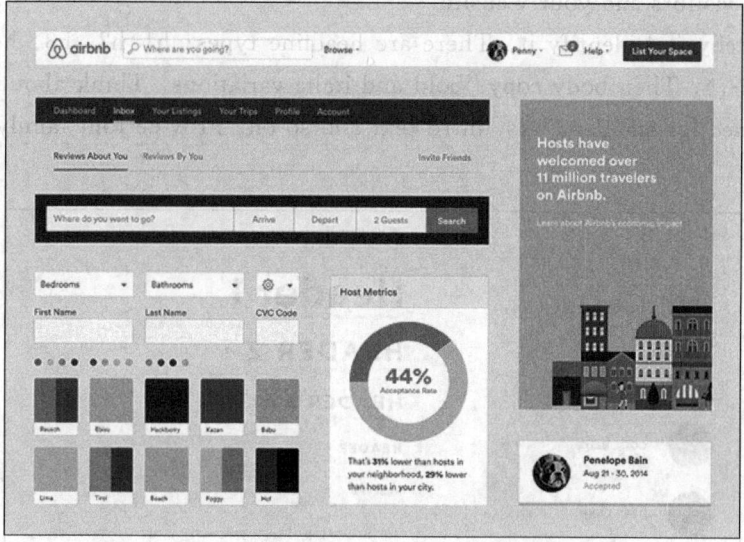

Figure 13-6   Airbnb UI Toolkit—Web by Derek Bradley

Why Is It Important?

It is extremely important when multiple designers are working on a big website or web App to ensure that they don't interpret too much and don't alter or adjust styles based on personal preference. In development, having defined elements of the website makes it easy for developers to reuse these elements. Moreover, it can make it easier because they will get what elements they have to code and will see exactly how they need to look from the start.

In order to make developers lives easier, it is the designer's duty to include all possible interactions such as hover, click, visit and other states for buttons, titles, links, etc.

Creating a Web Design Style Guide

1. Study the Brand

First, you need to study the brand so that you understand what it stands for. Get to know the story behind the brand, observe the team and figure out the vision, mission and values of the company. It is important to dig deeper into the brand so the style guide you produce will visually and emotionally represent the organization.

If you're a designer who can't code, simply open Photoshop and give your document a title and a short description of what the document is and what it is for.

If you can code, it is better to create an html document with pre-coded assets so they can be easily reused.

2. Define Typography

According to Oliver Reichenstein, typography is 95 percent of web design.

You must get typography right because it is one of the most important communication tools between visitors and your website.

Set hierarchy and identify it. There are headline types: h1, h2, h3, h4, h5 and h6 (See figure 13-7). Then body copy, bold and italic variations. Think about custom copy that will be used for smaller links, intro text and so on. Provide font family, weight and color.

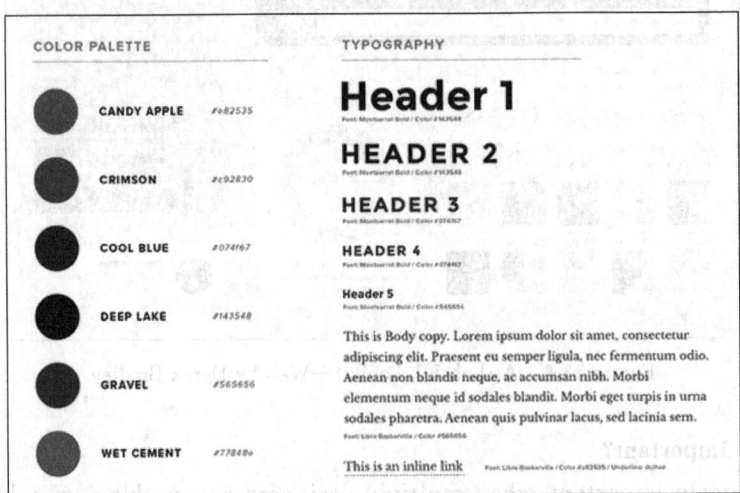

Figure 13-7　Style guides by Zech Nelson

3. Color Palette

It is incredible how humans perceive color and associate hues with known brands. Think of Coca-Cola, I bet you see that red now (See figure 13-8).

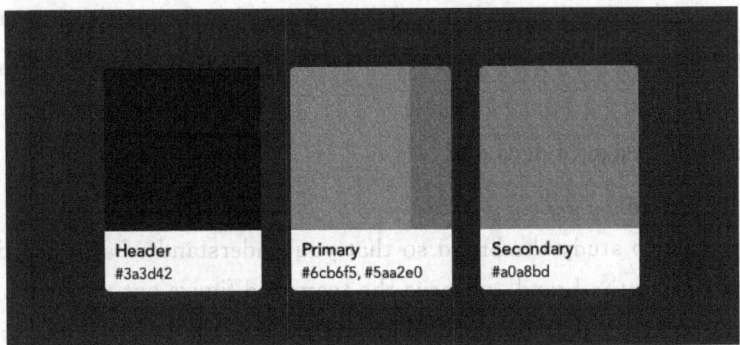

Figure 13-8　Guest Center color palette by Chloe Park

Begin by setting primary colors for your style guide that will dominate your website, dominant colors should include no more than three shades. In some cases, however, you will need secondary and even tertiary colors to illustrate your user interface, make sure you define them too. Also include neutral colors like white, grey and black for the primary brand colors to stand out.

4. Voice

The voice that I am referring to is actual copy. You have studied the brand before starting the style guide and found out that brand is youthful and trendy. If there are no directions for voice of the copy, you have to define it. It can be a simple example given showing that voice has to be professional yet funny and welcoming. Instead of stating "You've got 404 error" you can say "Oh boy, you've broken the interwebs. 404 error." If the voice were more corporate, you wouldn't do that. Brilliance hides in small things.

5. Iconography

Icons have existed for thousands of years and are older than text and words (See figure 13-9 and figure 13-10). Take advantage of using icons in your projects because they will give an instant idea to visitors as to what's going on and what will happen next. Picking the right icons will give more context to content than color palette, copy or graphics. When using icons, make sure to think about the target audience, religion, history, so you avoid misconceptions and misunderstandings. One more thing to mention, think about the brand and its values so you don't use hand-drawn icons on a large banking website.

Figure 13-9 Iconfinder is a great tool for finding awesome icons for your projects

Figure 13-10 NounProject is building a visual language of icons anyone can understand

6. Imagery

Pictures speak thousands of words (See figure 13-11). Make sure to include imagery that defines the style and direction of pictures the website should use. Once again, think about the values of the brand and its mission. For example, a water charity uses striking imagery that has strong emotion, good cause and calls to human emotion for them to be fortunate to have essential living commodities like water, food, electricity and education.

Figure 13-11　Some great websites for free imagery: 16 places to find the best free stock photos

7. Forms

Forms are what make your website or web App interactive and dynamic so the user can enter the data and you can then manipulate it and do the work.

Make sure to establish a hierarchy and include possible feedback from forms—active, hover, add error, warning and success messages including things such as a password being too weak, email being not valid or simple success messages e.g. "email was sent."

8. Buttons

Buttons are a mixture of color palette, forms and voice. Rely on these previously created assets to create consistent looking and functional buttons with different stated designs.

9. Spacing

How can spacing be in style guide? It is extremely important to mention the spacing. It can be in the form of a grid used for a layout; it can be spacing defined between headlines, buttons, images, forms and other elements.

Getting spacing right is important because it gives more breathing room to elements, and consistent use makes your work look structured and professional.

10. Dos and Don'ts

Last but not least: Make the Dos and Don'ts section much like an FAQ showing the most common pitfalls and give examples of how things should look and work instead (See figure 13-12).

Examples

Here are some of the best style guide examples to use as inspiration when creating

Figure 13-12　Twitter brand assets and guidelines

your own style guide. Keep in mind that these guides are highly influenced by the organization setup, their vision, mission and values and some decisions might be irrelevant or illogical in relation to what you are doing, so don't blindly follow the things done there (See figure 13-13～figure 13-17).

Figure 13-13　Spotify—Partner Brand Guidelines (PDF)

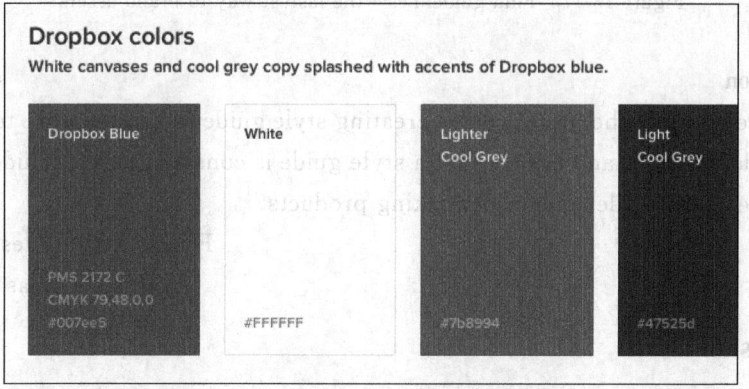

Figure 13-14　Dropbox branding and logos

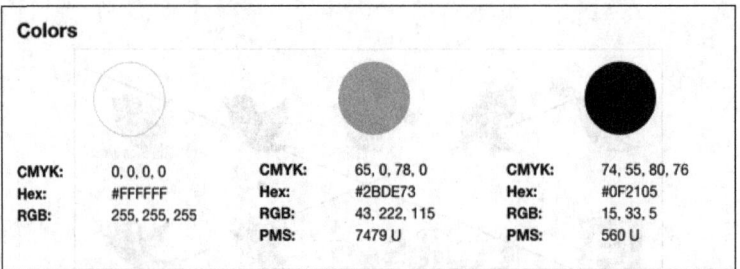

Figure 13-15　Kickstarter style guide

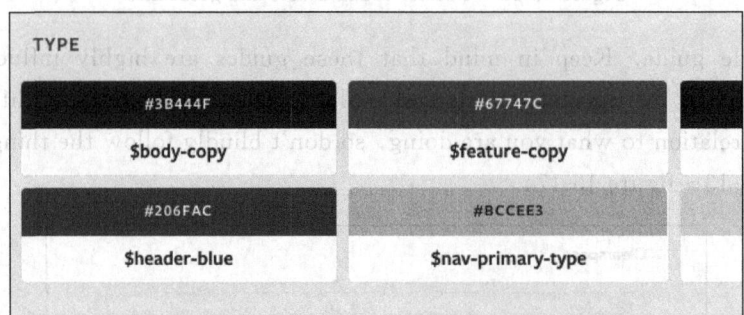

Figure 13-16　Lonely planet design guide

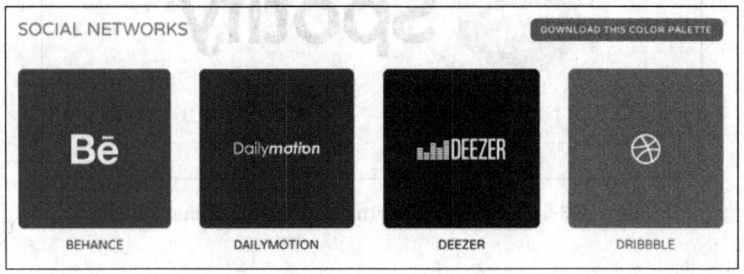

Figure 13-17　Find guidelines—the fastest way to brand assets

Conclusion

You have to study the brand you're creating style guide for, make sure to get different parts of the design right and ensure that a style guide is consistent and includes all possible scenarios when turning designs into working products.

From: http://designmodo.com

Author: Tomas Laurinavicius

New Words

Documentation *n.* 记录；证明某事属实的证据；参考资料；文献的编集，文件分类

Pre-design *abbr.* prelimiminary design 初步设计

Cohesive *adj.* 有黏着力的；紧密结合的

Visually *adv.* 视觉上；外表上；看得见地；形象化地

Emotionally *adv.* 感情上,情绪上,冲动地
Typography *n.* 凸版印刷术,排印,印刷样式

Exercises

Translation

1. A style guide is a collection of pre-designed elements, graphics and rules designers or developers should follow to ensure that separate website pieces will be consistent and will create a cohesive experience at the end.

2. It is extremely important when multiple designers are working on a big website or web App to ensure that they don't interpret too much and don't alter or adjust styles based on personal preference. In development, having defined elements of the website makes it easy for developers to reuse these elements.

3. Take advantage of using icons in your projects because they will give an instant idea to visitors as to what's going on and what will happen next.

4. Pictures speak thousands of words. Make sure to include imagery that defines the style and direction of pictures the website should use.

5. You have to study the brand you're creating style guide for, make sure to get different parts of the design right and ensure that a style guide is consistent and includes all possible scenarios when turning designs into working products.

Definitions

Style Guide

_____
_____
_____
_____
_____
_____

Have you ever design website by yourself? Talk about your experience.

_____
_____
_____
_____
_____
_____
_____
_____

Reading Material
11 Web Design Trends for 2016

Are you ready for 2016? Let's bring on the web design trends.

The new year will come with plenty of new techniques and trends, but the dominant theme is likely to be a continuation of things we have started to see at the end of 2015. More video, vertical patterns, Material Design-inspired interfaces and slide-style sites will grow in popularity.

And it's not hard for you to make the most of these concepts. Here, we'll ring in the new year with 11 web design trends (and plenty of great examples) that designers will be seeing a lot of in 2016. (Make sure to click the links as well and play around with some of these sites to really get a feel for them. Many of the trends are just as much in the user interface as the visuals)

2016 Web Design Trends
Vertical Patterns and Scrolling

A bigger leaning toward mobile—with some thinking mobile traffic could equal desktop traffic this year—means more sites are being designed with vertical user flows (See figure 13-18).

Figure 13-18 Vertical patterns and scrolling

A few years ago, we were all debating the end of the scroll in web design only to find it roaring back as an important interaction tool. Smaller screens lead users to scroll more and designers to create user interfaces that are much more vertical in nature.

More Card-Style Interfaces

One of the biggest elements to spring from Material Design has been the emergence of card-style interfaces (See figure 13-19). They are in everything from Apps to websites to printed pieces. Cards are fun to create, keep information organized in a user-friendly container and are engaging for users. The other bonus is that they work almost seamlessly across devices because cards can "stack" across or down the screen (or both).

Figure 13-19   More card-style interfaces

Hero Video Headers (Think Movie-Style Sites)

Websites design is going to the movies (See figure 13-20). Higher speed Internet connections and better video plugin integration is making it easier for more websites to include an immersive movie-style experience. Video clips are growing from small snippets to almost full-length preview clips. The images are sharp, crisp and in high definition,

Figure 13-20   Hero video headers (think movie-style sites)

creating a video experience online that is new to users, but familiar from other devices, such as televisions.

Tiny Animations

Animation has been one of the "it" trends of 2015. From hero-style animations that lead off a site design to those tiny divots that you almost miss, moving elements are everywhere (See figure 13-21). And they will continue to grow in popularity, even as they decrease in size. Animated user interface elements are a fun way to help engage users, give them something while they wait for content to load and provide an element of surprise.

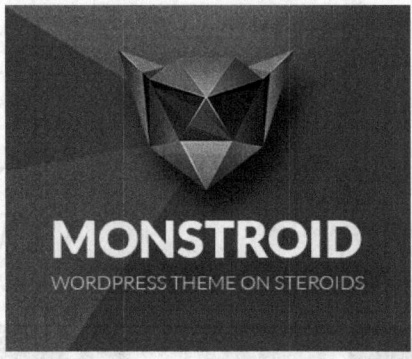

Figure 13-21 Tiny animations

The most important factor when it comes to animation is to make sure it serves a purpose: Why are you creating the effect and what exactly is it supposed to do?

Focus on Interactions

Going hand-in-hand with animation is interaction (See figure 13-22). As the staple of Apps and mobile interfaces, interactions create links between users and devices. Good interactions are often small—even micro in nature—and provide value to the user. From the simplest of alarms to a text message to a blip that it is your turn in a game, these small interactions shape how people interact with devices (and how loyal they are to associated

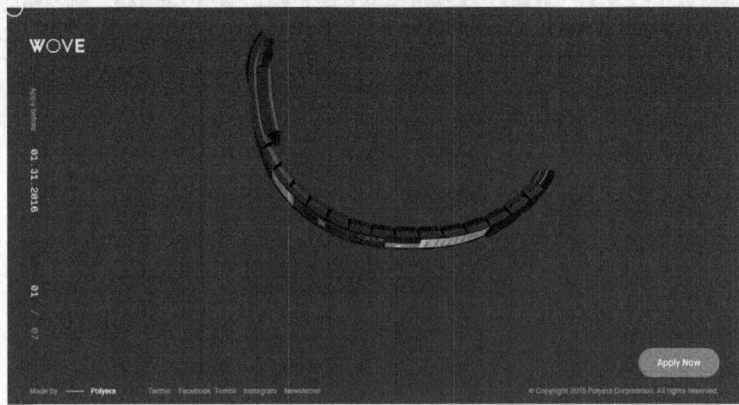

Figure 13-22 Focus on interactions

websites and Apps).

Even More Beautiful Typography

Streamlined interfaces have paved the way for the emergence of beautiful typography (See figure 13-23). (As has the addition of more usable web type tools such as Google Fonts and Adobe Typekit as mainstream options for creating expansive type libraries online)

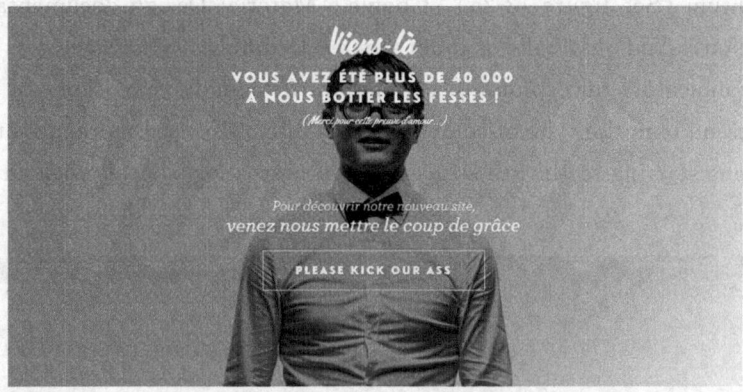

Figure 13-23   Even more beautiful typography

Big, bold typefaces will continue to rule because they work well with other trendy elements. This simple concept of lettering gives more room to other elements, while communicating the message with a highly readable display. The must-try trick is a simple pairing of a readable typeface and fun novelty option.

Illustrations and Sketches

Illustrations and sketches bring a fun element of whimsy to a site design (See figure 13-24). They can work for sites of all types and aren't just for children anymore. The illustration style has also started to grow in popularity when it comes to some of the

Figure 13-24   Illustrations and sketches

smaller pieces of website design as well, such as icons and other user interface elements. What's nice about this trend is that illustrations make a site feel a little more personal. Because an illustration or sketch style icon appears to be hand-drawn, it looks and feels personal for users. That can go a long way into creating a connection with them.

Bolder, Brighter Color (With an 1980s Vibe)

Big, bright color really started to emerge with the flat design trend and has continued to gain momentum (See figure 13-25). Google's Material Design documentation furthers that conversation. And just take a look around Dribbble, where color is everywhere. These are key indicators that color will stay big in the coming year. Some of the change to the big color trend is in the type of colors used. While 2015 used more monotone big color designs, usage is starting to shift to larger and brighter color palettes with an almost 1980s vibe to them.

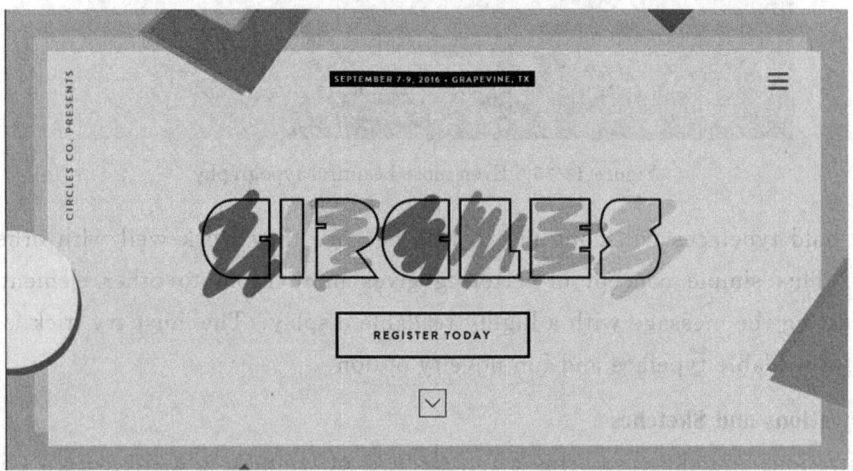

Figure 13-25 Bolder, brighter color (With an 1980s Vibe)

More Hamburgers and Iconography

Icons, icons, icons! From the debated hamburger icon to divots through design projects, iconography is big (See figure 13-26). More designers are releasing fun UI and icon kits that are easy to use, making icons easier than ever to work with. (And pretty affordable) One of the other big things designers are experimenting with is oversized icons thanks to SVG formats.

Reality-Imagination Blur

Is that site real or animated? Is the path predetermined or can I make choices along the way? The next step of gamification and design is emerging with a blurred line between what's real and what's created (or imaginary) in web design projects. And the results are pretty stunning.

From virtual reality to websites that let you make choices to find new content, this type of customization is personal and users seem to really like it. This trend also includes creating imagery that looks real, but you know that it is not (See figure 13-27).

Figure 13-26 More hamburgers and iconography

Figure 13-27 Reality-imagination blur

Websites with Slides

First there were sliders, so that websites could move images within a frame to showcase content. The next part of that evolution includes full-screen slides (See figure 13-28). Each slide refreshes the entire screen with new content; it can work with a click, scroll or timed effect. Users can navigate forward and backward for an experience that is almost physical. Expect to see plenty—and we mean a lot—of sites using this concept in the coming months.

Conclusion

Looking through the examples above it's easy to see that there's not just one web design trend that designers will focus on in the coming year. It's a combination (and culmination) of multiple trends from the past few years. Look even closer and you'll see that many of these sites use multiple trending elements from this list to create interactive and engaging websites.

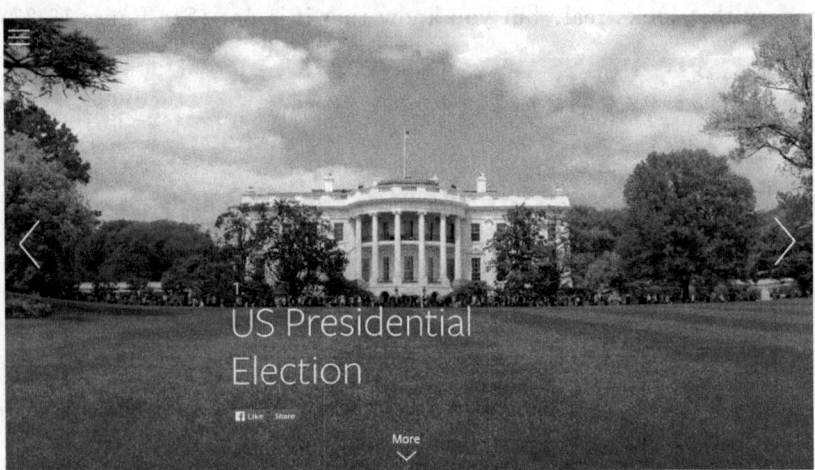

Figure 13-28   Websites with slides

What trends are you most excited about in 2016? Are there any we missed on this list? Join the conversation in the comments below.

From: http://designmodo.com

Author: Carrie Cousins

UNIT 14

Information Design

COMPETENCIES

After you have read this unit, you should be able to:
1. Discuss what is Information Design.
2. Find some information designs, which style you are favorite.

Text A

What Is Information Design?

Introduction

STC's Special Interest Group on Information Design (See figure 14-1) was founded in 1997. A scant 3 years later, it has over 2,700 members. That astonishing and rapid growth is testimony to the widespread interest in the topic and is deeply gratifying to those of us who have thought of ourselves as information designers for many years.

What do those 2,700 SIG members mean by information design? As Beth Mazur says about plain language in her article in this issue, "Ask 10 people and you'll get 10 different answers."

In part, the differences in those answers may reflect the backgrounds of the people answering the question. Information design, like many other aspects of technical communication, draws on many research disciplines and many fields of practice, including anthropology and ethnography, architecture, graphic design, human factors and cognitive psychology, instructional design and instructional technology, linguistics, organizational psychology, rhetoric, typography, and usability.

The Two Meanings of Information Design

In part, the differences in definitions may reflect an ambiguity between using design in a very broad sense and, at the same time, in a narrower sense (see Redish, *Document and information design* 1999). I and—I suspect—many others within the Information Design SIG use information design, perhaps at different times, to mean
1. The overall process of developing a successful document.
2. The way the information is presented on the page or screen (layout, typography,

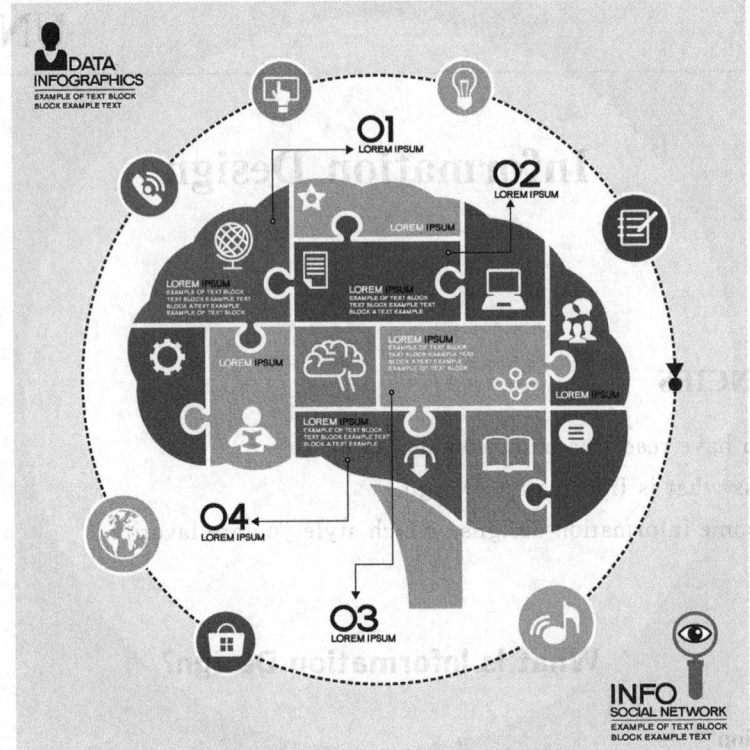

Figure 14-1　Information design

color, and so forth).

Using the same term for the whole and a part of that whole violates a guideline of good writing, but the fact is that the term information design means both. (A little later in this commentary, I briefly describe a historical reason for this dual usage, at least within the North American technical communication community)

Information Design as the Overall Process

My definition of document design or information design has always been, first and foremost, the "whole." Information design is what we do to develop a document (or communication) that works for its users. Working for its users means that the people who must or want to use the information can.

- Find what they need.
- Understand what they find.
- Use what they understand appropriately.

This definition comes with two additional points that information designers must always remember:

- Most of the time, most users of functional information are using that information to reach a personal goal—to answer a question or to complete a task.
- The users, not the information designer, decide how much time and effort to spend

trying to find and understand the information they need.

To develop a successful document (or any other type of product, such as a website, software application, or hardware device) requires a process that starts with understanding what you are trying to achieve, who will use it, how they will use it, and so on.

When I drew a model (flowchart, job aid) for that process in 1978, I called it the "document design process." Today it might well be called the "information design process." The model has been updated many times over the years based on experience, conversations with colleagues and clients, and changes that make it more appropriate for different media, but many characteristics have remained through all the permutations of the model, especially:
- The importance of the planning questions and of the front-end analysis;
- The role of iterative evaluation;
- The interaction and equal importance of writing and presentation (the other, narrower, meaning of information design);
- The fact that the specific guidelines that one uses depend on the answers to the planning questions (That is, there is no one best design for all situations).

Figure 14-2 is an example of a recent version of this model.

Information Design As the Presentation on Page or Screen

Information design in the narrower meaning of the way the information is presented on the page or screen is a part of the larger information design process. In this sense, information design encompasses layout, typography, color, relationship between words and pictures, and so forth.

The two meanings of information design are intertwined. Clear presentation on the page or screen is critical. However, the presentation that works for users is not just a matter of aesthetics. The best presentation for a specific communication depends on the situation—on the answers to the planning questions that the broader definition makes us think through.

Information design on the level of page or screen also depends on doing a good job of other parts of the broader process, such as selecting the right content and organizing so users can find what they need quickly. Information design as whole and as part must work together.

A Bit of History

How did I (and others) come to use *information design* in both the broad and narrow meanings? I can think of two reasons:
- Many STC people come to information design from a background in rhetoric and technical communication, which take the broad view, stressing users, content, organization, and writing, as well as presentation.
- The U. S. federal government funded a broad-view project and called it the

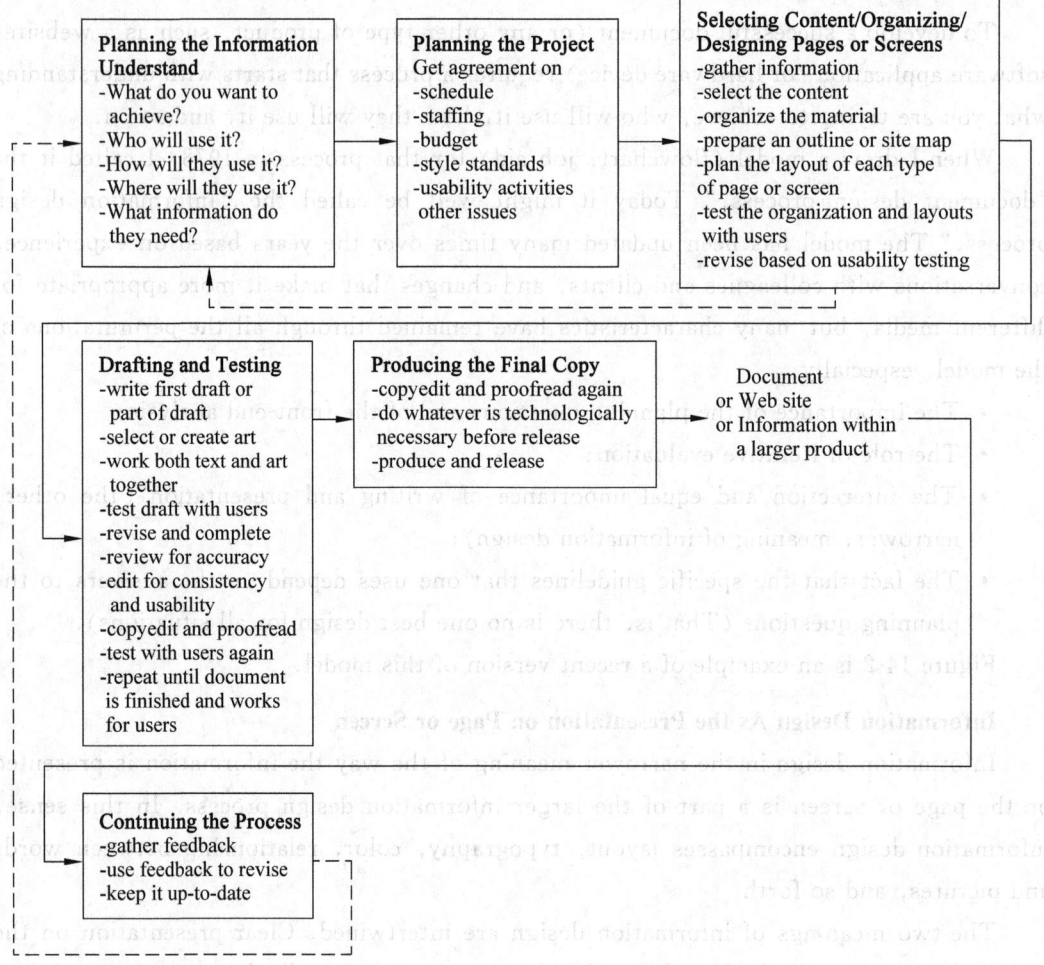

Figure 14-2　A model of the information design process. This is a visual of information design in the broad sense of doing what is necessary to develop information that works for users. The dotted arrows indicate that the process is iterative, not strictly linear. A dotted arrow should also connect the Drafting and Testing box back to the box on Selecting Content/Organizing/Designing Pages or Screens. Model © 1999, Janice C. Redish, based on versions of a similar model developed between 1978 and 1999 at the American Institutes for Research and at Redish & Associates, Inc.

Document Design Project. For an excellent treatise on the first of these reasons, read Karen Schriver's Dynamics in document design (1997). I elaborate a bit here on the second reason because many readers of Technical communication, especially those who have joined the field recently, may be unaware of this history.

Information design for the Web

The Web requires information design in the broad sense of the entire process described in Figure 14-2. We must not let excitement over technical possibilities or the super rapid pace of development eliminate the front end of the process. To develop a successful website, you must first consider the planning questions in the process, select the relevant content, and organize it into an appropriate hierarchy for ease of navigating quickly to the right place.

The Web also requires information design in the narrower sense of paying great attention to the mix of text and pictures and to presentation on the screen. Technical communicators know that for information on a page to be accessible, it must be chunked into small pieces, and the different page elements (such as headings, instructions, notes, screen shots) have to be clearly visible, separable, and easily identified. That's even more true on the screen where the amount of space available is smaller, where reading from the screen is slower and more difficult than from paper, where people have come to expect less text and more visuals. Learning to turn text into visual presentations (lists, tables, maps, pictures, fragments) is one of the most important skills for a technical communicator turned Web designer.

From: *What Is Information Design?*
Author: JANICE C. (GINNY) REDISH

New Words

Information Design 信息设计
Appropriately *adv.* 适当地
Document *n.* 公文;(计算机)文档,证件;*vt.* 记录;证明;为……提供证明
Evaluation *n.* 估价
Screen *n.* 屏幕;银幕;屏风;*vt.* 掩藏;庇护;检查;放映
Encompass *vt.* 围绕,包围;包含或包括某事物;完成
Rhetoric *n.* 修辞学;花言巧语;辩论法,雄辩术;华丽的文词
Elaborate *vi.* 详尽说明;变得复杂;*vt.* 详细制定;详尽阐述
Visible *adj.* 看得见的;显然的;可得到的;可察觉到的

Exercises

Translation

1. Information design, like many other aspects of technical communication, draws on many research disciplines and many fields of practice, including anthropology and ethnography, architecture, graphic design, human factors and cognitive psychology, instructional design and instructional technology, linguistics, organizational psychology, rhetoric, typography, and usability.

2. Information design is what we do to develop a document (or communication) that works for its users.

3. Information design on the level of page or screen also depends on doing a good job of other parts of the broader process, such as selecting the right content and organizing so users can find what they need quickly. Information design as whole and as part must work

together.

4. The Web also requires information design in the narrower sense of paying great attention to the mix of text and pictures and to presentation on the screen.

Definitions
Information Design

Text B
Physical, Cognitive, and Affective: A Three-part Framework for Information Design

A Definition of Information Design

Before offering a more comprehensive definition of information design (See figure 14-3), a consideration of design in general might be appropriate. According to Rowland, *Designing and instractional design* (1993):

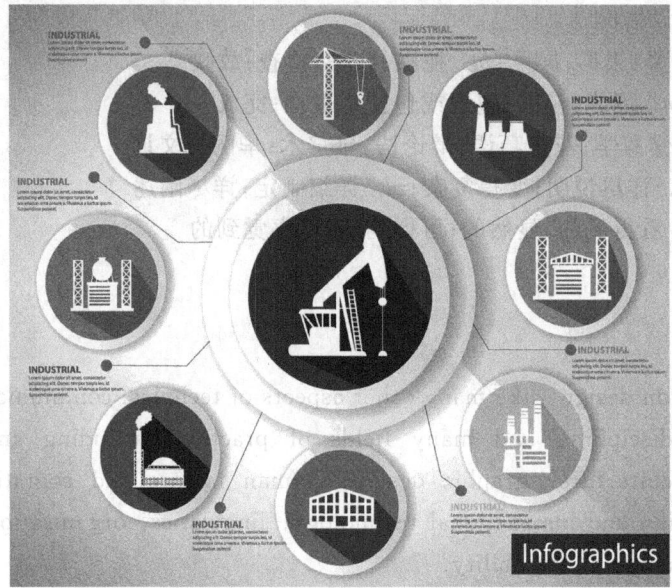

Figure 14-3   Information design

Some argue that a science of design is possible and represents an important goal. Cross, reporting on a number of studies in design, argues that design is quite different from science. While scientists focus on the problem, on discovering the rule that is operating, designers focus on the solution, on achieving the desired result. (p. 81)

He concludes that design is ultimately a series of personal choices based on a subjective sense of what is "right."

In other words, design is a problem-solving discipline. It considers more than the appearance of the designed product, but also the underlying structure of the solution and its anticipated reception by users. Because design is focused on solving problems, a design theory must provide more than a series of guidelines about discrete characteristics of the solution; it must focus designers on identifying problems and supplying a framework for identifying and considering the interrelated issues that must be addressed in a solution. Design must also help designers develop their instincts for choosing "right" solutions.

Table 1: Definitions of Information Design
- Information design is concerned with making information accessible and usable to people. (David Sless 1990).
- Information design is the intentional process in which information related to a domain is transformed in order to obtain an understandable representation of that domain. (Peter J. Bogaards 1994).
- Information design is the defining, planning, and shaping of the contents of a message and the environments it is presented in with the intention of achieving particular objectives in relation to the needs of users. (*ID news* 1999).
- Information design helps explain things and uses language, typography, graphic design, systems and business process improvement as its key tools. Information design is focused on users and is committed to using usability and other research and testing to find out whether its products actually achieve their objectives. (*Text matters* 1996).
- Information design is the art and science of preparing information so that it can be used by human beings with efficiency and effectiveness.
- *Most of these definitions were found on the website of the International Institute for Information Design.*

Table 1 lists many definitions that have been offered for information design. Some are no different from the definitions of document design that we have already seen, with their primary focus on text and pictures. Others take a broader view, focusing on defining the problem and designing effective solutions for problems in communication.

If information design primarily focuses on issues of appearance and text, it is not distinct from document design, nor does it solve the problem of the limited focus of document design in most current practice and research.

Information design must therefore have a broader focus, one that encompasses not only graphics, text, and reader goals, but also the goals of the sponsor who commissioned the text. Therefore, information design may be better defined as:

Preparing communication products so that they achieve the performance objectives established for them. This process involves:

1. Analyzing communication problems.

2. Establishing performance objectives that, when achieved, address those problems.

3. Developing a blueprint for a communication effort to achieve those objectives.

4. Developing the components of the planned communication effort solution.

5. Evaluating the ultimate effectiveness of the effort.

Some of the terms in this definition have specific meanings.

- Performance objectives are observable, measurable tasks and business goals that users should be able to perform, the conditions for doing those tasks, and the level of acceptable work (Mager 1997).
- A blueprint is a detailed design plan for a document that indicates not only the content to be presented, but the extent and format of the presentation (Kostur 1999).

Inherent in this definition of information design is the Analysis, Design, Development, Implementation, and Evaluation (ADDIE) model that is widely used in instructional design (Gustafson 1991) and is similar to models used in software engineering.

A Model of Information Design

This new model I propose approaches information design on three levels. This model is adapted from the three levels that theorists in education and instructional design consider when designing courses (Dick and Carey 1990).

- Physical, the ability to find information.
- Cognitive (intellectual), the ability to understand information.
- Affective (emotional), the ability to feel comfortable with the presentation of the information (comfort with the information itself might not be possible, depending on the message).

From: *Physical, Cognitive, and Affective: A Three-part Framework for Information Design*
Author: SAUL CARLINER

New Words

Framework *n.* 框架;构架
Appearance *n.* 外貌,外观;出现;露面
Product *n.* 产品;乘积;结果;作品
Guideline *n.* 指导方针;指导原则
Blueprint *n.* 蓝图,设计图;计划大纲;原本; *vt.* 为…制蓝图;为…制订计划

Exercises

1. In other words, design is a problem-solving discipline. It considers more than the

appearance of the designed product, but also the underlying structure of the solution and its anticipated reception by users.

2. Information design must therefore have a broader focus, one that encompasses not only graphics, text, and reader goals, but also the goals of the sponsor who commissioned the text.

3. A blueprint is a detailed design plan for a document that indicates not only the content to be presented, but the extent and format of the presentation (Kostur 1999).

Can you translate the following information design to English?

Reading Material
Audible Information Design in the New York City Subway System: A Case Study

1. Introduction

This paper presents a case study of the New York City subway system (See figure 14-4) as a means to articulate a new methodology for the analysis, simulation, and design of sound information systems. It is a hypothetical exercise, in that the new design we propose for the subway system is not intended for immediate application and would not be practical to implement using the existing equipment.

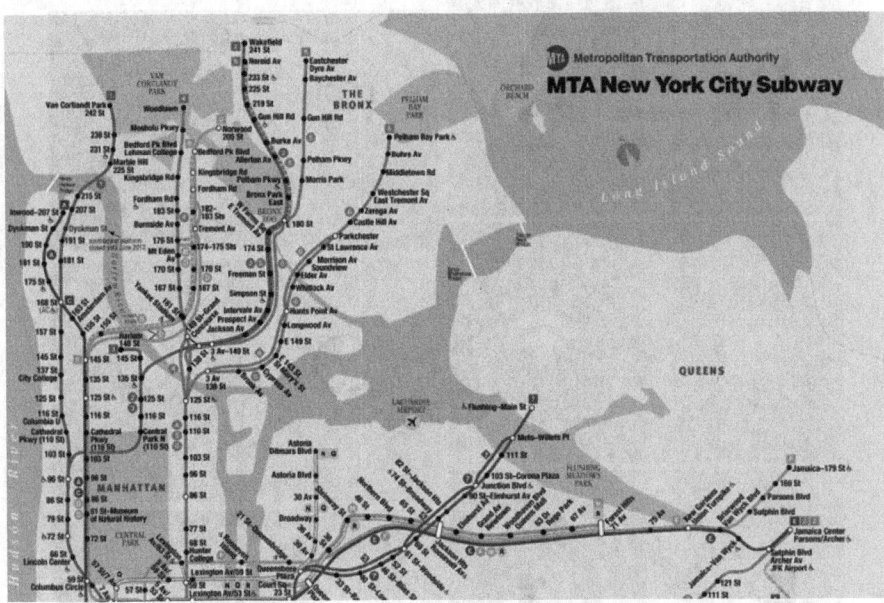

Figure 14-4　New York City subway system

While the New York City subway system is not a complex information environment, it nonetheless provides a very attractive site in which to study sound used as an information medium. At present, the use of sound is uniform across the hundreds of stations and thousands of trains throughout the system. More importantly, an audible signal is a crucial modality for the communication of several key pieces of information, including the success or failure of a turnstile transaction, and the arrival of a train in the station.

The New York City subway system thus presents some straightforward audible display design challenges: a few simple pieces of information need to be communicated quickly, unambiguously, and harmoniously by a small number of audible signals. How successful is the existing design at accomplishing this task, and how can it be improved?

As we will see below, the existing design fails to reach its potential for informing system users through sound. The design also has important ergonomic and aesthetic shortcomings that will be discussed in greater detail below.

Principles from music, information design, interface design, and the emerging field of auditory display science are applied to create a new system-wide sound design. This proposed design will be presented using audiovisual simulations. Our goal is to explore the notion that a unified, musically composed sound design not only improves the experience of subway system users, but also expands the possibilities for communicating critical information through sound.

2. Existing Audio Signals in the New York City Subway System

All subway stations posses at least one row of turnstiles, a token booth where subway tokens and Metrocards (electronic fare cards) are sold, and a train platform (track) area. Any station in which the token booth and turnstiles are not immediately adjacent to the track also has a designated "Off-hours waiting area" that is generally within sight of the token booth and turnstiles.

1) Turnstiles

The New York City subway system uses both token coins and newer electronic farecards (called "Metrocards") at its turnstiles. Table 14-1 shows the various conditions and signals associated with turnstile transactions. The turnstiles display short electronic text messages that visually indicate the specific user condition, and there is a small speaker inside the card reader that beeps audibly after each card swipe. Example 1: turnstile signals is a recording of the single, double, and triple beep sounds produced by the turnstiles.

Table 14-1 Existing mapping of turnstile conditions to audible signals

Transaction result	Specific user condition	Associated Sound
Success	Token OK	Plain beep
	Metrocard OK	
	Metrocard OK-reduced rate	
	Metrocard OK-funds low (one ride or less remaining on pay-per-use-Metrocard)	Triple beep
Swipe failure	Swipe again	Double beep
	Swipe again at this turnstile	
Card failure	Insufficient funds on Metrocard	
	Monthly, weekly, or daily Metrocard expired	

2) Waiting Area

All major subway stations and many smaller ones have waiting areas that are separate from the track platforms. Electronic display signs have been installed in these waiting areas to tell riders when a train is arriving. A text message on the sign indicates the destination of the train and its track designation (local or express). The text display is accompanied by a loud, pulsing whistle sound that is the same for all arriving trains. The sound can be heard in Example 2: arriving train signal.

While these electronic display signs are visible only in the area immediately in front of them, their signals are audible for hundreds of yards through stairways, connecting corridors, and on the train platforms. Many riders respond to the beep signal by breaking into a run in corridors or stairwells in hopes of catching the arriving train, even though the beep does not tell them the direction of the arriving train. Rider responses will be explored in more detail in section three below.

3) Train Platforms and Interiors

On train platforms, verbal announcements convey information about train delays or routing anomalies when necessary. No attention signal precedes these messages, nor are any other non-verbal audio signals routinely present here. Verbal announcements are also made aboard trains: as a train pulls into each station, the conductor announces the name of the station and any available connections. As the train prepares to leave a station, the conductor announces the next stop and recites a verbal warning to, "Stand clear of the closing doors," at which time a two-tone alert signal is sounded just prior to the doors closing. Example 3: subway train interior presents the audible signal heard inside the train cars.

3. User Survey

This section presents the responses of subway riders to the existing sound environment. Thirty-six subway riders were asked questions about their awareness of and feelings about the signals present in the system. While this survey is too small to be of statistical value, the rider responses nonetheless help to identify some shortcomings of the system and offer clues as to directions to follow in the redesign. Riders were asked questions about the helpfulness of three main signals in the system: the beeps of the turnstiles, the "train arriving" signal, and the "doors closing" signal. Figure 14-5 shows a summary of the results.

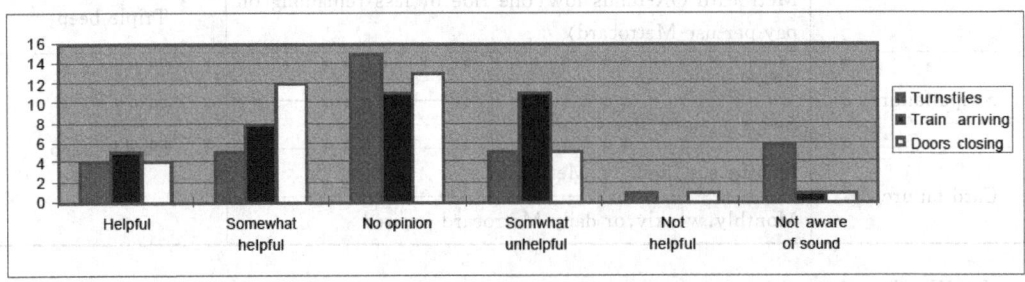

Figure 14-5　Summary of rider survey results

Respondents were also encouraged to offer opinions and observations about the quality of the sonic experience in the subway system. Regarding the turnstile beeps, four people said they could not tell the difference between the signals for successful and unsuccessful transactions. One rider said, "I hear a sound but I don't know what it means, so I just go through the turnstile and see if it works." Another person specifically commented that he liked the beeps and noticed that they meant different things. He especially appreciated the warning that his card was low on funds. Several people seemed to equate the "swipe again" signals with the fact that the Metrocards don't work well much of the time. Four of these people used the word "annoying" to describe this signal.

In response to the "train arriving" signal, seven people commented that you cannot tell which train is coming from the sound. Five people said that the signal is hard to distinguish from the combined sound of many Metrocards being swiped at the turnstiles. One woman commented, "It took me five years to figure out what the hell that sound is." Another person said the arrival beeps are too loud.

As for the "closing door" signal, five people commented that this sound made them feel safer. Six people called the sound annoying. Several people associated this sound with rush hour and stressful commutes. One person said, "I like it. It keeps me awake in the morning." Another person liked the musicality of it. One person was particularly enthusiastic about all the system's audible signals. "It's like Pavlonian conditioning," he said. "[The sounds] tell me my morning is going well."

From: *Audible Information Design in the New York City Subway System: A Case Study*
Author: Benjamin U. Rubin

UNIT 15

Architectural Animation

COMPETENCIES

After you have read this unit, you should be able to:
1. Discuss what is Architectural Animation.
2. Try to make an Architectural Animation by yourself.

Text A
Making of Phoenix & Vieques House Animation

Introduction

Hello Everyone! I am Viktor, architectural designer at the office of Messana O'Rorke. I would like to present two architectural walkthrough animations that our office produced for Global Architecture's exhibitions in 2013 and 2014.

I would like to thank Ronen for kindly hosting my article and to all the artists here for the substantial knowledge that you share. I have learned so much from you…

About "Arch-Anims"

I'm always interested in experimenting on the edge of graphic design-illustration-architecture-animation, and I was eager to create an architectural walkthrough that is not conventional and has its own style and narration. It seems to me that architects use virtual walkthroughs only to document their projects and don't think of them as individual artistic pieces. It is just not in their focus and usually before a deadline they throw together something that is just… there. Long, repetitive, uninteresting shots and medium quality renderings. It's informative but not engaging. Of course making a high-end movie is an option in about every 2 out of 100 cases.

Therefore, the best architectural videos are personal developments. For instance the best architectural animation ever-Alex Roman's "The Third and the Seventh". You can see the heart & soul that went in it and it is also enjoyable for nonprofessionals, because of the pure beauty of it.

However, I think that there can be great potential in architectural animation without having the "Big Shiny Yacht". I am going to show you my workflow that can be great when you have to act fast.

Making these videos was a great experience for me and fortunately the open-minded office of MO'R has always been very supportive of this kind of experimenting.

The Concept

The whole concept of the videos started with a DEADLINE over our heads (See figure 15-1). I made 6 renderings of Phoenix House for GA's exhibition of 2013. We submitted them, but they asked us to send them a quick animation of the project as well within 1 week. First, we were leaning towards an un-inventive SketchUP walkthrough. However, one of the partners at MO'R was in love with the purity of ambient occlusion passes of previous renderings and this gave us the idea. Making AO is fairly fast and easy and we already had the 6 renderings. I just had to stitch them together and we're done (hopefully within 1 week).

Figure 15-1 The concept

So our concept was to create a monochrome, maquette like, raw style with glitches, grain and other imperfections and to have the colorful renderings as glimpses of the real thing. (Two worlds if you like). We liked the idea of this juxtaposition, and how the images became accentuated climactic points in the animation. We basically tried to mimic the process when you are turning a maquette in your hand and looking for the best views. In the case of Phoenix House the raw animation was also a perfect way to show the secluded nature of the building.

As far as the story of Phoenix House Video is concerned, the beginning and ending framed the narrative. We wander in the desert, find a "cactus flower", it opens up for us, then closes itself up again and we leave it behind.

With Vieques we tried to raise the bid. We were to have the same concept as for Phoenix House, but we aspired to create a unique character to it. Here I made the fault of overstuffing the concept (just like the Transformers sequels). Luckily, MO'R has a reductive way of thinking so the excrescent sequences were simplified greatly.

The only new feature we had was light & shadow. Since Vieques House was designed as a tropical vacation house, light and shadow were very important. Therefore we wanted to introduce them as part of the story and have some playfulness within the monochromatic style. We were inspired by an YSL commercial. It is just so simple. Of course it is telling a totally different story, but we liked how the light is a part of it.

The client of Vieques House required a minimal living environment, where he could disconnect. A place that gives a strong shelter from the quickly shifting weather. Messana O'Rorke's response was to create a modern version of a 'fortress'. This gave the idea of the story-it is about conquering this fortress. At first it is just not welcoming at all. It is threatening from below but as you get closer and start to understand it, it becomes comforting and cozy, up until the point where the viewer just dissolves in the lap pool.

In comparison with the framed structure of the Phoenix House animation the structure of the Vieques House animation is concentric as we are getting closer and closer and closer to the subject.

Now, I am going to go through the making of Vieques House as it is more complex. I will also refer to Phoenix House at some points.

Modeling

The base model was made in SketchUP (See figure 15-2). I always use a combination of groups and layers in SketchUP. I only put the grouped entities onto different layers and leave all edges and faces on the default layer. This way there is no conflict. I always make sure not to have flipped surfaces because they cause a lot of headaches later on. I like to model all small reveals of doors, windows in this stage. I only use colors at the end of modeling to separate the different materials.

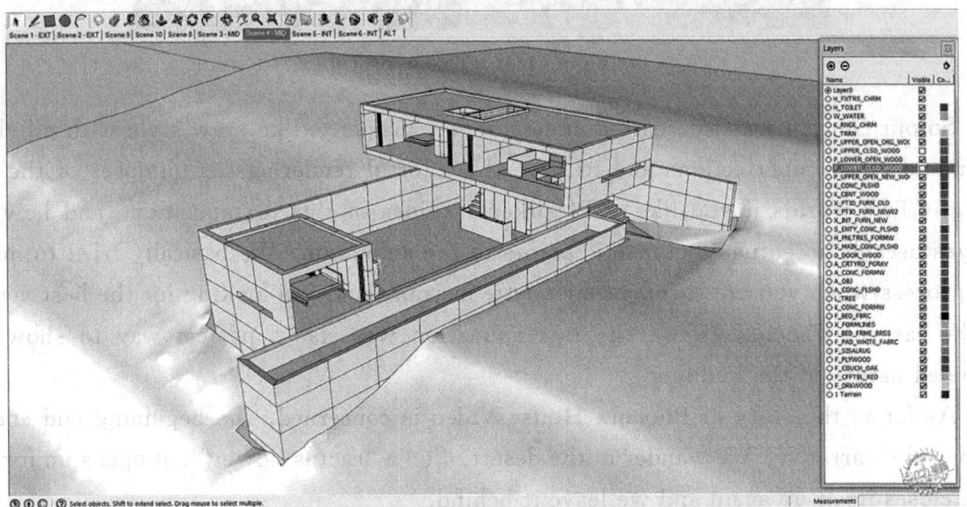

Figure 15-2 Modeling

Then in 3ds Max I made further enhancements. I chamfered some edges, made and imported a couple models. For the renderings I used 2d vegetation, because I had to do them fast. For the video I used VRayProxy trees and bushes.

Rendering and Post Production

The 6+6 rendered images are just not at a level that I should brag about. There is way better making-off's on this site regarding beautiful photorealistic renderings (See figure 15-3). I still have a lot to learn about materials and lighting of 3d scenes. I do most of the work in PS.

Figure 15-3 Rendering and post production

Cameras, Lights and Props

Animating the cameras was a relatively long process (See figure 15-4). I wanted all camera views to be interesting, but also to be coherent with the one before and after, therefore I was constantly looking for references in the shots (a corner of the building, the radio, the middle tree). I tried to balance steady shots with moving ones. I changed the cameras' focal lengths at certain points.

Figure 15-4 Cameras, lights and props

I only put one VRayLight in the scene. It circles around the building. We wanted the light to be artificial. Instead of imitating the sunlight the idea was to imitate a table light that you would use to enlighten a maquette.

I made a couple of copies of the light and controlled the speed of them separately for each scene (See figure 15-5). Wherever the camera moves fast the light moves slowly and vice versa. The constantly moving light was a good way to make the environment lively in comparison to Phoenix House.

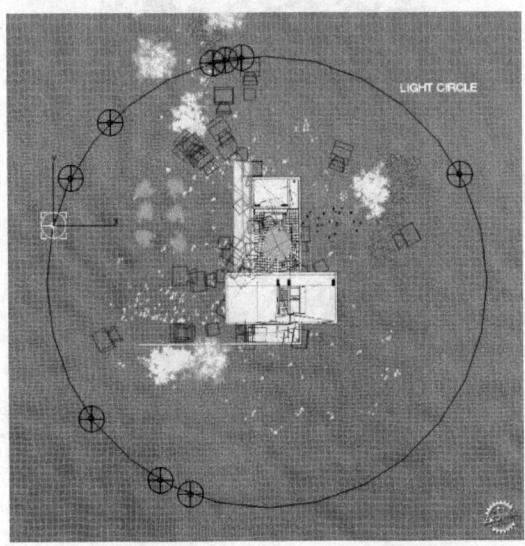

Figure 15-5　Cameras, lights and props

Afterwards I animated all the moving elements like the birds, the ball, the splash and the slippers (See figure 15-6). My favorite was the animation of the birds. I made one low poly bird, animated its wings with the Bend modifier. Then I scattered a couple copies, offset their keys and changed their trajectories. I refined them up until they looked good from the camera.

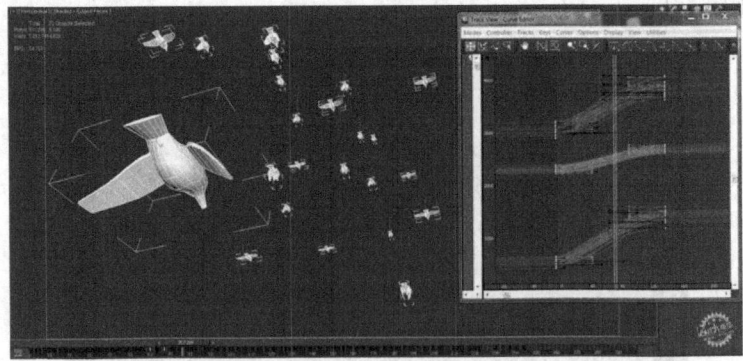

Figure 15-6　Cameras, lights and props

In Phoenix House the only animated props were the tumbleweed and the boots. I only put the boots in as Easter eggs and was about to delete them. However, the partners at Messana O'Rorke just loved them and they became signature elements. The comments that we have received always mentioned the boots (See figure 15-7). I really like them because it breaks the "architectural seriousness" of the animation with self irony at a climatic point. I hid an Easter egg in Vieques House as well. If you find it you must have enormous Waldo/Wally experiences.

Rendering of the Sequences

I made draft renderings and created the final look of a couple frames in PS before I started rendering whole sequences (See figure 15-8 and figure 15-9). When we were happy with these reference images, I started rendering.

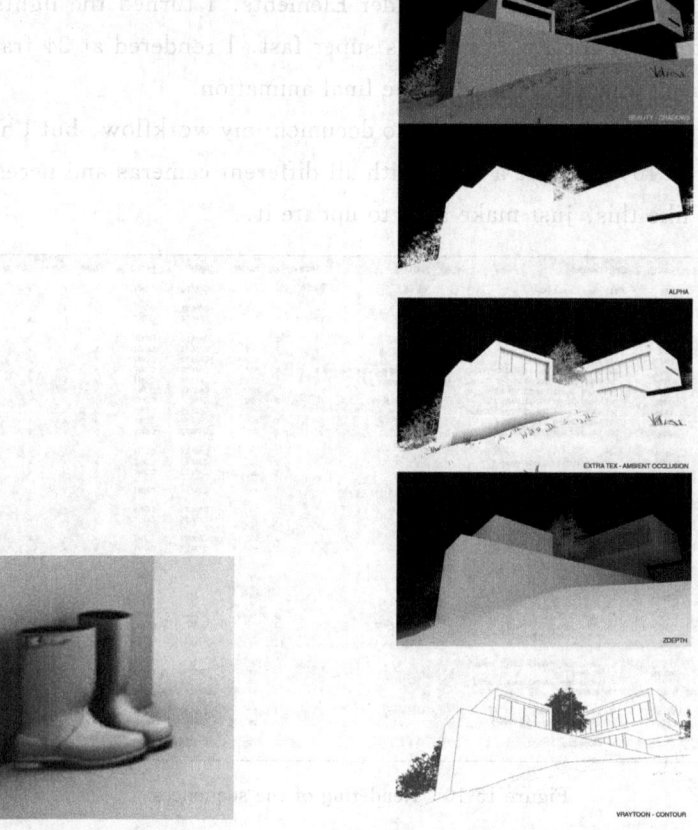

Figure 15-7 Boots   Figure 15-8 Rendering of the sequences

I used V-Ray with Render Elements: Beauty, Alpha, Zdepth and ExtraTex passes. ExtraTex render element is I think the best way to create ambient occlusion. You just have to add to it the VRayDirt map that you usually use for an AO material.

I only had direct light in the scene so the frames rendered relatively fast. Although, I had troubles with the anti-aliasing. Its calculation is based on the beauty pass so whenever

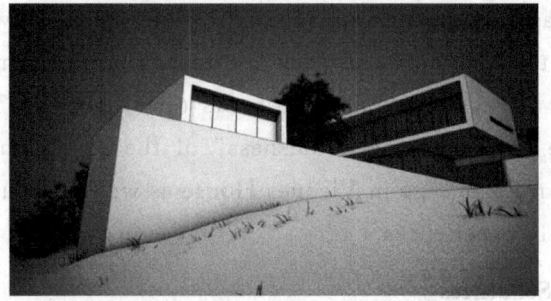

Figure 15-9 Rendering of the sequences

a detail was in shade it didn't use enough samples there and the additional passes had zigzagged edges. Therefore I had to increase the AA sampling.

I rendered the contour separately using VRayToon, because I couldn't find a way to incorporate the contour pass into the Render Elements. I turned the lights off for these sequences so fortunately the rendering was super fast. I rendered at 24 frames/second in order to have a more imperfect look for the final animation.

Usually I am just not patient enough to document my workflow, but I had to do it this time (See figure 15-10). I made a table with all different cameras and necessary settings. If you do a table like this, just make sure to update it.

CAMERA NAME	NOTES	LIGHT	FRAMES	FRAM QT	LAYERS	NATURE	TREE 00	AO	ZDEPTH	PATH1	PATH2	DIFF	RENDER ELEM.	OUTLIN	CORRECTIONS	
CAMERA 00	monumental entry	light 360	0-299	300	Wood Closed, INDI	1,2,4,8	5'	3'	127'	CAM 00	CONT	x	x	x		**check:**
CAMERA 01	monumental w/ birds	light 360	0-220	221	Birds, Wood Closed	2,4,8	5'	3'	127'	CAM 01	CONT	x	x	x		path
CAMERA 02	detail corner	light 720	0-149	150	Smooth grass and terrain	-	5'	3'	16'	CAM 02	CONT	x	x	x		light
																frames
CAMERA 10	SIGNATURE	light 180.2	0-160	161	Wood Closed	2,4	0'	3'	110'	CAM 10	CONT	x	x	x		camera view
CAMERA 11	panning wormseye	light 180.1	0-220	221	Wood Closed	2,3,4,5	0'	3'	140'	CAM 11	CONT	x	x	x		zdepth
CAMERA 12	corner w/ 1st splash	light 180.7	130-299	170	Wood Closed	3,6,8	0'	3'	start 120'	CAM 12	CONT	x	x	x		layers
CAMERA 13	round the back	light 180.2	0-299	300	Wood Closed, Doors1, Radio1, Water3	3,9, 2 & 10 in middle, 5 at end	0'	3'	127'	CAM 13	CONT	x	x	x		adaptive dmc: 2,3
CAMERA 14	from end of wall	light 360	0-299	300	Wood Closed, Doors1, Radio1, Water3	2,5,9 hide tree	0'	3'	127'	CAM 14	CONT	x	x	x		**contour**
CAMERA 15	thru door	light 180.3	0-140	141	Wood Closed, Doors2, Water3	2,3,9		3'	90'	CAM 15	CONT	x	x	x		light: on off
CAMERA 16	side view of pool	light 180.3	0-100	101	Wood Closed, Doors2, Water3	1,5,8, unhide tree		3'	100'	CAM 16	CONT	x	x	x		render elements
CAMERA 17	peak into yard	light 180.4	100-260	161	Wood Closed, Doors2, Water3, Radio3	2,7		3'	80'	CAM 17	CONT	x	x	x		vraytoon: active inactive
CAMERA 18	thru courtyard	light 180.3	0-140	141	Wood Closed, Water3, Radio4	2,5,7		3'	80'	CAM 18	CONT	x	x	x		adaptive subdiv:0,3
CAMERA 19	central tree	light 360	0-299	300	Wood Closed, Water3, Radio4	2,5,7		3'	50'	CAM 19	CONT	x	x	x		save rgb save channels
CAMERA 20	SIGNATURE	light 360	140-240	101	-	11		3'	40'	CAM 20	CONT	x	x	x		
CAMERA 21	panning dining table	light 180.2	0-121	122	Radio4, Wood Closed, Water 3	1,8		3'	60'	CAM 21	CONT	x	x	x		
CAMERA 22	radio shot	light 360	0-299	300	Radio4	-		3'	32' ? 25?	CAM 22	CONT	x	x	x		
CAMERA 23	panels fade away	light 180.5	0-110, 40-150	302	Wood Closed and Wood Open	3,9 at beginning, 2 at end		3'	40'	CAM 23	CONT	x1, x2	x1, x2	x1, x2		
CAMERA 24	staircase from above	light 360	140-240	101	Delete kitchen	-		3'	30'	CAM 24	CONT	x	x	x		
CAMERA 25	ball splash	light 180.8	0-220	221	Wood Open, Ball2, Water2	2		3'	85'	CAM 25	CONT	x	x	x		
CAMERA 26	into living window	light 180.8	0-150	151	Wood Open/Water CLosed EDIT POLY, Ball3, Water3, Radio 4	10,4		3'	70'	CAM 26	CONT	x	x	x		
CAMERA 27	living light"water"	light 360	100-249	150	Wood Open	10		3'	60'	CAM 27	CONT	x	x	x		
CAMERA 30	SIGNATURE	light 180.8	0-100	101	Wood Open/Water CLosed EDIT POLY, Ball3, Water3, Radio 4	1,8, 10, 4		3'	75'	CAM 30	CONT	x	x	x		
CAMERA 31	pan above pool	light 720	0-200	201	Wood Closed and Open EDIT POLY, Ball3, Water3, Radio4, ,BLANKET, Slippers1	8		3'	25'	CAM 31	CONT	x1,x2	x1,x2	x1,x2		
CAMERA 32	pan next to pool	light 360,	0-200	201	Wood Closed and Open, Ball3, Water3, Radio4, ,BLANKET2, SLippers1	3,9, 10, 4		3'	15'-62'	CAM 32	CONT			x1,x2		
CAMERA 33	ball in water	light 720	110-259	150	Wood Open,Ball3, Water 3	VrayPRoxy047		3'	50'	CAM 33	CONT	x	x	x		
CAMERA 34	turn into guest	light 180.4	0-150	120	Wood Closed/open, Water 3, Radio 4, BLANKET2	-		3'	10-48	CAM 34	CONT	x1,x2	x1,x2	x1,x2		
CAMERA 40	SIGNATURE	light 360	100-220	121	Wood Open, Water3, Ball1, Slippers1, , BLANKET2	2		3'	90'	CAM 40	CONT	x	x	x		
CAMERA 41	panning at the end	light 360,180.2	0-120	121	Wood Open, Water3, Ball1, Slippers1, , BLANKET	2		3'	80'	CAM 41	CONT	x	x	x		
CAMERA 50	SIGNATURE	light 180.8	90-190	101	Wood Open, Water3	5,6, 1		3'	50'	CAM 50	CONT	x	x	x		
CAMERA 51	ending splash	light 180.3	0-299	300	Wood Open, Slippers2, Water3	2,5,6,7, 1		3'	50'	CAM 51	CONT	x	x	x		
CAMERA 60	SIGNATURE	light 180.3	0-100	101	Wood Open, Water3	1,5,8		3'	90'	CAM 60	CONT	x	x	x		
				5632												

Figure 15-10 Rendering of the sequences

Composition

When I had all the render passes (around 32,000 individual images) I started putting them together in After Effects (See figure 15-11 and figure 15-12). I used the AO pass as the base and multiplied all others on top with different opacity. Then I animated the lens blur effects using the Zdepth pass. These lens blur glitches were elemental parts of the story, so I paid much attention to them. The lens blurs were also great to hide a couple weird-looking camera movements.

Figure 15-11 Composition

Figure 15-12 Composition

Afterwards, I pre-composed the sequences and added grain, sepia filter and vignetting and oh ... a little chromatic aberration. Since there is no such effect in After Effects as chromatic aberration I used a "manual" method that I found here:

(I cannot really get used to plugins (that is just me) so I am always happy if there is a manual alternative). Chromatic Aberration was great because it gave a little color to the monochrome images (See figure 15-13).

Figure 15-13 Composition

Editing

Once I had all the sequences exported from AE, I started the editing part in Premiere Pro (See figure 15-14). This was my favorite phase because all the previous effort became tangible here. At this point you see how the sequences work together and you can modify/enhance/fine-tune the mood to a great extent with the sounds and music.

Figure 15-14　Editing

The sound effects gave so much life to the animation. The ambient effects like the whistling wind in Phoenix House or the chirping birds in Vieques House were great for setting up a mood. I really like the juxtaposition of the graphic environment and the lifelike sounds. I made the camera sound effects (zooming, flash recharging, etc.) loud to accentuate the rawness of the animation.

Since Vieqes House is a Puerto Rican vacation house we found lounge music with a tropical mood to be perfect.

The music of Phoenix House was a tribute (See figure 15-15). We always talked about Phoenix House as an architectural "Clint Eastwood". It is in a dreary environment, in solitude. Hard as rock. The strong horizontal lines of the facade and the strong horizontal lines of Clint Eastwood's face are just remarkable. For the startling resemblance see the next image. (I tagged both of them not to confuse you.)

Therefore we had to pay homage to the spaghetti westerns with the music of Phoenix House.

Finally here is the breakdown of Vieques House：

Video: http://v.youku.com/v_show/id_XMTQ0MjgxMTYwMA==.html

And some frames of the videos (See figure 15-16~figure 15-18)：

Figure 15-15 Editing

Figure 15-16 Vieques House

Figure 15-17 Vieques House

Figure 15-18　Vieques House

Here are some views from the Phoenix House too (See figure 15-19～figure 15-21):

Figure 15-19　Phoenix House

Figure 15-20　Phoenix House

From: www.ronenbekerman.com/
Author: Viktor Nassli

Figure 15-21　Phoenix House

New Words

ArchitecturalAnimation 建筑动画
Experiment *n.* 尝试；实验，试验；*vi.* 尝试；做实验，进行试验
Narration *n.* 叙述，故事
Nonprofessional *adj.* 外行的；无职业的，无专长的
Overstuff *v.* 装填过度，给（软椅、沙发等）加厚软垫
Monochromatic *adj.* 单色的，单频的
Cozy *adj.* 舒适的，安逸的，惬意的
Concentric *adj.* 同一中心的，同轴的；*adv.* 同一中心地，同轴地
Model *n.* 模型；模式；模特儿；典型
Combination *n.* 结合；联合体
Conflict *n.* 冲突；矛盾；战斗；相互干扰；*vi.* 冲突；抵触；争斗；战斗
Enhancement *n.* 增强；提高；增加；改善
Render *v.* 渲染
Coherent *adj.* 连贯的；一致的；条理分明的；清楚明白的
Sequence *n.* 顺序；连续；片段插曲；*vt.* 使按顺序排列，安排顺序
Incorporate *vt.* 包含；组成公司；使混合；使具体化；*vi.* 合并；包含；吸收；混合
Composition *n.* 作文，作曲；创作；构图，布置；妥协，和解

Exercises

Translation

1. Therefore, the best architectural videos are personal developments. For instance the best architectural animation ever – Alex Roman's "The Third and the Seventh".

2. So our concept was to create a monochrome, maquettelike, raw style with glitches, grain and other imperfections and to have the colorful renderings as glimpses of the real thing. (Two worlds if you like)

3. I always use a combination of groups and layers in SketchUP. I only put the grouped entities onto different layers and leave all edges and faces on the default layer.

4. Then in 3ds Max I made further enhancements. I chamfered some edges, made and imported a couple models. For the renderings I used 2d vegetation, because I had to do them fast. For the video I used VRayProxy trees and bushes.

5. I made a couple of copies of the light and controlled the speed of them separately for each scene.

6. I used V-Ray with Render Elements: Beauty, Alpha, Zdepth and ExtraTex passes. ExtraTex render element is I think the best way to create ambient occlusion. You just have to add to it the VRayDirt map that you usually use for an AO material.

7. I used the AO pass as the base and multiplied all others on top with different opacity.

8. At this point you see how the sequences work together and you can modify/enhance/fine-tune the mood to a great extent with the sounds and music.

Definitions

Architectural Animation

_____
_____
_____
_____
_____
_____
_____
_____

Can you summarize the process of Architectural Animation?

_____
_____
_____
_____
_____
_____
_____
_____
_____

Reading Material
Architecture Software

In contemporary architecture practice, proficiency in an ever-widening array of architecture software is becoming increasingly important. For almost every job in the field, it is no longer enough to bring a skilled mind and a pencil; different jobs may require different levels of expertise and different types of software, but one thing that seems universally accepted is that some level of involvement with software is now a requirement.

While software has opened a huge range of capabilities for architects (See figure 15-22), it also presents a challenge: universities have taken wildly different approaches to the teaching of software, with some offering classes and access to experts while others prefer to teach design theory and expect students to pick up software skills in their own time. New architecture graduates therefore already face a divide in skills—and that's not to mention the many, many architects who went to school before AutoCAD was even an industry standard, and have spent the past decades keeping up with new tools.

Figure 15-22 Architecture software

The Internet has therefore been a huge democratizing effect in this regard, offering tutorials, often for free, to anyone with a connection—as long as you know where to look. That's why ArchDaily wants your help to create a directory of the internet's best architecture tutorial websites. Find out how to help (and see our own short list to get you started) after the break.

In the comments, we'd like you to tell us your favorite sources for software tutorials. Just like our own list below, please let us know which of the categories the source focuses on:

Pre-production modeling and drawing (software such as AutoCAD, Sketchup, Rhino and—for the sake of simplicity—BIM programs such as Revit and ArchiCAD).

Image production (such as the V-Ray plugins for various software).

Post-production image manipulation (such as with Photoshop).

To start off the list, and give you an idea of the type of tutorials we're hoping to feature, ArchDaily staff (with the additional input of some friends) have put together the following short list:

General Purpose Tutorial Sites

Lynda.com: You may have heard of this site, which offers over 3,500 courses and hundreds of thousands of individual video tutorials in everything from photography and business to architectural software. What many students don't know is that their university may be able to provide them with a free subscription.

Visualizing Architecture: Alex Hogrefe has created a comprehensive list of tutorials for creating compelling images, split conveniently into four sub-categories. Most of the tutorials focus on techniques that can be simply achieved using just SketchUp and Photoshop.

Ronen Bekerman: Ronen Bekerman's blog is, above all, a fantastic place to see case studies. Bekerman regularly features contributors who showcase their own work, explaining how they created a single render from the modeling stage to post-production.

Pre-Production (Drawing, Modeling, BIM)

Autodesk's Youtube Channel: It almost goes without saying that Autodesk offers a wide range of resources for their own software. Their Youtube channel contains a number of instructional videos alongside showcases of new features and promotional videos—the list can be overwhelming at first, so unless there's something specific you're searching for keep an eye out for anything labeled "Getting Started."

Bond-Bryan BIM Blog: Bond Bryan's Rob Jackson has been publishing on the company's "BIM Blog" since 2013, focusing on BIM-related news, case studies and guidance for using ArchiCad, the BIM tool used by his company.

Nick Senske on Youtube: Created for the course he runs at UNC Charlotte, Senske's video tutorials largely focus on modeling in Rhino.

Plethora Project: Jose Sanchez's series of tutorials focus on a number of tools that are perhaps less "standard" in architecture, including the Unity3d game engine, Autodesk's Maya software for animations, and C#, Python and Javascript. However, the site also includes the more usual Rhino and Grasshopper tutorials, meaning there is something for almost everyone here.

NYCCTfab on Vimeo: New York City College of Technology's Department of Architectural Technology Fabrication Lab has created an astonishing number of videos on modeling software, including Revit, Rhino and Grasshopper—they even have a series of videos on GIS.

Production (rendering and other forms of image creation)

Simply Rhino Webinars: Although not the most comprehensive of tutorial platforms, this Youtube channel has a series of videos about V-Ray for Rhino totaling over five hours.

Visual Dynamics Website: This V-Ray reseller is gradually adding sets of tutorials for the software in 3ds Max, Rhino and Sketchup, among others. So far, only the 3ds Max tutorials are particularly developed, but watch this space for more.

Official V-Ray Website: In a similar vein, the official V-Ray website has a range of tutorials, mostly focusing on 3ds Max and Maya (See figure 15-23).

Figure 15-23   Architecture software

Post-Production (Adobe Photoshop and other image manipulation software)

Tutorials: London-based visualization studio Vyonyx offers a small set of tutorials, largely focusing on how to achieve certain effects in Photoshop. They also include a small number of tutorials focusing on modeling software such as Rhino and 3ds Max.

ARQUi9 Visualisation on Youtube: Another visualization studio who are sharing their knowledge online, ARQUi9 have only five videos to date, but their tutorials are clearly presented and cover useful techniques on Photoshop from adding people to images to creating convincing reflections in water.

From: www.archdaily.com/

UNIT 16

Visual Communication

COMPETENCIES

After you have read this unit, you should be able to:
1. Discuss what is Visual Communication.
2. Discuss what is type basic.

Text A

Type Basics

Same Size For All

To optically align all characters on a line, they cannot have exactly the same mathematical height (See figure 16-1). For example the triangle on this drawing has to be higher than the rectangle. If this is not the case, the triangle will for sure look smaller than the rectangle. While creating a typeface, you want all the letters to have the same height.

Figure 16-1 Same size for all

Also round forms have to exceed the baseline to be optically the same. If the circle would have exactly the same mathematical height as the rectangle, it would look smaller than the square. This doesn't only count for basic forms like triangles, circles and squares. It's essential in type design, because they apply to every single character in a typeface. Then it even doesn't matter if you're designing a latin, cyrillic or greek font. It's a basic principle for any kind of shape.

Fluent Shapes

Designing type is like driving a car (See figure 16-2). If you drive a car, you always take the curve in a natural way. If you draw a curve (of a character) on paper, this is exactly the same. The curve starts smoothly, never out of a sudden. While driving a car, you don't start turning the wheel when you are already in the beginning of the curve. A while before you arrive in the curve you anticipate by leading your car gently in the right direction. Think about driving a car when you are sketching type on a paper.

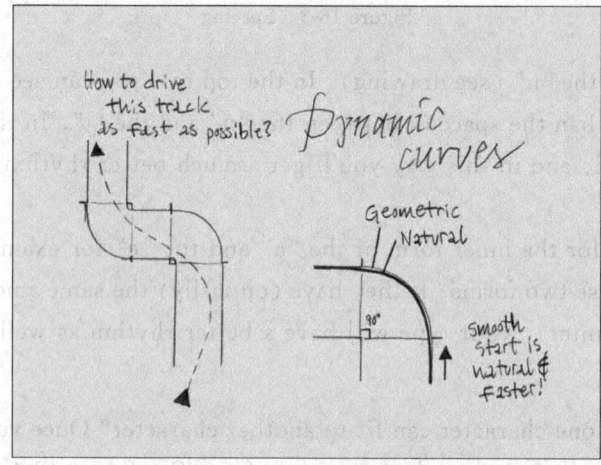

Figure 16-2   Fluent shapes

Spacing

Some words about spacing type (See figure 16-3). Much more important than the shapes of the characters, is the rhythm of the type. A typeface with beautiful characters which are badly spaced is extremely hard to read. However, if the shapes of the letters are not that good, but when they are all perfectly spaced, the type will be fairly easy to read. Defining the rhythm is more important than defining the shapes.

The white spaces inside and in between letters are defining the rhythm, much more than the black shapes of the letters. When you manage to create a good rhythm in your line of text, your type gets more readable and gives a balanced end result. While creating the black shapes, you have to take the white spaces into consideration. Because the white spaces are more important than the black shapes. However, white cannot exist without black. Changing a white shape, inevitable will have an influence on the black shape. From that perspective, one colour cannot be more important than the other.

For example, there has to be a relation between the space inside an "n" and the space

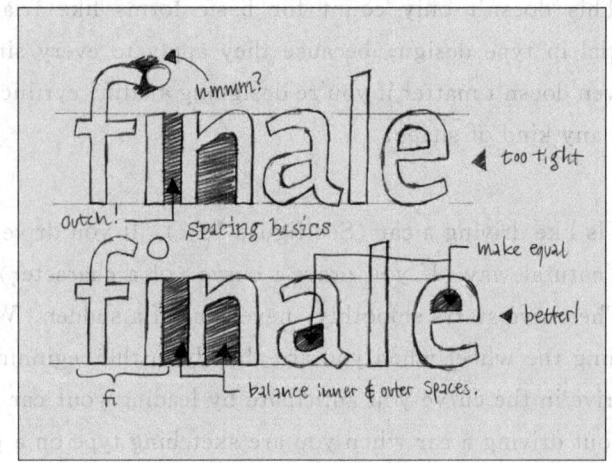

Figure 16-3 Spacing

between the "i" and the "n" (see drawing). In the top row you can see the space inside the "n" is much bigger than the space in between the "n" and the "i". In the bottom row they are much more equal, and in this way you'll get a much better rhythm and more harmony in your line of text.

The same goes for the inner form of the "a" and the "e" for example. There is a big relation between these two forms. If they have (optically) the same amount of white inside the character (=counter), your type will have a better rhythm as well.

One For All

What defines if one character can fit to another character? Once you made a decision, how to apply this to all the other characters in a font (See figure 16-4)?

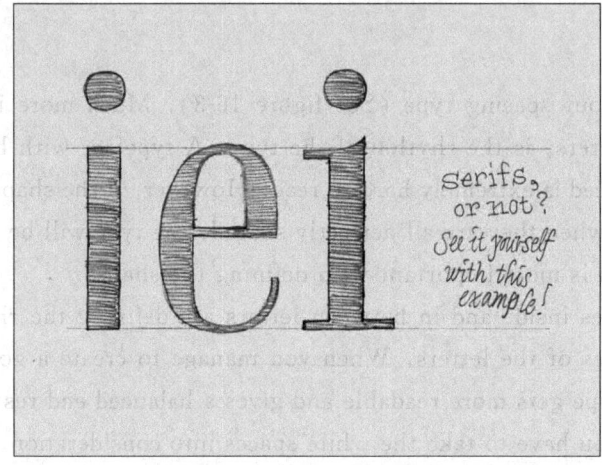

Figure 16-4 One for all

Starting point: "e" (in the center of the drawing). Imagine you sketched this "e", you like it a lot, and now you want to design more characters fitting to this "e". Where to start? Should it be a serif or a sans serif for example?

First try: "i" on the left. Sans serif. The black part is as thick as the black parts of the "e". Same x-height. So this should work you think.

Second try: "i" on the right. Same thickness, the character has the same x-height, but now it has serifs.

The bowl of the "e" is not only having a certain thickness, but the "e" also has contrast. The "i" on the left has no contrast at all. Therefore these two characters don't belong to each other. The "i" on the right however has the same kind of contrast as the "e", just because it has serifs. Just those tiny serifs make sure there are thick and thin parts, like the "e" has. This means that the starting point, the "e", already defined that the rest of the font cannot be a sans serif typeface.

Of course, every so called rule is there to be broken. Mentioning this, doesn't mean you can't make a font which has an "e" combined with an "i" like the one on the left. Everything is possible of course. But now you realize better what you are doing, also when you don't do it. Still get it?

Proportions

Which x-height to define? Which descender depth? Defining these proportions are essential, and very strongly connected to the purpose of the type. The proportions within a certain typeface are influencing the way your type will work & look. For example, it's impossible to create a space saving newspaper typeface with an extremely wide body width (See figure 16-5).

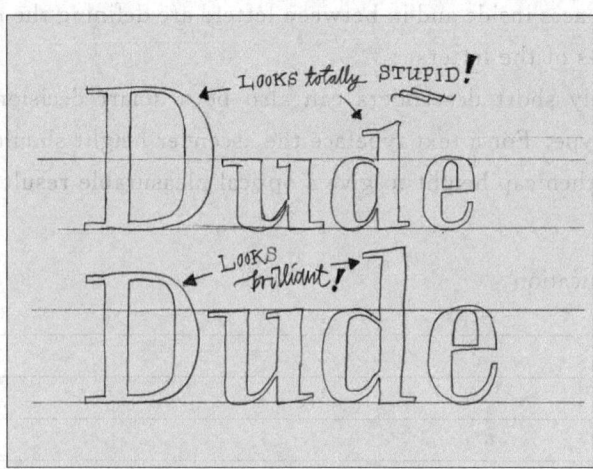

Figure 16-5 Proportions

Extremely short descenders will give a strange look to a text typeface. Even worse, they might not be visible at all anymore. But extremely short descenders can also be a smart decision, while creating a display or headline type. For a text typeface the ascender height should be as big or, even better, bigger than then cap height to give a optical pleasurable result (see drawing).

From: http://www.typeworkshop.com

New Words

Visual Communication 视觉传达
Type *n.* 类型
Typeface *n.* 字体，字样，打字机字体
Form *n.* 表格；方式；形状；形式；外形
Sketch *n.* 素描；草图；梗概；*v.* 速写；草拟；简述
Serif *n.* 衬线体；衬线，截线（衬线指的是字体起始末端的细节装饰）
Proportion *n.* 比，比率
Descender *n.* 下降者，下降物，下行字母

Exercises

Translation

1. To optically align all characters on a line, they cannot have exactly the same mathematical height.

2. If the circle would have exactly the same mathematical height as the rectangle, it would look smaller than the square.

3. Much more important than the shapes of the characters, is the rhythm of the type. A typeface with beautiful characters which are badly spaced is extremely hard to read.

4. The white spaces inside and in between letters are defining the rhythm, much more than the black shapes of the letters.

5. But extremely short descenders can also be a smart decision, while creating a display or headline type. For a text typeface the ascender height should be as big or, even better, bigger than then cap height to give a optical pleasurable result (see drawing).

Definitions

Visual Communication

_____
_____
_____
_____
_____

You can find more type basic at www.typeworkshop.com. Can you summarize the type basic?

Can you design a type with your style?

Reading Material
Style Tiles and How They Work

When you engage in a new client project how do you get started? A solid process plays a critical role in the project's overall success, yet this process is one of the deepest darkest secrets of our industry. Evolving from print, identity, and advertising the web retains many methodologies and deliverable relics from disciplines that produce very different products.

When we supply detailed mockups that represent set widths, we can imply that we're executing the final design. Clients can feel disconnected from the process, which gives them a false sense of completion, detaching them from the final product. So why don't we more closely design our own process to work within clients' expectations and emotions? We must evolve our deliverables to make clients a more active participant in the process.

Websites are so much more than just usable interfaces: they tell a story. The style tile is a design deliverable that references website interface elements through font, color, and style collections delivered alongside a site map, wireframes, and other user experience artifacts. Style tiles are based on visual preference discussions with the client. They're sample options that spur discussion with stakeholders on a common visual language. Containing sample UI style swatches, a style tile illustrates how a designer translates a stakeholder's brand to the web. When a client uses the word "friendly" or "clean" to describe the site they want, the style tile visually represents those adjectives. Style tiles offer a catalyst for discussions to clarify and refine the client's preferences and goals.

Emotional Connection

Style tiles are a flexible starting point that define a style to communicate the web in a way that clients understand. A style tile is more refined than a traditional identity mood board and less detailed than a website mockup or comp. When an interior designer redesigns a room they don't build multiple options of the designs they're proposing, they bring color swatches, paint chips, and architectural drawings. Style tiles act as paint chips and color swatches for the interface that we can execute on any device or at any dimension. It's a truly responsive solution to visual design.

A mood board can provide a great jumping-off point for client discussion, but is often too vague to help clients make a clear leap from discussion to website. Mood boards are a good way to dig deep into a brand identity, but when it comes to bringing the identity to a complex web system, such a weak connection can make it hard for a client to understand and imagine the outcome. By contrast, style tiles make a great visual design artifact. They help a designer communicate how they will apply the styles across a larger web system, which includes desktop and mobile experiences.

Ask Questions to Extract Adjectives

The style tile process teases out the passion behind a brand, revealing nuggets of descriptive goodness all while connecting the client to the project. The first step in the style tile process is to question the stakeholders. You can use a survey or ask the questions in a design kickoff meeting. First, be sure to have the stakeholders list and rate their goals for the site's visuals. Having them define their goals up front reinforces the priority of each style decision throughout the process. Next, ask questions that will encourage adjective-rich answers in your survey. Metaphor questions like the ones described in this Adaptive Path article are strategic and help break the ice. For example: "If your website was a vehicle, what vehicle would it be and why?". This is a great question: there are social and cultural perceptions that surround different automobile brands and types of transportation. The adjectives associated with these brands may be very different. Your client will describe a Toyota Prius differently than an SUV.

Semantic differential survey questions are a really good way to understand the client's aesthetic preferences. You can set up word pairs that are opposite of one another and ask clients to select a point on the scale between the two to help describe the way they envision the site. Do they envision the site as modern or old-fashioned, or somewhere in between? These questions help rate how closely the stakeholder relates to a word that describes the site's potential style. Illustrative, photographic, and typographic are all words that a stakeholder can rate to help you get a sense for their preferences. Often I'll pair an example site with each word so that the stakeholder can see the relationship. MailChimp is an example of "illustrative" while NPR is an example of "typographic."

The answers you get are key to forming the emotional bond between a two-dimensional visual design concept and the passion that the client feels for their brand. Listen carefully, sort and dissect the stakeholder's responses, and draw clear connections between the visuals in your style tiles and the client's actual words. The more literal you can be, the more your client begins to feel connected to the process, which builds trust, and paves the way to a smoother approval process.

Once your stakeholders have filled out your survey or answered your questions during a kick-off meeting, analyze what they've given you. Study their answers and highlight adjectives to compile a list. Have some adjectives been used more frequently? Those words go to the top of your list. Themes will begin to emerge, and from this you can start to formulate an online brand vision. This can be a short statement that sums up your findings, or it might state that all of the stakeholders are in disagreement. Whether the online brand vision is clear or disjointed, it provides you with a jumping off point to discuss how to move forward with your client as you present the tiles.

In a recent project, the Phase2 Technology design team worked with The Washington Examiner to create a 2012 election campaign microsite to serve up-to-the-minute political information. The site goal was to extend the Examiner's historic brand with more of a patriotic tone to energize readers for the upcoming election. Using adjectives the Washington Examiner team provided, Phase2 interpreted the newspaper's brand by exploring three different stylistic options for the client to choose from. The styles reflected interpretations of three variations on their current online brand.

The three tiles presented to the client are below (See figure 16-6～figure 16-8).

Figure 16-6 The first three stile tiles we presented to the Washington Examiner

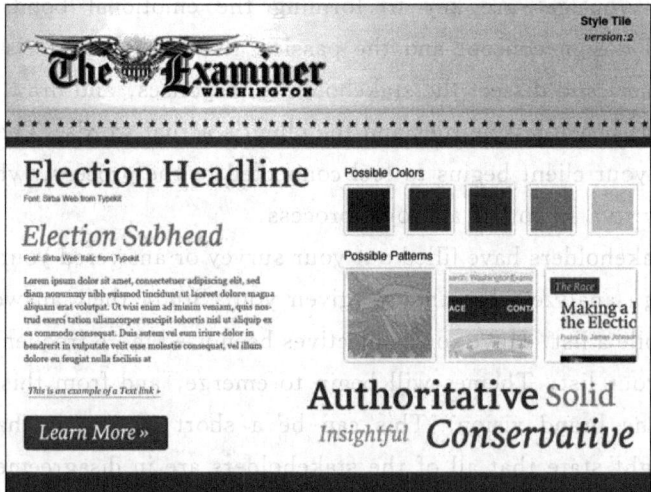

Figure 16-7　The first three stile tiles we presented to the Washington Examiner

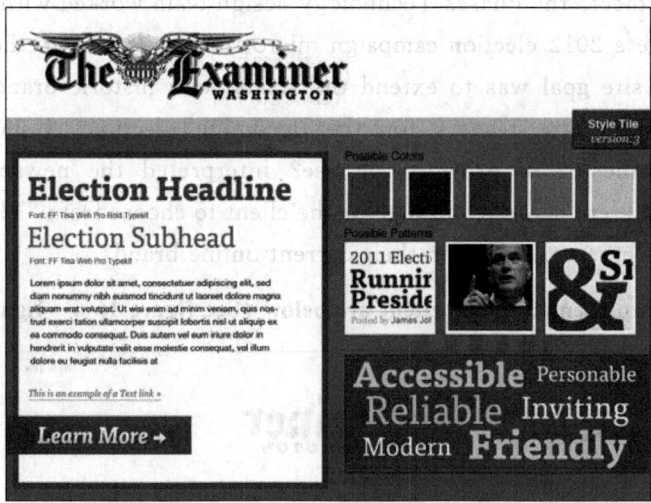

Figure 16-8　The first three stile tiles we presented to the Washington Examiner

Iteration Nation

There was some overlap in the adjectives that the Washington Examiner stakeholders used to describe their brand, which helped us to create a clear brand vision. The word "patriotic" dictated a red, white, and blue color scheme and their rich history in publishing led us to choose several slab serif typefaces which were developed for readability and the publishing industry. Words like "current" and "modern" coupled with the fact that the site was specifically for the 2012 campaign spurred us to explore texture and depth in the presidential candidates' brands. Beyond the adjectives that were most popular, "clean," "strong," and "friendly" dictated three directions that the overarching vision could evolve into. The "clean" tile was bright with a lot of white space, the "strong" tile featured brushed aluminum and the stars from their logo, while the "friendly" tile included large hits of vibrant color.

During the iteration period, the stakeholders decided they wanted the first tile but the red stars from the second tile and the typeface from the third tile. During this round, they decided that they preferred a friendly slab serif typeface, so we chose Adelle and they loved it. This final tile translated directly to the final design of the site (See figure 16-9).

Figure 16-9 The style tile that the Washington Examiner approved

The Way It Was

It's common to present multiple comps to a client during the design process. Clients like to see options, and multiple comps make stakeholders feel like they're getting what they paid for. Design is sales and we love to make our clients happy, but presenting multiple, fully visualized comps hurts the process more than it helps it. Because it's human nature for people to mix and match, this allows clients to sabotage the best solutions to their design problems based on transitory stylistic preferences. In the end, you have a Frankencomp, a mishmash of interface elements conceived outside the website's goals.

Process and Approach Affect the End Result

Design is a tricky practice because everyone has an opinion on aesthetics. Clients are a major part of the design process: without them you'd be making websites for free and that's not a design job, it's a hobby. Style is preference-oriented while design is goal-oriented. It can be daunting to help your client understand how the two are separate, but style tiles can be a key component in the web design process that allows you to involve your client on an interactive, iterative level. When you expose the design process deliverables in iterative chunks, the client is able to provide more feedback, feel more involved, and become a valuable collaborator in the final design.

Design Is About Trust

The style tile redefines the roles in the client/ designer relationship. People go to counselors when they need to solve life challenges. Clients go to designers when they need to solve communication problems. If you consider the designer as a counselor who guides the client to a solution, then trust builds with each iteration. Would you trust a counselor if you walked into a room and they pulled out your fully developed recovery plan based only on your previous history? You would walk out! An organization's brand and the way they communicate can be delicate matters, as delicate as a family relationship issue or marriage. The approach, tone, and process that you take as a designer has a tremendous influence on the relationship you build with a client. Having direct access to the client, educating them on your plan for the process, and incrementally diving into the design are all parts of the style tile process that help to establish invaluable trust.

Responsive Design

Designing for the web is no longer designing for just a 960-pixel width. Designing sites to act responsively across multiple screen widths and devices changes the relevancy of design comps for client interfaces but also for team communications. Creating a mockup for every possible device or screen size is inefficient and confusing to a client. Style tiles are the cornerstone of a solid design system that sets client expectations and communicates the visual theme to all the project team members. Designing a system rather than site pages gives your team the tools to create a living, breathing website. From a client-approved style tile you can begin to build other visual assets, such as component style guides that address frequently used elements. For more thoughts on design systems check out sweet systems.

Designing Our Design Process

As web designers we craft experiences for users, but we often overlook the need to design the experience that clients have during the web design process. Design thinking can improve how we tackle challenges, involve our clients, and present deliverables. Style tiles expedite project timelines, involve stakeholders in the brainstorming process, and are an essential artifact in the responsive design process. Involving stakeholders early on and mixing and matching styles with a deliverable that is void of layout can have a dramatic emotional effect on the entire team and the project's outcome. For a quick cheat sheet on how to get started integrating Style Tiles into your process take a look at StyleTil. es.

http://alistapart.com/article

Author: Samantha Warren

UNIT 17

Online Game

COMPETENCIES

After you have read this unit, you should be able to:
1. Discuss what is Online Game.
2. Discuss your favorite Online Game.

Text A

Angry Wingless Birds are Taking Over

Wingless birds (See figure 17-1) have become a gaming sensation. Even Britain's Prime Minister David Cameron (See figure 17-2) admitted to a mild addiction.

Figure 17-1　Angry wingless birds are taking over

Figure 17-2　For the birds…David Cameron and John Hamm

Every day, millions of man hours are spent playing Angry Birds (See figure 17-3). Could this fiendishly silly game really become bigger than Mickey Mouse? Paul Kendall finds out.

Figure 17-3　Angry Birds

One night about two years ago, a Finnish video games designer called Jaakko Iisalo found himself home alone with time on his hands. His wife had gone out for the evening and, as usual, when there was nothing requiring his immediate attention, the 30 year-old settled down in front of his games console.

Iisalo, a self-confessed "games geek", would happily spend all his spare time immersed in the world of electronic make-believe if left to his own devices.

While he messed around, his brain chewed over a project he'd been set at work.

His employer, a small mobile games developer called Rovio, was short of funds and had recently drawn up a make-or-break business plan, which, essentially, involved developing a game for the hot new gadget of the day: Apple's iPhone.

Iisalo and the company's other developers had already put forward a number of ideas, all of which had been rejected by Rovio's directors for being either too complicated, too simplistic or too boring.

What would hit the spot? Iisalo knew it had to be something fun, something with a strong central character. Suddenly, an idea began to form in his head.

Switching on Photoshop, the designer started sketching a flock of fat, round birds with big yellow beaks, thick eyebrows and intense, slightly crazed expressions on their faces. They had no legs to speak of, but, despite this drawback, were racing manically along the ground towards some sort of castle.

"I didn't think it was that special at the time," Iisalo says now. "I didn't even mention it to my wife when she came home."

But the following week, when Iisalo presented the screen shot to his bosses at work, it caused quite a stir. The mechanics still needed work—the object of the game was still not clear at this stage—but there was something about the cross-eyed birds that everybody in the room found irresistible.

"As soon as I saw those characters I liked them," recalls Niklas Hed, Rovio's co-founder. "Straight away, I had a feeling that I wanted to play the game."

Two years later, millions of other smartphone users have had the same feeling. Angry Birds has become iPhone's most popular App, in other words, the piece of software that has been installed on the most number of handsets worldwide (quite an achievement when you consider that it's one among 300,000 applications on offer) and has quickly spread to Apple's iPad and other types of phones as well.

The game has been downloaded 50 million times. The Prime Minister, David Cameron, has admitted to a mild addiction, as have a variety of other supposedly busy people, from Dick Cheney to Mad Men actor Jon Hamm.

Last year, two brothers, Rodrigo and Gustavo Dauster, competed against each other in a two-month marathon session to see who could score the maximum number of points. (Gustavo is now writing a book entitled Angry Birds Yoga)

Mothers bake Angry Bird (See figure 17-4) cakes and stitch Angry Bird Halloween costumes for their children, and a sketch on an Israeli comedy show, which featured an Arab-Israeli style peace conference between birds and pigs, has been viewed more than four million times on YouTube.

Figure 17-4 Angry Birds

In total, the game notches up 200 million minutes of play time every day, which is close to the number of minutes viewers in the United States spend watching the average prime-time television programme. Versions of the game are being developed for the PlayStation, Xbox and Wii.

There is a line of Angry Birds soft toys, Mattel is working on a board game and before long there will be a cartoon series, and, if all goes well, a film.

"Suddenly it's ubiquitous," says James Binns, head of the games media brand Edge International. "There have been other iPhone games that have sold a bunch, but it's the first one that everybody is talking about. It reminds me of the Rubik's Cube. You see people playing it all the time."

One of the things that makes the game so popular is its simplicity. Taking advantage of Apple's touch screen technology, Angry Birds doesn't require the player to master any controls. In fact, there are hardly any instructions at all; once the game starts, a child can work out what to do.

To the right, on the main screen, are a collection of sniggering green pigs, sheltering under a structure made out of wood, concrete, steel or ice. To the left are Iisalo's legless, cross-eyed birds, whom you must launch through the air at the pigs, using a catapult. Points are scored for destroying the forts, which become increasingly elaborate, and squashing the pigs. The only thing a player needs to operate the catapult is their finger. When I tried the game for the first time, my friend's five-year-old daughter showed me how to play.

But if that was all there was to it, Angry Birds wouldn't be the hit that it is. As the game unfolds, you realise that there's a science to the bird-flinging. Certain trajectories are more effective than others and certain birds (there are seven different types) need to be drafted in to break certain materials.

Hit the pigs' various shelters in the right place, with the right bird, and you are generously rewarded. Get it wrong and you are forced to start the level again with the sound of porcine laughter ringing in your ears.

Like many of the best video games, Angry Birds hides a keen intelligence underneath its wacky exterior. In contrast, the people who work at Rovio couldn't be less wacky if they tried. The office, in Espoo, just outside Helsinki, is thoroughly bland; a large open-plan room with regulation desks, white boards and pot plants.

A splash of colour is provided by the Angry Birds soft toys that are perched on top of computer towers and filing cabinets. But next to the towers about 40 people sit in almost total silence, staring at their screens. They are nearly all men in their mid to late twenties and they take their jobs very, very seriously.

When they go out to a bar after work on a Friday they bring their iPads and iPhones with them and play games. At lunch, the canteen is abuzz with industry talk.

These people haven't become successful by accident. Angry Birds (See figure 17-5) was the product of a very deliberate strategy—devised by Niklas Hed and his cousin, Rovio's CEO, Mikael—that combined business acumen with technical expertise.

"This was our most calculated game," says Niklas—an intent 30 year-old, with blond hair and a whispy goatee beard—when we sit down to talk in one corner of the office.

"We had done 50 games before Angry Birds. We knew we were able to make the best games in the world, but the problem was that you had to do loads of versions to support all the different handsets. So our development time and overheads were getting worse and worse."

Rovio needed a solution and the iPhone provided one. After the phone's launch in 2007, Rovio realised that their industry was about to change completely. For the first

Figure 17-5   Angry Birds

time, users from all over the world would be able to download games from the same place: Apple's online App Store. So a manufacturer only had to produce one version of a game, reducing costs dramatically.

Rovio was perfectly positioned to take advantage. It had learnt a lot from the triumphs and failures of its past games. It also had copious notes from focus groups it had organised over the years, during which Niklas and his colleagues had watched people playing games from behind a glass screen and recorded what the players found difficult, what excited them, what they found boring.

The information from these sessions had then been used to produce a blueprint of the "perfect" mobile game. The checklist ran to several thousand words, but, one of the main things they learnt was that each level had to feel achievable.

"It's important that players don't feel that the game is punishing them," Niklas says. "If you fail a level you blame yourself. If the pigs laugh at you, you think: 'I need to try one more time.'"

They also knew it was important that any game they designed could be played in short bursts—occupying those periods of "downtime", such as queuing for a coffee or waiting for a bus, that had formerly been devoted to staring into space or, perhaps, reflecting on life.

"You have to be able to play the game right away," Niklas says. "We didn't want any loading times."

It was this principle that led to the introduction of the catapult, the game's central feature. Players know immediately what to do with it and it makes the game more intuitive.

The game also had to appeal to both video game "virgins" and hard-core enthusiasts. "We knew it had to be simple but it couldn't be too simple," Niklas says.

"That's when we started building layers in the game: different kinds of birds (See figure 17-6), certain birds affecting different blocks. And these were things we didn't tell you about—you had to figure them out on your own." (Iisalo chose birds as his protagonists because there are so many varieties. He chose green pigs for no other reason than that he found them funny)

Figure 17-6 Angry Birds

Finally, and crucially, Rovio put together a remarkably canny strategy for getting to the top of the iPhone chart. This was where Mikael Hed's commercial nous—a business degree from Tulane University in New Orleans and years working for his entrepreneur father—paid off.

If they wanted to get noticed among all the competing Apps (there were 160,000 at the time) he realised they would need a strong brand; to put a face to their product. Which is why the game was called Angry Birds and not, for example, "Catapult".

"We recognised what we were building," Mikael tells me, with the same intent manner as his cousin, when we speak later in the day. "We looked at the App Store and realised the power of the brand." Apple chose products with a clear identity as their "Featured Apps" and these in turn, enjoyed massive sales.

Rovio can't take all the credit for this strategy. Angry Birds was published by Chillingo, a company based in Macclesfield, which had good contacts at Apple and had already taken unknown brands and made them No 1. But Rovio does deserve credit for choosing Chillingo in the first place.

You have to admire their determination. Nevertheless, my time at Rovio has turned out to be considerably less fun than I was expecting. It's been more like a business meeting. Even Ville Heijari, the company's head of marketing, who refers to himself as "Bird Whisperer" in his emails, and whom I was expecting to be relatively entertaining, is super serious.

"Everything was aimed at eliminating luck," he says during a tour of the office. "You could make a game according to your own tunnel vision and then, fingers crossed, if you get lucky, people will pick it up. But we didn't want to depend on luck."

As we look over the shoulder of one of Rovio's designers, Heijari tells me about the game's intricate programming. A "physics engine" has been built into the game that applies basic rules of gravity, velocity, mass and so on to every material. Things don't fall apart exactly as they would in the real world, of course, but everything in the Angry Birds universe—stone, glass, wood, steel—performs in a consistent fashion.

Rovio's designers are constantly having to think of different structures for the birds to destroy. Since launching the game with 63 levels in December 2009, Rovio has added another 147, at the rate of about 15 every three or four weeks, in a ploy to keep the game at the top of the charts.

They released special themed versions of the game at Hallowe'en and Christmas last year, and are publishing a Valentine's edition—with exploding chocolate boxes and pink hearts. There will also be a game to accompany the new animated film, Rio, in April.

After winning over iPhone and iPad users, the game was rolled out onto other smartphones last October, where it was downloaded one million times in the first 24 hours, and to PCs and Macs last month. Now Rovio is busy working on console versions and promising future Angry Birds permutations.

Heijari won't give away any details and he won't say how the plot will be expanded in either the games or a prospective cartoon series. But he assures me that this is just the "first glimpse" of the Angry Birds world. "There are a lot of storytelling opportunities," he says.

So, has it made the directors millionaires? Niklas's answer is typically deadpan. "No, not yet. I think it's somewhere there in the future but we're just concentrating on growing the brand," he tells me. "The focus is not [on money] at all. It's all about building the infrastructure, making operator deals, opening new platforms…"

At the moment, the company is privately funded by Mikael's father, Kaj, but this could change. Last January, another mobile phone games developer, Ngmoco, was sold to a Japanese firm for $400m.

Rovio certainly doesn't lack ambition. At a conference in Munich last month, Peter Vesterbacka, the company's head of business development, boasted that Angry Birds was "bigger than Mickey Mouse". He was referring to the number of times the two terms were searched for on Google, but said he intended eventually to be "larger than the brand itself".

In fact, Rovio no longer describes itself as a games developer. It sees itself as a media company focused, as Mikael puts it, on "building really strong brands" of which Angry Birds is only the first.

The soft toys, phone cases, comics and even the movie are not an after thought. They were part of the plan from the very beginning. Whether the comics and the movie will ever come to pass is a moot point, but you can be sure that Rovio will leave no stone unturned.

It is Friday and, as my visit comes to an end, I ask Heijari whether the team is going out for their traditional Friday night drink/games session. I feel journalistically obliged to tag along. But it's not to be. People are going home first, he tells me, and meeting up later, by which time I will have to be at the airport.

OK, I say. I'm secretly elated. I'd rather go to a bar, have a beer on my own and maybe play a little bit of Angry Birds on my phone.

From: http://www.smh.com.au/technology

New Words

Developer *n.* 开发者
Flock *n.* 兽群，鸟群
Worldwide *adj.* 全世界的；*adv.* 遍及全球地
Trajectory *n.* ［物］弹道，轨道；［几］轨线
Expertise *n.* 专门知识或技能；专家的意见；专家评价，鉴定
Checklist *n.* 清单；检查表；备忘录；目录册

Exercises

Translation

1. His employer, a small mobile games developer called Rovio, was short of funds and had recently drawn up a make-or-break business plan, which, essentially, involved developing a game for the hot new gadget of the day: Apple's iPhone.

2. Switching on Photoshop, the designer started sketching a flock of fat, round birds with big yellow beaks, thick eyebrows and intense, slightly crazed expressions on their faces. They had no legs to speak of, but, despite this drawback, were racing manically along the ground towards some sort of castle.

3. Angry Birds was the product of a very deliberate strategy—devised by Niklas Hed and his cousin, Rovio's CEO, Mikael—that combined business acumen with technical expertise.

4. For the first time, users from all over the world would be able to download games from the same place: Apple's online App Store. So a manufacturer only had to produce one version of a game, reducing costs dramatically.

5. The game also had to appeal to both video game "virgins" and hard-core enthusiasts. "We knew it had to be simple but it couldn't be too simple," Niklas says.

6. "Everything was aimed at eliminating luck," he says during a tour of the office. "You could make a game according to your own tunnel vision and then, fingers crossed, if you get lucky, people will pick it up. But we didn't want to depend on luck."

7. After winning over iPhone and iPad users, the game was rolled out onto other smartphones last October, where it was downloaded one million times in the first 24 hours, and to PCs and Macs last month.

Reading Material
Apple Buys Star Wars Tech Firm Faceshift to up Its VR Game

As the virtual-and augmented-reality wars heat up, Apple is making sure it stays competitive with occasional acquisitions such as AR pioneer Metaio and 3D sensor outfit PrimeSense.

Now it's adding another company to its quiver, Swiss-based Faceshift (See figure 17-7), whose motion capture tech allows animated avatars to double the facial movements of real actors. The tech was used in the new Star Wars movie (See figure 17-8), out on December 18.

Figure 17-7   Faceshift makes technology that allows an actor's face to be replicated on an animated avatar

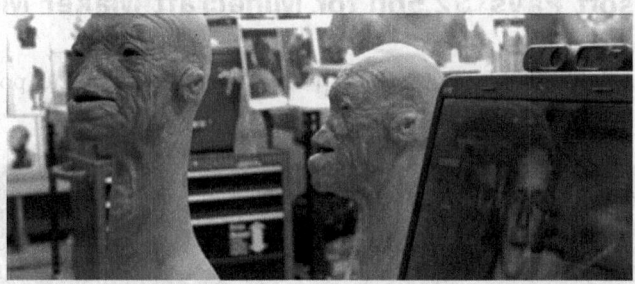

Figure 17-8   In the upcoming Star Wars film, Faceshift tech is used to make non-human characters appear more human

Rumours of the Apple purchase had surfaced earlier in the year, but TechCrunch cited unnamed sources on Tuesday in confirming the report. Apple declined to confirm the acquisition to TechCrunch, simply saying "Apple buys smaller technology companies from time to time, and we generally do not discuss our purpose or plans."

Many analysts believe 2016 will be a watershed year for AR/VR tech. Samsung just released its low-priced Gear VR goggles, which use a Samsung smartphone to power VR content that ranges from games to entertainment. And next year Sony will release

PlayStation VR, Microsoft is expected to release a developer kit for its HoloLens augmented reality glasses, and Facebook-owned Oculus Rift also should also finally be released in a consumer friendly form.

According to Digi-Capital, AR and VR combined are expected to be a $US150 billion business by 2020, as entertainment companies, media giants and the gaming industry look to exploit the new technology to lure in consumers. Interestingly, of that sum, the vast majority—$US120 billion—will be generated by augmented reality, whose technology isn't as developed and whose existing hardware is aimed mainly at enterprise customers ranging from doctors in surgery (whose monitors pop up in their field of view) to oil workers on remote platforms (who can follow repair instructions out of the corner of their eye).

There's no telling just how Apple might be planning to use its latest purchase in future products, especially since Apple is not at the moment a video game company and Faceshift's tech would seem perfect for that sort of application.

Apple's extreme secrecy when it comes to projects currently extends to its much-rumoured development of a car. While Apple has never confirmed its interest in making automobiles, its recent hiring spree of auto-world veterans would suggest the tech company is—much like Google—interested in having a hand in the upcoming makeover of the transportation industry.

From: http://www.smh.com.au/technology

Reading Material
Microsoft Pays $2.5bn for Minecraft Maker Mojang

Microsoft has bought Mojang, the Swedish firm behind the popular video game Minecraft (See figure 17-9), for $2.5bn (£1.5bn).

Figure 17-9　Minecraft players can create intricate virtual worlds

The title, which has sold over 54 million copies, allows players to build structures with retro Lego-style blocks, as well as explore a large map and battle others.

The deal was announced by Xbox chief Phil Spencer.

Mojang, whose three founders will leave the company, assured fans that "everything is going to be OK".

Some analysts have speculated the deal is designed to attract more users to Microsoft's Windows Phone devices.

The acquisition comes a year after Microsoft bought the handset and devices division of Finnish mobile phone firm Nokia.

Minecraft is one of the top-selling Apps on both Apple's iOS store and Android's Google Play, and has recently been released for the Xbox One and PlayStation 4, further boosting sales.

Last month, it was the third most popular console game, according to market research firm NPD Group, despite being on sale for a while.

The game's developer, Mojang, which was founded in 2009, brought in over $100m in profit last year, and employs about 40 people.

Microsoft said the Mojang team would join its game studio, which is responsible for titles such as Halo, Forza and Fable.

The tech giant's chief executive, Satya Nadella, said: "Minecraft is more than a great game franchise—it is an open world platform, driven by a vibrant community we care deeply about, and rich with new opportunities for that community and for Microsoft."

Opposition to Sale

Mojang's founder, Markus "Notch" Persson, has previously criticised Microsoft, and commented to Reuters that the market for Windows phones was "tiny" and not worth developing Apps for (See figure 17-10).

Figure 17-10 Minecraft encourages users to build their own versions of the game, such as this Hunger Games title

Minecraft has a large and enthusiastic cult following, many of whom have reacted angrily to what they see as a corporate takeover of a communally-spirited independent company.

"Makes me sick, and sad," wrote one user on a popular Minecraft forum. "It would kill the gaming community," EvilBatsu added.

Others expressed concerns about whether fans would be able to exhibit their skills.

"Not only will it cost more money to play the game it will cost people their jobs too. Many people play Minecraft and upload it to YouTube as their career, but if Microsoft takes over there will for sure be copyright issues."

However some enthusiasts made the point that Microsoft could devote larger resources to upgrading and expanding the game.

In a statement, Microsoft said it would maintain Minecraft across all its existing platforms, with a "commitment to nurture and grow it long into the future".

It added that the acquisition was expected to be concluded by the end of 2014.

In an announcement confirming the deal on its website, Mojang reassured gamers, saying: "Please remember that the future of Minecraft and you—the community—are extremely important to everyone involved. If you take one thing away from this post, let it be that."

With regard to Microsoft, Mojang said: "There are only a handful of potential buyers with the resources to grow Minecraft on a scale that it deserves."

The firm added that "Notch" had decided that he "doesn't want the responsibility of owning a company of such global significance".

Developer Notch on Selling Minecraft (See figure 17-11):

Figure 17-11　Minecraft

"I've become a symbol. I don't want to be a symbol, responsible for something huge that I don't understand, that I don't want to work on, that keeps coming back to me. I'm not an entrepreneur. I'm not a CEO."

Why Minecraft?

James McQuivey of analytics firm Forrester, noted that "Minecraft is one of the most important gaming properties in the world" (See figure 17-12).

Figure 17-12　Many Minecraft enthusiasts build detailed structures, such as this house

"Not only is it profitable, but it continues to increase in profits years after its release, largely due to the passionate fan base that invests in building out their own Minecraft worlds."

"That helps explain why Microsoft would want Minecraft and would want to ensure it is always available on Microsoft's gaming platforms."

Prof Mark Skilton, from Warwick Business School, said the acquisition was about building a "strong customer base" for Microsoft.

"The online gaming industry is fast moving from niche collective enthusiast to mass market and Minecraft is a logical move as big business follows the traffic numbers in the digital world."

Last month, Amazon bought Twitch, a site which allows users to watch other people play video games, for $970m (£597m).

From: http://www.bbc.com/news
Author: Joe Miller

参 考 文 献

[1] http://money.cnn.com/2006/01/24/news/companies/disney_pixar_deal/index.htm.
[2] http://www.economist.com/blogs/graphicdetail/2015/12/graphical-history-disney-films-and-company-walt-created.
[3] http://www.latimes.com/business/la-fi-china-animation-20110817-story.html.
[4] http://edition.cnn.com/2014/02/27/business/tencent-wechat-unseats-sina-weibo/index.html?hpt=hp_c2.
[5] http://gizmodo.com/5982787/7-lessons-you-can-learn-from-shooting-with-a-camera-phone.
[6] Wang BoQiao. Digital art in China[J]. Technoetic Arts, 2012, 10(2-3): 145-149.
[7] http://money.cnn.com/2015/10/13/investing/hillary-clinton-wall-street/index.html.
[8] Curtis Carter. Dadaism [M]//Michael Kelly, Encyclopedia of Aesthetics. New York: Oxford University Press, 1998: 487-490.
[9] https://en.wikipedia.org/wiki/Marcel_Duchamp.
[10] http://www.bbc.com/news/entertainment-arts-14901992.
[11] http://news.bbc.co.uk/2/hi/entertainment/3689655.stm.
[12] http://www.theguardian.com/artanddesign/2010/mar/21/warhol-can-sold-world-review.
[13] BRANDEN W. JOSEPH. My Mind Split Open: Andy Warhol's Exploding Plastic Inevitable[M]// Grey Room. Charleston, South Carolina: Nabu Press, 2002, 80-107.
[14] https://en.wikipedia.org/wiki/Montage_(filmmaking).
[15] http://www.rogerebert.com/reviews/great-movie-taxi-driver-1976.
[16] http://news.bbc.co.uk/2/hi/programmes/click_online/8421468.stm.
[17] http://windows.microsoft.com/en-us/windows/windows-media-player-12.
[18] http://createdigitalmusic.com/2010/05/makers-of-pianoteq-talk-piano-modeling-developing-for-linux/?utm_source=feedburner&utm_medium=feed&utm_campaign=Feed%3A%20createdigitalmusic%20%28createdigitalmusic.com%29.
[19] http://www.adobe.com/about-adobe.html.
[20] http://www.adobe.com/about-adobe/fast-facts.html.
[21] https://helpx.adobe.com/after-effects/how-to/adobe-character-animator.html.
[22] http://pluggedin.kodak.com/pluggedin/post/?id=687843.
[23] http://news.bbc.co.uk/2/hi/technology/7846575.stm.
[24] http://www.bbc.com/news/magazine-11564766.
[25] http://news.bbc.co.uk/2/hi/science/nature/128906.stm.
[26] Heinz-Otto Peitgen, Hartmut Jürgens and Dietmar Saupe. Chaos and Fractals[M]. Springrt-Verlag New York, 2004.
[27] http://news.bbc.co.uk/2/hi/uk_news/1919330.stm.
[28] http://www.hypergridbusiness.com/2014/09/5-ways-virtual-reality-will-change-education/.
[29] https://hbr.org/2014/03/dont-compare-virtual-reality-to-the-smartphone/.
[30] http://www.bbc.com/news/technology-22013676.
[31] http://mashable.com/2012/12/19/augmented-reality-city/#yV4S3I_ccsqG.
[32] http://readwrite.com/2010/08/19/can_augmented_reality_help_save_the_print_publishing_industry.

[33] http://www.bbc.co.uk/news/uk-england-merseyside-14252101.
[34] http://strangelibrarian.org/2010/01/geolocation-augmented-reality-qr-codes-libraries/.
[35] https://www.technologyreview.com/s/425258/gps-app-keeps-drivers-eyes-on-the-road/.
[36] http://qz.com/75181/mobile-advertising-is-soaring-while-newspapers-continue-their-inexorable-decline/.
[37] http://www.spherelondon.co.uk/8-reasons-to-join-the-digital-media-and-advertising-industry.
[38] http://thecdm.ca/program/digital-media.
[39] http://ignorethecode.net/blog/2010/01/21/realism_in_ui_design/.
[40] http://usabilitypost.com/2008/10/13/experience-vs-function-beautiful-ui-not-always-best-u/.
[41] http://designmodo.com/mobile-apps-gradient-effect/.
[42] http://designmodo.com/ghost-buttons/.
[43] http://designmodo.com/create-style-guides/.
[44] http://designmodo.com/web-design-trends-2016/.
[45] JANICE C. (GINNY) REDISH. What Is Information Design? [J]. Technical Communication, 2000, 47(2): 163-166.
[46] SAUL CARLINER. Physical, Cognitive, and Affective: A Three-part Framework for Information Design [J]. Technical Communication, 2000, 47(4): 561-576.
[47] Benjamin U. Rubin. Audible Information Design in the New York City Subway System: A Case Study [D]. New York University.
[48] www.ronenbekerman.com.
[49] www.archdaily.com.
[50] http://www.typeworkshop.com/index.php?id1=type-basics&id2=&id3=&id4=&id5=&idpic=19#pictloader.
[51] http://alistapart.com/article/style-tiles-and-how-they-work.
[52] http://www.smh.com.au/technology/technology-news/how-angry-birds-really-took-off-200m-minutes-a-day-spent-playing-it-20110208-1akt5.html.
[53] http://www.smh.com.au/technology/technology-news/apple-buys-star-wars-tech-firm-faceshift-to-up-its-vr-game-20151126-gl9b0i.
[54] http://www.bbc.com/news/technology-29204518.
[55] Tony Feldman. An introduction to digital media [M]. London; New York: Routledge, 1996.